Getting Real About Sex Ed

Getting Real About Sex Ed

What Today's Students Need

SHAFIA ZALOOM

HARVARD EDUCATION PRESS
CAMBRIDGE, MASSACHUSETTS

Paperback ISBN 979-8-89557-059-3

Cataloging-in-Publication Data available from the Library of Congress.

Published by Harvard Education Press,
an imprint of the Harvard Education Publishing Group

Harvard Education Press
8 Story Street
Cambridge, MA 02138

Cover Design: Joel Gendron

The typefaces in this book are Minion Pro and ITC Stone Sans.

Contents

Foreword

About fifteen years ago, born out of my work on children's moral development, I became deeply troubled by our country's epic failure to prepare children for caring and ethical romantic love, sex, and relationships in their adult lives. I had heard too many stories from teens and adults about their own experiences with sexuality education that were alienating and comical. Who, I wondered, was doing this work well? What did *well* look like? How might *well* be scaled?

I was introduced to Shafia Zaloom by a mutual friend, Peggy Orenstein. Peggy was working on a book about girls and sex, and she described Shafia as a kind of guru, a deeply wise and skilled practitioner.

My first conversation with Shafia was a blast of fresh air. Hardheaded, softhearted, and funny, Shafia clearly had a deep understanding of young people's developing sexuality, a keen sense for how to talk to children about sex, and a nuanced, mature, compelling vision for what healthy sexual and relationship education should look like. Several times over the years, I invited her to speak to my class at the Harvard Graduate School of Education (HGSE). My students loved her. In recent years, she has taught courses on sexuality education at HGSE as well as consulted and presented to numerous organizations across the country. I am thrilled her voice is reaching such a wide audience.

Now, Shafia has packed her wisdom into this book. Levelheaded, insightful, and attuned to young people with varying gender identities and sexual orientations, Shafia shows us how to prepare children to have healthy, joyful, caring, and safe relationships, sex, and intimacy when they are mature. She describes the work from elementary school through high school. She takes up, for example, how rich discussions about the human body, boundaries, healthy touching, and consent in elementary school lays the foundation for safe, caring relationships later in life. She deftly uses actual scenarios, drawn from her vast experience consulting in schools nationwide, to capture the opportunities and challenges in this work and squarely take on tough, complex situations. What to do, for example, when a teen is inappropriately touched by another student but doesn't want to discuss it with an adult, or when teens fling derogatory remarks like "that's so gay" and write off adults' admonishments by claiming they're only kidding, or when school adults come upon two students engaged in sexual activity on an empty bus. As is inevitable in such a complex field, there are moments where readers, including myself, may reach different conclusions than Shafia. My own reaction to some of these candid everyday scenarios spurred reflection on how I would address them with young people—exactly the intent of this book. Her thoughtful consideration of every issue is evident throughout, and her expertise provides invaluable guidance for educators and parents alike.

In *Getting Real About Sex Ed: What Today's Students Need,* Shafia effectively draws not only on her own experience but on her deep knowledge of social-emotional learning and resilience. She illuminates how social-emotional learning and skills—e.g., empathy, self-awareness, and self-regulation—are at the heart of high-quality sexuality education and how, conversely, high-quality sexuality education is a powerful way of developing social-emotional awareness and skills. At many points, this book not only takes up how to prepare young people for healthy romantic relationships and sex but also how to prepare them to be good friends and community members and have caring connections of many kinds. Shafia's strong moral compass is evident throughout. She knows that sexuality is rife with potential both for many kinds of harms and for expressing the deepest forms of tenderness and respect.

It is a travesty in this country that we have typically entrusted the teaching of one of the most profound, fraught, complicated, and wonderful domains of human experience to adults who have not been given adequate training, support, or resources by our educational systems. Sexuality education is also commonly relegated to a few days or weeks in a health education class, and the focus is too often solely on abstinence or disaster prevention—how not to get pregnant or contract STIs. Adults' knowledge about how to help teens around a wide range of issues of sexuality and romantic relationships is also far too thin. Making matters worse, opposition to comprehensive sex ed and to supporting LGBTQIA+ teens is increasingly fierce in many parts of the country.

Elevating the profession of sex education, shifting public attitudes, and providing comprehensive, developmentally appropriate learning about sexuality will require work on many fronts. Yet the most urgent need is often right in the classroom, where educators—no matter their subject or training—are routinely confronted with real-world questions and scenarios related to gender, sexuality, and relationships. Too often, teachers find themselves unsure how to respond and miss opportunities for meaningful dialogue. This book serves as an essential roadmap, offering educators evidence-based strategies, practical tools, and clear language for navigating these daily situations with confidence and care. Modeling healthy communication and boundaries empowers educators to turn everyday challenges into teachable moments that build students' empathy, self-awareness, and lifelong skills. We are fortunate to have such an important and timely resource.

—Richard Weissbourd
Senior Lecturer on Education
Faculty Director, Making Caring Common
Harvard Graduate School of Education

1

The Sexuality Education Our Students Deserve

Last Spring, I was in Louisville, KY to facilitate a Sexual Violence and Sex Trafficking Prevention training on behalf of the Nest Foundation for the Department of Juvenile Justice. Group home staff from all over the state had gathered to participate. Many folks don't realize that prevention within this context is actually comprehensive sexuality education (CSE). At the time, national antisexuality education and anti-LGBTQIA+ surveillance was building, so my defenses were up. After all, I am a progressive health educator who promotes social justice, particularly the inclusion of LGBTQ+ young people. I am also a woman of color. Still, as someone who teaches about being open and accepting of others, my own biases had surfaced, and I braced myself for resistance to messages about healthy sexuality education for all students, whatever their identity. I assumed that if I were to meet any pushback, it would certainly be in the South.

When I arrived at the training facility, the morning welcome was warm and inviting. The care and love participants had for the youth was obvious and immediate. As we talked about cultivating physical and emotional safety within group homes and the partnership between those homes and public schools, the topic of gender emerged in concrete ways.

Kelce, at the end of the second row, raised his hand. A man of impressive size, he openly shared about his experience when charged with keeping a young trans woman, Brooks, safe. Brooks identified as male to female (MTF) trans and had been assigned to an all-male juvenile-offender teen group home based on her biological characteristics. Today, some states restrict young people to group homes based on their gender assigned at birth. Brooks presented as very feminine and many of the male residents found her beautiful. There were also several rehabilitating sex offenders among them, and like most places, there was transphobia at the school they attended.

Kelce acknowledged that dealing with Brooks brought up his own biases and his lack of experience with trans people. "You know, to be honest, this was really hard for me. I grew up as a good 'ol boy in rural eastern Kentucky. This isn't something I had experience with or learned about in positive ways. And, I knew I needed to keep her safe. So, I just kept saying, 'help me to understand. . .' and she was open to working together. I learned more from her than many of the other residents, and by the time she finished the program, she was 100% female to me."

I asked Kelce to describe how he worked to keep Brooks safe, particularly at school. He and the school counselor, who was sitting next to him in the training, had established daily communication and invested a tremendous amount of care and time in supporting Brooks, as well as working to keep her safe while using the bathroom, etc. Kelce was aware that his physical stature could be perceived as intimidating and how this could impact Brooks but could serve as a shield for her as well. His description of his partnership with the school counselor and their commitment to Brooks was beautiful and inspiring for all of us.

During a break, I talked to Kelce one on one, and he described how he and Brooks arrived at the name she would use as a resident in the home. Her chosen name was feminine, yet she was living in an all-male group home, so he was concerned about the negative attention this might attract. They had a conversation about how to stay true to who she is and also identify a name that would carry less baggage. They landed on her last name, which felt gender neutral.

I asked Kelce what gave him the openness to support Brooks, given the strict gender norms he grew up with. He said, "My mom. Yeah, I grew up as a good 'ol boy and all the stereotypes that go along with it, but I was raised by a single mother who taught me to live from my heart. So that's what I did. I opened my heart."

Kelce went on to provide invaluable locals-only information about the best spots to sample the "real deal" Kentucky fried chicken and fried green tomatoes it's famous for and which distilleries would provide the best whiskey. He told me about the Louisville Slugger, and Mohammed Ali Museums, as well as Colonel Sanders's wife's fried chicken recipe (which the Colonel took credit for) and his own hunting and fishing expeditions. His kindness and compassion overturned the assumptions I'd brought because we all have our biases, and endeared me to Kentucky. I ate plenty of authentic Kentucky fried chicken before catching the plane home, but what really filled me up was the humble pie I had to eat. Kelce had modeled that when we lead with curiosity and heart, we find humanity that has the power to transform all of us. I got to experience the very lesson I was there to teach. What I was left with is the realization of what it always comes down to: LOVE. That is what this book is about. Love. A radical love—for our students, our learning communities, and ourselves.

Educators ask me:

"Isn't it inappropriate for teachers to talk to little kids about sex?"

- Childhood sexuality education is not intercourse education like many people assume. The focus for childhood sexuality education is on families, feelings, friends, and what's fair.

"Isn't teaching them about sex going to make them want to try it?"

- This is common, yet misinformed, thinking. In fact, the opposite is true. Numerous studies have found that CSE programs encourage young people to delay intercourse, reduce the frequency of intercourse, and reduce the number of sexual partners they have.[1]

"How can I be expected to guide young people in matters of sexuality when I never had that education myself?"

- You've identified the very problem we're trying to solve. There are lots of great training programs for educators on how to approach and teach this topic with students of all ages. We have to start somewhere and that could be with you.

"I could get fired for teaching about sex in my class, even though I know it's important. What can I do?"

- This is an unfortunate conundrum that discounts teacher's expertise in child and adolescent development and the creativity that is teaching. Teachers and schools need to decide if they will teach according to the mission of their district (which always includes citizenship and youth development—a big part of sexuality education) or adhere to the limiting laws of their state. Even if you face limits in how much you can cover, there are ways to discuss sexuality education without using semantics that are prohibited. As an educator, you are modeling many aspects of sexuality education all of the time: how you communicate about boundaries, how you respect and care about others, and how you hear and see students for who they are.

WHAT IS COMPREHENSIVE SEXUALITY EDUCATION?

Sexual development is an essential, multifaceted part of the human experience. It is a vital aspect of well-being, and comprehensive sexuality education (CSE) supports young people in developing into sexually healthy adults. Comprehensive sexuality education means learning about the cognitive, emotional, social, interactive, and physical aspects of sexuality. CSE supports and protects sexual development. It gradually equips and empowers children and young people with information, skills, and positive values to understand and enjoy their sexuality, have safe and fulfilling relationships, and take responsibility for their own and other people's sexual health and well-being. It enables young people to make choices that enhance the quality of their lives and contribute to a compassionate and just society. All children and young people have the right to have access to age-appropriate sexuality education.[2] School-based CSE ideally begins in preschool or kindergarten and is scaffolded across a student's education until graduation from high school. It is best offered within the context of a comprehensive health curriculum and is most effective when its messages are reinforced by parents and the community.[3]

Thirteen years ago, The Sexuality Information and Education Council of the United States (SIECUS) convened a national task force of experts in the fields of adolescent development, health care, and education to create a framework of key concepts, topics, and messages that all sexuality education programs would include. This vital resource, *Guidelines for Comprehensive Sexuality Education, 3rd Edition, Kindergarten through 12th Grade*, has become one of the most influential publications in the field and a trusted resource for educators, curriculum developers, and school administrators.[4] Although the guidelines are adaptable to the needs and beliefs of different communities, they are based on specific values and an ideal vision of sexuality education. The task force agreed on the goals of sexuality education, which is to promote adult sexual health (for a list of values inherent in the guidelines and life behaviors of a sexually healthy adult, see *Guidelines for Comprehensive Sexuality Education*) and support young people in developing a positive view of sexuality. It should assist young people by providing them with the information they need to take care of their sexual health and help them acquire skills to make decisions now and in the future. The goals fall into four areas: (1) information; (2) attitudes, values, and insights; (3) relationships and interpersonal skills; and (4) responsibility. The fundamental principles that underscore the importance and benefit of sexuality education include being part of a comprehensive health program, well-trained teachers, community involvement, a focus on all youth, and a variety of teaching methods.

WHAT'S THE VALUE OF COMPREHENSIVE SEXUALITY EDUCATION?

There are decades of research, including studies from government and international organizations, that emphasize the importance of sexuality education to students' mental, emotional, and physical health, as well as community health. The US Department of Education partners with the US Department of Health and Human Services through the Centers for Disease Control and Prevention (CDC), which promotes CSE across elementary, middle, and high school age classrooms, because it is proven that age-appropriate sex education develops a safe and positive view of sexuality, builds healthy relationships within educational spaces, and provides information that encourages informed, safe, positive choices about sexuality and sexual health.[5] These organizations—in particular, the CDC through its Youth Risk Behavior Survey and many federally recognized nonprofits such as SEICUS's National Sex Education Standards—recognize that school connectedness, which sex education programs promote, reduces health-risk experiences and behaviors, including loneliness, depression, anxiety, and suicidal ideation.[6] Moreover, this aligns with the American Academy of Pediatrics' evidence-based conclusion that access to CSE promotes healthy sexuality, which is a core developmental milestone for adolescent health.[7] National, state, and local polls consistently find that the majority of parents want schools to provide comprehensive education about sexuality.[8] Many states mandate that topics such as abstinence, STIs, HIV/AIDS, contraception, and disease prevention methods are covered in school programs. Numerous studies have also found that CSE programs help young people delay intercourse, reduce the frequency of intercourse, reduce the number of sexual partners they have, and increase their use of condoms and other contraceptive methods when they do become sexually active.[9]

CSE is increasingly recognized as a human right. International organizations such as the World Health Organization (WHO), UNESCO, the Joint United Nations Programme on HIV/AIDS, and the International Conference on Population and Development recognize that sex education is an obligation of the government and that it must be evidence based and must not be biased, ideologically motivated, or censored.[10] Internationally, there are four primary evidence-based standard-setting documents for international sexuality education: (1) *Advocating for Comprehensive Sexuality Education* (2009, 2010); (2) *International Technical Guidance on Sexuality Education*; (3) *It's All One Curriculum: Guidelines and Activities for a Unified Approach to Sexuality, Gender, HIV, and Human Rights Education*; and (4) *Standards for Sexuality Education in Europe*. Collectively, the documents represent collaboration among academics, practitioners, activists, community members, and UN officials. All four documents are voluntary; however, each of the documents went through a lengthy process to ensure quality, acceptability, and ownership at the highest levels.[11]

It's All One Curriculum has been in high demand since its first publication in 2009 (the second version was published in 2011). Requests have come from over 150 countries and every state in the United States from various government agencies, international NGOs, and community organizations supporting young people. This includes requests from very conservative regions like strict Islamic settings in northern Nigeria and Aceh Province in Indonesia, polygamous communities in Utah, and abstinence-only schools in Nevada. Teachers in these settings report that the curriculum is opening up safe ways to talk about challenging topics like coercion, power, gender equity in relationships, and human rights.[12]

In the Netherlands, sex education has remained largely nonstigmatized and nonpolitical. It is no wonder that their statistics for unintended pregnancies and sexually transmitted infections are some of the lowest in the world.[13]

WHAT DOES THIS MEAN FOR SCHOOLS?

Parents are, and professionals believe ought to be, the primary sexuality educator in a child's life; however, they are not the only ones. While parents play a critical role in fostering healthy sexuality, schools (whether public, independent, or faith based) remain an important setting for teaching sexual health. Schools have access to young people at critical developmental stages and most have a core mission of fostering the positive development of young people.[14] Faith-based institutions, community-based organizations, and schools all play an important role. CSE is mission driven. Whether a public, independent, or faith-based school, all of the schools I know of commit to encouraging character development, cultivating citizenship, and building community in some way. In other words, they address who we are as individuals and together—and how we treat each other—because it matters. Here are a few examples that demonstrate how almost every school incorporates language about equitable, responsible, and safe communities, all tenets reinforced by CSE.

Mission language pulled from various public school districts in different states:

- Goal Area: Create a climate and culture that makes each student feel valued, supported, and respected. (Flathead County, MT)
- Mission: Ensures a safe and inclusive environment empowering a community of learners. (Washington & Benton Counties, AR)
- Board Policy: Each [community member] has a legitimate expectation to have a barrier-free learning environment counteracting the contemporary and historical impact of bias, prejudice, and discrimination, which for generations, has produced a predictability of learning outcomes based on race, class, socioeconomics, gender, ethnicity, sexual orientation, gender identity, cognitive/physical ability, diverse language fluency and religion. (Hamilton County, OH)
- Mission Achievement: Prioritizing relationships and focusing on the safety and social and emotional well-being of students and staff. (Maricopa County, AZ)
- Vision: A dynamic, progressive, and collaborative learning community embracing change and diversity where every student will graduate with the skills needed to succeed in postsecondary education and the workplace. (Lake County, FL)

Mission language pulled from various independent schools in different states:

- Core Values: We value responsibility, honesty, compassion, diversity, and respect, acknowledging that our actions have a profound impact on others, on the environment, and on the community as a whole. (Middlesex County, MA)
- Mission: An inclusive and equitable community that celebrates diversity and multiculturalism. (Cook County, IL)
- About: Instills kindness and nurtures a sense of belonging and community. (Richland County, SC)
- Mission: Create transformative learning experiences that empower a diverse community of students to lead lives of intellectual curiosity, personal integrity and compassionate contribution to a more just world. (Bernalillo, NM)
- Values: Acceptance of and appreciation of each person's dignity. (Milwaukee County, WI)

Mission language from various faith-based schools in different states:

- Core Value: Believes that the authentic development of each student unfolds within a safe and supportive environment. (Marion County, IN)
- Core Value: Encourage our students to become open to growth, intellectually competent, loving, religious and committed to justice. (Douglas County, NE)
- Commitment: Creating a community where all community members—students, families, faculty and staff (or employees)—are seen, heard, and their dignity respected. (San Francisco County, CA)
- Guiding Principles: Emphasizes the development of sound character, integrity, and personal honor. (Harris County, TX)
- Core Value: Nourishing the whole child—mind, soul, and heart—we seek to cultivate abundant growth in each student. (New York County, NY)

In addition to this mission-driven endeavor, schools have an opportunity to address this learning on a unique level. Young people spend the majority of their waking hours in schools; therefore, educators can consistently and simultaneously have conversations with students who are most likely expressing and exploring sexuality with each other. Encouraging direct and honest dialogue about shared knowledge is a powerful way for students to practice and strengthen their communication skills and support accountability for relationship behaviors.

"WHO AM I?"

Understanding the concept of identity is an essential and complex developmental task for young people, shaped by individual characteristics, family dynamics, historical factors, and social and political contexts. As social scientist Charles Cooley indicated, other people are the looking glass in which we see ourselves.[15] Beverly Tatum deconstructs this process and recognizes the significance of intersectionality, which impacts this marked undertaking as well: "This 'looking glass self' is not a flat one-dimensional reflection, but multidimensional. 'Who am I?' depends in large part on who the world around me says I am. Who do my parents say I am? Who do my peers say I am? What message is reflected back to me in the faces and voices of my teachers, my neighbors, store personnel? What do I learn from the media about myself? How am I represented in the cultural images around me? Or am I missing from the picture altogether?"[16] Schools are undeniably a huge factor in this process. How we reflect children and teach them to recognize the effect they have on each other is an essential part of youth development. Identity is multifaceted—a young person's experience of their sexual identity will be affected by other aspects of identity, such as socio-economic status, nationality, religion, race and ethnicity, and/or ability. Choices made in adolescence ripple throughout one's lifespan.[17]

The process of socialization for young people begins at home. Once they begin to attend school, their sources of socialization multiply. Schools contribute to the messages young people receive about how to be, what rules to follow, what assumptions to make, what to believe, and especially who we may look up to or look down upon. Schools consciously and unconsciously reinforce messages about who we and others are in the world—about who is valued and who is not.[18] In addition to intentional programs and curricula, schools socialize young people with hidden curricula, the socialization of what we model without directly teaching it, especially when it comes to sexuality education. What can we talk about? Who isn't included? What impact does the omission of certain aspects of identity have? If we are caring for and affirming all children, we must include conversations about gender and sexuality that will meet the myriad needs that are a part of their whole selves and full humanity.

This means implementing CSE programs and training teachers in all of the ways we address these issues in educational spaces in and outside the confines of classrooms. School educators and officials, students, and families need knowledge about CSE, yet we allow our ideologies to get in the way of the science that serves and centers students. Debbie Roffman, an author and sexuality educator for over forty years, says, "As a culture, we virtually worship knowledge about practically every other aspect of human existence. All we really need to do to bring this topic into the twenty-first century is to simply decide to apply the same standard to learning about sexuality—Knowledge is good! Knowledge is the cornerstone of responsibility! Knowledge is the key to a fulfilling life!—as we do all others. We have to stop thinking emotionally about the topic and start thinking educationally."[19]

WHAT DOES THIS MEAN FOR ME AS AN EDUCATOR?

These days, children are given implicit and explicit messages about sexuality before they're even born (think gender reveal parties) and will continue to be socialized on sexuality throughout their lives. We are constantly modeling behaviors that signal our values in all our interactions and relationships, including sexual ones: how we dress according to our gender, how we show respect to our students and colleagues (Do you actively listen when a student is sharing something important to them?

Do you ask colleagues before borrowing something of theirs?), the language we use when addressing classrooms (Do you use gendered language like "you guys" when addressing a gender-varied bunch?), and how we deal with conflict or disrespect (How do you address derogatory language like "fag" or "bitch" if you hear it in the hallway or when you're driving the track team in the school van?). Sometimes our silence speaks louder than words. If we keep the well-being of our students at the center of our work in educational spaces and believe in the mission of the school we are contracted with, then we need to figure out how to address these topics not just in the classroom but in all aspects of school culture. The challenge is that we live in a sexually unhealthy culture and in many cases haven't had the benefit of this education ourselves.

Discomfort with sexuality is really just a learned association—it's how we've been socialized given the shame- and avoidance-based sociopolitical history of sexuality in American culture. To be effective, it's important to understand your own general comfort level and attitudes towards sexuality, how they may impact your teaching, and to recognize your own strengths and limitations with this topic so that you may ask for assistance when needed.

If you aren't comfortable with or don't feel prepared to talk about these issues, there are many wonderful and impactful professional development digital and in-person tools available (many are included in appendix C). To get more comfortable with the topic, start talking about sexuality with friends, family, and colleagues. Apply for a professional development training. Encourage others to do the same. Every educator I've met has a story of when sexuality has shown up in their work—whether it was a "you can't play" moment around gendered recess games, a kid who was made to feel uncomfortable because everyone has a crush and they don't, or a teen who is inspired to create a zine that addresses coming of age as a girl in a sexist context as part of a literature portfolio. These kinds of experiences represent an opportunity; it's an opportunity for our own personal and professional growth so that we can empower young people with the knowledge, skills, and capacities to advocate for themselves and each other and build caring, equitable communities together.

Educators tell me, "There's no time!" Yes, time is a precious commodity in schools, but we have to start somewhere, and it may not require as much time as many educators think. Ideally, all schools will work towards establishing a fully integrated CSE program with a full-time health teacher. In the meantime, it's important to remember that research shows that the amount of time spent on sexuality education is not nearly as important as the quality of the experience.[20]

WHO THIS BOOK IS FOR

Anyone who works with and impacts the lives of young people in schools—kindergarten through grade twelve—can benefit from this book. It is a resource for anyone interested in guiding and educating young people towards bodily autonomy, effective sexual and relationship communication, critical thinking, informed decision-making, and authentic connection that will contribute to their overall well-being and humanitarian citizenship. *Getting Real About Sex Ed: What Today's Students Need* is a resource for classroom teachers, educational nonprofit care-taking adults, policymakers, and researchers. Most of the educators I consult with seek an approach to these issues that is free of stigma and shame, age appropriate, accessible, compelling, relatable, realistic, and meaningful. The concrete language and strategies for how to arrange information and scaffold skill building over time, as well as cultivate capacities for action through exercises and practice, meet this need. Case studies illuminate social power dynamics and meaning as young people and educators grapple with ethical quandaries and interpersonal dynamics that hone skills for managing the complexities of human relationships.

Policymakers may resource this writing to better understand what public health messaging within this context will best serve young people. Whether in the realm of education or other public health contexts, policies may be informed by the depth and breadth of information as well as case studies. This combination will provide perspective on the political and financial capital needed to implement healthy sexuality and relationship education for students, as well as professional development for teachers and administrators that will impact education and public health initiatives in the realms of physical and mental health, community responsibility, youth development, and digital, interpersonal, and sexual citizenship.

Researchers can gain a greater understanding of what resonates and feels meaningful to young people, which will help focus their efforts on identifying data that will ultimately enforce the value of healthy sexuality and relationship education, discover how educators and public health policy makers may further support young peoples' physical and mental health, and acquire a deeper knowledge of what actually matters to young people and encourages them to thrive.

QUALIFICATIONS AND COMPETENCIES

Teaching lessons about sexuality requires certain competencies. Ideally, all teachers would have effective training in a broad base of knowledge in human sexuality content and issues.[21] Competencies include being able to maintain clear adult/student boundaries, the ability to engage in culturally responsive guidance and instruction, experience with addressing sensitive issues, comfort with teaching health-related topics in a way that encourages all voices and perspectives no matter the nature of one's own personal beliefs, and knowledge and practice in how to create safe spaces for youth that are conducive to sharing with openness and honesty.

WHAT ROLE DO PARENTS AND CARETAKING ADULTS PLAY?

It is misinformed to assume that friction between parents, communities, and schools is inevitable. The vast majority of adults support public school involvement in sexuality education.[22] In fact, parental involvement, including an open dialogue about sexuality education, can minimize objections and excusals and increase parent-child communication. While abstinence-only-until-marriage proponents might present CSE as a controversial issue, all evidence suggests that CSE is a mainstream value in the United States. A vast majority of people in the US support CSE. Public support for sex education is overwhelming—regardless of political affiliation, religion, and/or regional demographics.[23] In 2017, 93.5 percent of parents felt it is important to have sex education taught in middle school and 96 percent felt it is important to have sex education taught in high school.[24] In my experience, the majority of parents are supportive and appreciative that their child is being taught CSE and enjoy our partnership. Parents have a tremendous amount of wisdom to share about their kids and how they navigate the world. I have also experienced parents who felt hesitant, trepidatious, and in some cases, completely disagreed with what and how I was teaching CSE. I have learned the most from these parents, especially if they are receptive to my outreach and invitation to dialogue about their concerns. Parents, like most of us, want to feel seen and heard.

However, it is possible that communication with parents on this topic will be challenging. *Strategic Questioning* by Fran Peavey provides helpful strategies for transforming conflict into connection, even across differences. Strategic questioning is "a way of talking with people with whom you have differences without abandoning your own beliefs and yet looking for common ground which may enable both parties to co-create a new path from the present situation. In every heart there is ambiguity; in every ideology there are parts that don't fit."[25] See appendix C for more on this invaluable resource.

Parents often want support when it comes to talking to their children about sexuality, especially because the vast majority didn't receive CSE themselves. Parent education is a wonderful way to affirm the parent-school partnership and appropriately share the responsibility of educating young people in CSE concepts. Parents also have the sole responsibility of teaching something teachers cannot, and that is their family's values. I emphasize this with parents and encourage dialogue about what will be discussed in classes. Parents and caretaking adults typically don't like surprises and appreciate communication. Normalizing these conversations with informational correspondence goes a long way. I also engage caretaking adults in take-home assignments as students get older, especially in middle and high school.

WHAT ABOUT RESISTANCE AND LIMITATIONS?

Because many states have modified their statutes around education, many teachers are afraid of responding to the developmental needs of their students within this context because it may invite scrutiny, defamation, job insecurity, and even abuse from other adults. It is important to recognize that there is a difference between childhood sexuality and adult sexuality. Restricting teachers from talking to their students about the cognitively congruent realities of life puts political ideology above student health. Politics puts adult needs at the center of this issue, not children. Some teachers are anxious about teaching "sexualized" concepts, especially during childhood. What's important to understand is that CSE is not about SEX, it's about science. Teachers know this, yet their professional expertise in the development of young people and scaffolding of learning across developmental stages is dismissed. One of the primary roles of a teacher is to help children feel that they belong, and these limitations ask teachers to ignore aspects of their students that make them feel like they don't. Teachers must then be cautious, and as a result, we take away their capacity to work their magic: the magic of creating educational spaces in which all children enjoy feeling seen, heard, and safe.

To keep opposition in perspective and reinforce and capitalize on existing community support for programs, you can be proactive by using key strategies such as prevention, diffusion, and self-care.[26] When cultivating and/or maintaining support for your program, consider establishing an advisory committee in the spirit of community participation and partnership. Community participation can be a vital strategy that helps shift the ways in which communities deal with adolescents and their sexual health as community adults partner with young people and with program planners to create appropriate solutions to community problems.[27] Reflect the many community constituencies by inviting folks who have expertise in the community's culture and priorities: parents, community members who are not parents, community health representatives, elders, spiritual leaders, elected officials, business folks, teachers, administrators, and students.[28] Consider inviting folks from any groups from which you anticipate resistance. Identify your allies and create opportunities for connection and dialogue about the value and vision you have for CSE in your school. It's important to build a network before issues surface.

Debbie Roffman conducts training across the country on how to manage and diffuse resistance. She encourages educators to first identify what kind of opposition the school is confronting. In an effort to get a better understanding of the problem, Roffman encourages us to listen closely for what someone is afraid of and offers five categories of obstacles and strategies tailored to each:

Reluctance: Is someone hesitant because of their own lack of CSE? Is their reluctance because they are unsure about what and how it will be taught? Hear the person out (as long as they are being respectful), ask clarifying strategic questions, offer transparency (not necessarily concession) and information, and reassure them to dispel their fears.

Resistance: Listen, explain, and problem solve. What is it exactly that the person has issues with? How can students be centered in the dialogue to problem solve? Share how different points of view will be encouraged and respected. Offer to communicate with the adult(s) about what's being taught so that they may weigh in at home and offer their perspective as well.

Opposition and Organized Opposition: Is this one person who, despite attempts at seeing and hearing them, is still adamant about their child not attending? Encourage alternatives for learning. Make it clear that nobody is going to force anyone to participate and that the school won't stop someone from holding their child home for the day; however, if you work in a school that requires CSE for graduation, you'll want to ask about the guardian's plan for the student to meet that requirement. Organized opposition is typically a digital petition of sorts. It's important, in this case, to respond to the strategies of the folks opposing, not the content. Whatever folks in opposition are saying in digital spaces, do not comment. Instead, focus on how they are going about getting what they want and offer to talk in a way that doesn't create unnecessary angst or discord. Antibullying strategies are best used in this context.

Outside Agitation: Are these accusations coming from outside of the school community? Does the organization and its representatives have children at the school? This is typically not the case, so respond assertively and nondefensively.

Recently, many divisive concept laws, legislative, and executive actions that restrict teaching and discussions in schools and workplaces regarding race, gender, sexuality, and US History have been put in place. In a 2024 conversation with Michael Tafelski from the Southern Poverty Law Center, we discussed how these statutes can be challenging to understand because many are vague with inconsistent language and definitions. As in all situations, it's important to document and keep a paper trail of incidents. Be astute and aware of the legal and political dynamics in your state and consider asking questions of your school district's legal counsel or, if you are in a private school, the school's General Counsel. Request their legal opinion on where the boundaries and risks may be. Build a record of those conversations and your lessons so that you have documentation should there be any dispute.

CSE While Laws May Shift and Change

What if you are dealing with actual state statutes that restrict CSE? This puts educators in the position to decide whether they will teach from the mission and values of their district and/or school or in line with the laws of their state. Most educators I know work in schools because they care about the healthy development and education of young people. Finding a balance between job security and teaching what you know is in the service of student well-being is tricky and tough. It will be influenced by a number of variables and circumstances; only the individual educator can calculate how to maintain that balance and their choices should be respected.

These limiting state statutes deny young people and their families the human right to receive CSE in all the ways that it is meant to affirm and encourage respect and honor for various genders and sexualities. It also puts educators in the position where they have to choose between providing an equitable educational experience for *all* children—each and every one—and their own well-being. Is it possible to provide this type of equitable educational experience within the confines of the restrictions? It is far from ideal; at the same time, it's possible to talk about sexuality without talking about sexuality. This is actually something we do as a culture all of the time—sex is everywhere and nowhere all at once. If we talk about all of the building blocks and nuances of CSE with vocabulary that isn't currently labeled as "woke" or "liberal," we may circumvent the limitations. I recently conducted another Sexual Violence and Sex Trafficking Prevention workshop for educators working in a school district in Texas. We spent two days discussing reproductive anatomy, bodily autonomy, setting boundaries, harm-reduction strategies, a wide range of feelings including joy, attraction, and love in the myriad ways people of many identities express it, interpersonal and communication skills, different types of relationships, intimacy, and how to authentically connect with all kinds of folks who represented a varied tapestry of what's real in young people's lives. Due to state statutes, I was not to "teach gender." Yes, it was deeply disappointing, disheartening, and in many ways, I felt like a sellout. At the same time, we discussed aspects of CSE in a variety of meaningful ways. Discussing these topics without "teaching gender" required strategies suggested throughout this book. The overall approach to these community conversations focuses on mutual respect, care, and dignity for all students. Teaching and cultivating capacities for self-regulation, empathy, authentic connection, consent, community care, and love are the foundation for understanding how people want and deserve to be treated within their various identities.

The widespread assumption that teachers have it easy is an insidious myth that minimizes the care and investment educators put into teaching generations of other people's children. In fact, teaching is deeply challenging, and teachers who work in regions that restrict what and how they can teach have it particularly hard. I know sexuality educators—folks who are some of the most thoughtful, big-hearted, brilliant, altruistic humans I've ever met—who have suffered verbal abuse, public exploitation, and defamation just for doing their jobs: meeting the needs of their students with guidance and curricula that has been proven through decades of research and science to support student well-being. Their courage and resilience is an inspiration to be honored.

When educators meet obstacles, it is important to practice self-care by connecting with other educators and taking time out by reaching out to others. Opposition typically represents a small minority, yet it can still take its toll. Who can you ask for support? Who are your allies? Cultivate social capital and find affirming ways to restore yourself.

HOW TO USE THIS BOOK

This book is organized by grade to be cognitively congruent with the developmental needs of specific age ranges while allowing for some variation in rates of development. "Cognitively congruent" is a phrase that Roffman created to inspire a paradigm shift away from the term "age appropriate" when it comes to sexuality education. Roffman has explained to me that "age appropriate" within this context implies "too much too soon" might be harmful, and reflects adult irrational fears regarding sexuality education. "Cognitively congruent" puts the child at the center instead of erroneous adult thinking and misplaced anxiety. Roffman's phrase enables adults to understand that it is the child's cognitive development that determines "readiness" for information, not necessarily social, emotional or physical factors.

As educators, much of our expertise is anchored in our professional understanding of child and adolescent development and how to scaffold learning in a way that builds upon itself and cycles back again and again. Our chosen methodologies should fit the objective, which must be aligned with the age, interest, needs, and abilities of the learners.[29] As we spiral learning towards young adulthood, we facilitate building knowledge and skills that will empower young people to be healthy, educated young adults.

Each chapter will address the following aspects of sexuality to demonstrate how CSE can be scaffolded across student development to deepen understanding, build skills, and cultivate capacities that encourage growth and effective practice. These different domains are bodies, gender and sexuality diversity, feelings, relationships (consent, communication, and decision-making), connection (intimacy and love), and safety. Each chapter features case studies gathered through my interviews of many parents, teachers, school counselors, administrators, and educational nonprofit employees from many different counties in many different states. These real-life scenarios focus on the *in-betweens* of academic instruction time, the moments that require all teachers to provide guidance in the hallways, right before dismissal, on the play yard, during passing periods, etc. I chose to focus this book on these moments because I have found that educators are confronted with issues of gender, sexuality, and relationships far more than they are prepared to address through their training. Whether teaching in a progressive state or a conservative state, all teachers are confronted with these moments multiple times during the day, every day. Because so many of us didn't receive CSE ourselves, it can be challenging to respond to these moments productively. Many of us, in fact, have been socialized to respond with fear and avoidance versus care and constructive guidance. There are many curricula (some you'll find in appendix C) for direct CSE teaching. I find it provides support and guidance for the organic, spontaneous moments throughout the school day that many folks, no matter what role they play in a school, are looking for.

Bodies: We experience and express our sexuality through our bodies. *Bodily autonomy*—or the understanding that our bodies belong to us and that we have rights and responsibilities to make our own choices about our bodies and have the skills to claim those rights—is an important aspect of healthy sexual development. Knowledge is the cornerstone of responsibility and empowerment. Children are capable of learning about their bodies and how to begin taking care of them. Appropriate vocabulary, hygiene, and personal space are all important early concepts. When children know the correct anatomical terms for all parts of their bodies, including their genitals, how they work, and how to take care of them, they feel more comfortable and confident in asserting and protecting themselves. The kid who learns to say, "I don't want a hug, but we could go out to the swings together," can become a teenager who learns to say, "I'm not comfortable with you posting that pic of me in the bathing suit, but the one of us hanging out at the mall is okay," can become a young adult who says, "I don't appreciate you resting your hand on my lower back. I keep my work relationships professional." This frees us to enjoy our bodies and share them with others on our terms.

Gender and Sexuality Diversity (GSD): GSD is a construct created by psychologist and educational consultant Jennifer Bryan. GSD includes everyone and recognizes the centrality of gender and sexuality in all human beings. In the school setting, adults and kids alike have a gender identity and sexuality. These are inherently diverse (biodiversity) and essential aspects of our identity.[30] Gender identity is a person's psychological sense of self: who they know themselves to be in their alignment—or lack thereof—with physical characteristics of different genders. It's a person's deep internal sense of being female, male, a combination of both, somewhere in between, or neither, resulting from a multifaceted interaction of biological traits, environmental factors, self-understanding, and cultural expectations. The old way of thinking is built on a binary idea of gender: male and female. Today, most people embrace a broader definition of gender, one that recognizes a spectrum between the binaries.[31]

Sexual orientation and gender are culturally typically conflated; however, they are quite separate. The founder of Gender Spectrum and author Stephanie Brill (with Rachel Pepper) say it beautifully in *The Transgender Child*: "Gender and sexual orientation are two distinct, but related, aspects of self. Gender is personal while sexual orientation is interpersonal. While these are two separate aspects of each person, they are defined by gender, so it can feel confusing. A person's sexual orientation reflects the gender(s) of those they are attracted to."[32] So, if gender describes who you are, sexual orientation refers to who you have romantic feelings about or who you might want to be intimate with. It's an enduring emotional, romantic, sexual, or affectional attraction or nonattraction to other people. Sexual orientation can be fluid and people use a variety of labels to describe their sexual orientation.[33] For a resource list of terms and definitions, see appendix C.

As educators, it is our responsibility to teach to the whole child—each and every one who sits in our classrooms—and to affirm who they are and the family structures and communities they come from. We are also charged with providing them with the information and skills they will need to transition into and navigate the realities of the world we all live in. That includes the myriad ways people express themselves and relate to each other. There has been an incredible effort over the last few decades to create safer schools for LGBTQ+ students. Recent politics threaten this progress and the well-being of all students as a result. We must continue to center students in our work and stand for LGBTQ+ kids and families as we strive for caring and loving educational spaces for all. Michael Sadowski puts it well: "Safety is an essential baseline for skills to meet the needs of LGBTQ students effectively . . . but is not a sufficient goal in itself.[34] It is imperative that we not essentialize and further the 'othering' of LGBTQ youth by isolating LGBTQ 'issues,' but rather integrate LGBTQ learning into all that we provide, so that we go beyond safe spaces (albeit important) to create an overall learning culture of inclusivity and equity that 'is palpable in every hallway and classroom of the school.'"[35]

Feelings: Our feelings are one of the primary aspects of what make us human. Learning to identify, express, and harness our feelings—even the most challenging ones—can help us create positive, satisfying lives.[36] Connecting with and naming feelings in ourselves and observing and connecting with feelings in others is an essential building block for healthy decision-making. The current mental health crisis is the result of many complicated factors, of course, and building skills alone will not solve all those issues, but it will help young people recognize and better cope with some of the challenges they are facing. In 2023, the CDC released The Youth Risk Behavior Survey, which documents record levels of sadness and anxiety in teen girls. Adolescent girls reported record levels of depression, suicidal thoughts, and sexual violence, as did LGBTQ+ youth. Reporting focused on the experience of girls specifically, as well as LGBTQ+ youth; however, it is suspected that gender differences may mask the aggressive and violent behavior in boys that can signal depression as well.[37] Feeling skills are essential for well-being throughout childhood, adolescence, and adulthood, and like all skills, developing them takes practice. Ultimately, it is in our student's best interest to aspire towards a variety of feeling skills—which Marc Brackett, founding director at the Yale Center for Emotional Intelligence, and his team have distilled in *Permission to Feel*. Those skills include recognizing one's own emotions and those of others—not just in the things we think, feel, and say but facial expressions, body language, vocal tones, and other nonverbal signals—understanding those feelings and where they come from, naming emotions with nuanced vocabulary, expressing feelings in accordance with cultural norms and social contexts in a way that informs and invites empathy from the listener, and regulating emotions instead of having them regulate us.[38]

RELATIONSHIPS (CONSENT, COMMUNICATION, AND DECISION-MAKING)

Consent: Consent is the foundation of all relationships. It protects the fundamentals of human dignity and is what holds everything in a relationship up. Consent laws are in place to protect people when they may not be able to protect themselves. Consent in all relationships is about asking permission. It's an agreement, anchored in a mutual understanding, for something to happen. Sexual consent recognizes that our bodies and our sexuality belong to us, so we get to choose what happens to them, and we must take responsibility for how we honor other people's rights to do the same. Young people need to understand their rights and responsibilities when it comes to consent. The child who says, "I'm not comfortable with a 'hi' kiss, do you want to fist bump?" could become the middle school kid who says, "I meant what I said, I need to study for my test, but I'd love to hang out later," could become the older teenager who says, "Stop trying to convince me, I'll tell you when I'm ready." The knowledge, especially in regard to identity and power, skills, and practice that empowers a young person to stand up for themselves takes time and lessons that start early and continue as they move into adulthood. I know many people my age who are still working on whether they truly want to say yes or no.

Communication: Lessons in effective communication give language and voice to students to talk about their bodies and sexuality for themselves and with others. The capacity to not just know about important concepts like consent but to put them into practice requires language, skills, and practice. Context is everything in relationships and contributes towards the emotional embodied experiences we have in them. How we understand ourselves, each other, and express that is an essential component of getting our needs met, meeting the needs of others, and building connections within relationships. How we communicate with someone makes a difference—it can be the pathway to greater intimacy, which is a cornerstone of feeling connected and an overall sense of well-being.

Decision-making: The neuroplasticity of child and adolescent development presents an incredible opportunity. Young people's brains grow from the back forward. Cognitive development in biological females is not complete until early to midtwenties and for biological males, late twenties to early thirties. *Myelination*, the process by which the brain organizes itself by insulating neuropathways to establish patterns of behavior based on a young person's behavioral choices, is in process. Being intentional and bringing attention to this development is invaluable in learning how to make decisions that positively contribute to our well-being. Knowledge, critical thinking, awareness of social interpersonal power dynamics, context, and potential consequences and benefits are all aspects of informed decision-making that keeps us healthy, safe and receptive to learning. This practice primarily happens during the school years of a person's life, so what better time than to intentionally address it?

CONNECTION (INTIMACY AND LOVE)

Intimacy: In a culture that all too often pushes young people to disconnect, evade vulnerability, and prioritize performance, kids are looking for more connection. Human beings need connection to thrive. We have a desire to be close to other people—we are social animals. Human connection contributes to our overall well-being. The psychological and physical health benefits of social contact can outweigh many risk factors and actually increase our longevity. Having positive relationships with family, friends, and community helps us recover from stress, anxiety, and depression. It promotes healthy eating and physical activity, improves sleep, well-being, and quality of life. It can help prevent serious illnesses like heart disease, stroke, dementia, anxiety, and depression.[39] Feeling connected to others cultivates joy in our lives through reciprocity, empathy, care, and love.[40]

Love: There are not many conversations about the meaning of love in our culture right now. Through teaching over thirty years and working with thousands of students, I have yet to meet one who doesn't long for intimate connection and love. Yet, there is a cynicism about love, especially its power as a transformative force, that seems to currently pervade among them. My students tend to associate love with vulnerability, which they mistake for weakness. I believe this comes from a misunderstanding or lack of knowing about what love is, what the practice of it looks, sounds, and feels like, and how critical it is to living a fulfilled and enriched life. Many people think that CSE is about health and skills, which is certainly true, but it's really about cultivating the capacity to love and be loved. We must open our students' eyes, minds, and hearts to the promise of love.

Facilitate lessons in discovery that deepen student understanding about what they may figure out about love so far in their lives—all of us know that love evolves as we journey through life. Have students construct questions that express curiosity about the unique experience of romantic love through Love Interviews. I have heard student-conducted interviews on new love, mature love, unrequited love, unspoken love (grandparents revealing first love that was never known to family), and everlasting love. Deconstruct love songs and what they represent universally, yet consider Leo Tolstoy's famed quote: "If it is true that there are as many minds as there are heads; then there are as many kinds of love as there are hearts." The look in a student's eye when the epiphany strikes: it is in how we express it in relationship with a special someone else. Identify acts of love such as listening deeply with focused attention, expressing appreciation for the positive ways someone impacts their life, or empathetic support when someone shares their pain: "I don't know what to say right now, and I'm so glad you told me." Discuss love languages and consent. The possibilities are endless and paramount.

In his 2024 Convocation speech to Harvard Graduate School of Education graduates, faculty speaker Irvin Scott recognizes how love inspires those of us who teach. A "Love for TEACHING. Love for STUDENTS. Love for FAMILY AND COMMUNITIES."[41] Embrace this love and share it with students.

SAFETY

The American Academy of Pediatrics states, "Children and teens who feel in control of their bodies are less likely to fall prey to sexual abusers, and if they do suffer abuse, they are more likely to tell a trusted adult—which can make all the difference in stopping the events and subsequently helping them recover from this painful experience."[42] Group-based instruction in classrooms has been found to be an effective strategy to reduce adolescent pregnancy, HIV, and STIs.[43] If that instruction includes refusal skills during CSE before college matriculation, students are at lower risk of experiencing sexual assault at college as well.[44] These harm reduction skills and strategies are an essential component of CSE. Students have the opportunity to acquire knowledge and practice with skills that build confidence and cultivate the capacity to assert oneself and make informed choices that help keep themselves, their friends, and their partners healthy and safe.

These dimensions of sexuality instruction will all contribute to a comprehensive, positive, and proactive sexuality education that addresses all the needs of the person's developing sexuality: learning about love, desire, intimacy, friendship, and commitment; enhancing self-esteem; improving relationship skills (beyond disease prevention only); clarifying one's values; examining gender roles and stereotypes; recognizing and appreciating diversity; developing skills in life planning, problem solving, and healthy living; becoming a critical consumer of media messages;

exploring spiritual aspects of sexuality; and achieving personal success and happiness, within or outside of a sexual relationship.[45]

CREATING SAFE, HEALTHY LEARNING ENVIRONMENTS FOR ALL STUDENTS

The Psychology of Space

When establishing trust with and among students, pay attention to the physical classroom environment. Historically, traditional individual desks and rows were strategic in promoting individual work and achievement. Since conversations about adolescence are meant to foster connection and encourage effective communication skills between and among each other, consider moving furniture around. Ask students to assist in creating large circles where everyone can see each other, cluster chairs and/or desks together in smaller groups, or angle chairs and desks so that neighbors can turn and talk to each other. Think about how physical obstacles may translate into emotional ones and arrange your classroom accordingly. If you are introducing a sensitive topic, for example, students may benefit from the grounding security of a desk in front of them. If you facilitate a discussion that you hope will lead to connection through solidarity, remove the desks and stick with chairs in a circle or have everyone sit on the floor. To reach the diverse range of learning styles that are a part of every classroom, take time to write keywords and concepts on the board, have students take turns with leadership roles during dialogue, and combine pedagogical approaches—dyads, triads, small groups, role play, presentations, larger group discussion, hand building, artistic expression, individual reflection, and personal writing etc.—to allow for various modalities that address all learning preferences. Be clear, direct, and concrete with various cues and structures for neurodiverse learners.

Cultivating Care and Dignity in Community

A requisite for building a class environment that allows for healthy vulnerability includes class guidelines and concrete expectations for behavior. Many educators refer to these as a *Creed for Caring*, a *Class Constitution*, or *Class Commitments* etc. If you are challenged for time, you may want to interview students outside of class and ask what they need to feel safe in class. You may synthesize their feedback and share it with your class. Establish what each guideline means with examples so as to ensure students' understanding and accountability. If you have more time, you may engage your students in creating the guidelines. You could have everyone write three things they need to feel open and inspired on a post-it to put on a wall. Go over the requests together as a class and come up with a shared language for recognizing the shared needs of the class.

When beginning with elementary age students, encourage asset-based affirmations versus dos and don'ts. And recognize that this may be tricky for multilingual learners. Investing time in understanding cultural contexts and different cultural associations with language is essential. Discuss that safety looks and feels different to different people. Again, a culturally responsive approach is important. Here are some examples of what typically comes up.

For elementary age students:

- Take turns: Everyone gets to share their voice and participate.
- Listen with care: Understanding helps us help each other.
- Treat others with respect: Everyone deserves to feel safe.
- Work together: Cooperation builds community.
- Make a mistake, learn, and love (yourself and other people): We're all growing, it's never too late to make it right.

To communicate these ideas you could project images of certain animals like a turtle (goes into its shell), a tiger (gets big and roars), a gazelle (runs and hides), and a shark (strikes) and then ask, "How do they keep themselves safe? What are the different ways they protect and defend themselves?" and "How does this connect to the different ways people respond to different situations when they may feel unsafe?" or "What about this information can help us understand each other better and share commitments to safety at school?"

Contemplating community, its significance and value, is critical. In an ever more individualistic society, ideas of citizenship, interdependence, and valuable social connectedness within communities is eroding. Competition stemming from that merit-based individualism and getting ahead or being perceived best at any cost creates obstacles to learning. When students are competitive above all else, it is difficult to foster an environment of cooperation. Common guidelines such as these keep us on track in the spirit of community.

For middle and high school students:

- Personalize your knowledge: Encourage students to speak for themselves by using "I" statements.
- Suspend judgment: Acknowledge how many people fear being judged for what they may say. Acknowledge that you are working together to create a space where students can be honest and sincere in the interest of learning how to make the community a healthy one for all.
- Respect the process: This is an exploration. Be patient and generous with each other. Be present and engaged through active listening and not interrupting.
- Listen to understand: Be attentive to what someone else is saying. This is the respect that all of us deserve and should expect for ourselves. Many times, we immediately think of what we want to say in response to someone else's sharing. Suspend that initial impulse and hear each other out entirely. Use this opportunity to learn from your peers. If you agree with what they are saying, it gives you more to consider. If you don't agree, it can further define what you think is right. You benefit either way.
- Lean into discomfort: Conversations that have to do with difficult topics and sexuality can be uncomfortable. It's important to be resilient when confronted with awkward and challenging situations. These situations can yield the most growth.
- License to fumble and use the word *ouch*: Acknowledge that these conversations may be challenging and that it's okay to make mistakes.

If someone says something that is offensive to another, simply say the word *ouch*. Pause in that moment to address the issue.

- Confidentiality: It is unrealistic to expect that no one will repeat personal sharing that takes place in the classroom; however, it is fair to expect of students to not violate others' vulnerability by gossiping, trash talking, mocking, or ridiculing what others have said. While we actually want the learning to leave the room, it's the personal sharing that stays private.

Be prepared to deal with conflicts as they arise. Be open and direct with your intervention. Avoid engaging in a deep teach when you may use the moment as a lesson for all that could be experienced as public humiliation and shame, recognize the behavior, and start with "I notice . . . " Do not give more attention than necessary to the behavior (public humiliation is unproductive), and default to meeting with the student or students during a break, small-group activity, or after class. Move to resume. You may need to pivot towards a different structure for the activity while you restore what's been compromised (typically trust) among students.

Due to the sociopolitical history and stigmatization of sexuality in the US, many young people are not used to discussing healthy sexuality in constructive ways. Should this happen with topics that may be uncomfortable for students, here are a few suggestions:

- Elementary aged students: "I get how this might feel silly or embarrassing, which makes sense since it's a grown-up kind of thing, and we need to find a way to focus. What might we do?"
- Middle school aged students: "Sometimes people laugh in classes like this because they feel uncomfortable or they've only heard about this topic as something funny or negative to talk about. I want to remind us that we're in a classroom and we're going to take it down a notch so we can focus on learning."

If you are asked a gratuitous or inappropriate question, maintain your position as the adult in the room and narrate what's happening with "I notice . . . " If the question is for humorous effect (typically included in anonymous question boxes), you could say, "This question feels like it may not be serious, and I take this class and your questions seriously, so I'm going to answer it as best I can" or "I wonder what the person who wrote this question is going for by asking it, so I'm going to respond to it (in this way)," or "Responding to this question doesn't feel productive to me but I will say (this)."

When you discuss healthy relationships with your students, it's possible that there are some social dynamics among students that you don't know about. Students may use class as an opportunity to bring this up and put a fellow classmate "on trial." Do not allow this to happen. Emphasize using "I" statements, and be clear that we don't use specific names to discuss others in class settings. If there is an issue, they are welcome to bring it to you after class.

As students get older, teachers may assume they get it by now when it comes to value-laden class guidelines and expectations and conclude that there isn't a reason to take valuable class time to re-establish parameters for how to treat each other. But messaging may become inconsistent if students are no longer in self-contained classrooms. It is always a good idea (even with adults) to be explicit and clear about community norms and values to develop caring classrooms and students. I frequently facilitate workshops for high school seniors about sex and drugs in college, and I always open by establishing guidelines. When I ask them, "How many of you have been taught to respect yourself and those around you your whole life?" Every single hand goes up. When I follow with, "Okay great, who can give me a definition?" there is a pause and then all of the hands go down. Through our exploration, it is revealed that most assume *respect* means treating others how you want to be treated. There is value in this; however, it isn't exactly respect. Especially within the context of relationships, respect is treating others how they want to be treated. This critical nuance is essential to the capacity for practicing consent. Be consistent with creeds for caring. The fundamentals can make all the difference.

Disclosure

When we create safe spaces and facilitate classroom conversations that feel more personal, there is the possibility of student disclosure. To manage disclosure, include parameters as a part of your class guidelines. Be concrete and specific about how people may share publicly. You may say, "Even though we commit to a certain level of confidentiality, our classroom is still a public space. If class brings up something deeply personal, hold onto it and we can discuss it individually after class," and follow with, "Another reason is that I, and all adults who work with students here, are mandated reporters [to whatever local social services requires], which means depending on the nature of what you share, if I think it is harmful, I am obligated to report it, and I wouldn't want you to create a situation where you don't have choices." It is also possible that students may ask you personal questions that you don't want or aren't appropriate for you to discuss. For instance, "When did you lose your virginity?" It is important to model being open while maintaining privacy and student-teacher boundaries. You may say, "I appreciate your question, the topic of virginity is an interesting one that we can talk about, and it is not something I choose to speak publicly about, not only because it's private but also because it is in the interest of our relationship as student and teacher."

It is important that all educators know what they are mandated to report, how to make a report, and to which organizations (Child Protective Services and/or a division of your local police department). These organizations offer training and welcome questions on the phone as well. If a student does in fact reach out to you with a disclosure, it is important to open with your responsibility as a mandated reporter and elaborate on what you would have to report. Some students will choose to speak hypothetically or about "a friend." Be sure about your responsibilities to hearsay or suspicion. You may say, "I appreciate you telling me. That was really brave. In the interest of your well-being and our relationship as teacher/student, it's important that we find you the best support. I don't have those skills or training, but I know how to get you to someone who does. How about talking about some options?" You can certainly offer nontherapeutic emotional care and listen to how your student is feeling. In response you may mirror language (not interpret what you think they are telling you or feeling) and assess who they would be comfortable talking to on your campus. Many school counselors are a tremendous source of guidance and support. They may offer consistent language that educators can use when receiving a disclosure. This keeps the student at the center of the situation so that they may be supported in the best possible way.

Culturally Responsive Teaching

We live in a multicultural nation, a pluralistic society. This diversity is a reality, not a choice—how we respond to it is. US schools are increasingly ethnically, racially, and economically diverse; therefore, culturally responsive teaching is mandatory in respect to the humanity and rights of diverse students.[46] This book assumes that we, as educators and people who care about children, believe in the intrinsic worth of every student. This means that, for those devoted to teaching the whole child, we must honor an asset-based perspective that respects and embraces cultural differences as a resource. Culture is ever evolving, so the components of culturally responsive teaching must be congruent as a dynamic, dialectical, and interwoven process as well.

Celebrated and distinguished professor of education at University of Washington, Geneva Gay, writes: "Since how someone thinks, writes and speaks reflects culture and affects performance, aligning instruction to the cultural communication styles of different ethnic groups can improve school achievement."[47] It is not enough to appreciate multiculturalism, we must actively embrace all that it requires. We cannot teach what we don't know, so it is critical that we reach out with cultural humility to build community within our classrooms and beyond, including our student's families. Co-construct curricula with students that contextualizes information, makes the abstract concrete, makes various facts understandable, and allows for multiple linguistic and social styles.

In this book, we will revisit time and again how we may guide students to self-reflection, self-regulation, and a critical consciousness; Through these they may identify and start to understand contextual dynamics and possible responses and results in ways that validate and affirm various identities. This cultivates an organic process that encourages students to develop their unique voice, develop skills for social citizenship, and how to live in community with each other and us. The pedagogical possibilities for this are continuous and included in this book, especially the value of story. Stories—those of teachers, parents, administrators, policy makers and students—anchor the writing of this book. Other culturally responsive practices you'll find or options through which you may teach include:

Honing linguistic heritages	**Visual images and symbols**	**Direct questioning**
Communication styles and tools for resonance (call & response, snaps, stand up/sit down) Small group work/dialogue	Media: digital recordings, film, photographs, audio recordings, literature, music Tactile and kinetic modalities Movement/performance	Deductive reasoning Storytelling Contextualizing/stage-setting Collaborative & negotiated problem-solving

The culturally responsive relational processes we model and facilitate in our classrooms will lead to positive self-concepts, pride in one's ethnic identity, and ultimately improve academic achievement.[48] Gay writes, "These relational competencies must encompass knowing, valuing, doing, caring, and sharing power, resources and responsibilities. Hence developing sociocivic skills for effective membership in multicultural communities is an important goal of culturally responsive pedagogy as improving the academic achievement and personal development of students of color."[49] This overlaps with the approaches and benefits of CSE. As you read the following chapters, I hope it is evident that culturally responsive CSE is a benefit to all students.

Being Restorative

Restorative justice is a process that builds community and cultivates relationships among a group of participants. It contextualizes interpersonal dynamics and promotes equity with how it holds people accountable to "right a wrong" in the spirit of our shared humanity.[50] This invaluable community endeavor recognizes how we are all connected and disrupts the systemic inequalities and injustices that affect many American youth, especially young people of color. Kids mess up. We all do. When we move away from zero tolerance policies that lead to fear-based compliance and isolation and instead focus on a nuanced understanding of harm, the needs of those harmed, and those who caused the harm, we work towards true repair and learning. We support our commitment to deepen the resilience, compassion, and empathy that will support relationships among each other and learning communities.

The tenets of restorative practices overlap and intersect with CSE. A professor in the School of Education at the University of California, Davis, and codirector of the Transformative Justice in Education Center, Maisha T. Winn, poses an essential question: "What can teachers and staff *do* to address discipline in their classrooms? How can classrooms be organized physically in ways that facilitate restorative justice?"[51] Her book, *Justice on Both Sides*, answers these questions brilliantly. CSE focuses on the information, skills, and capacities that support this work.

This book is all about how we may authentically connect with our students and support their connections among each other. Transformative justice is a critical approach to how we approach the causes and consequences of harm within the community—I find many educators think of it as *interventive,* which is true. CSE supports the restorative *preventative* measures that empower young people to access their feelings, be accountable for their behavior, and communicate their needs and honor those of others. Both restorative justice and CSE value how we bring our humanity to relationships while being in and connected to community.

Neurodiversity

We all have a learning style that best serves us and poses challenges given different educational contexts. This natural variation in cognitive function contributes to our individuality. For students who have identified learning differences, learning disorders or disabilities, difficulty reading social cues, and understanding concepts (such as empathy) may require a variety of concrete approaches and supplemental direct instruction. Many of the interviews I conducted to write this book revealed how neurodiverse students are integrated into classrooms with support that ranged from Independent Education Plans (IEPs) and neuropsychological evaluations to one-on-one paraprofessional support in addition to general classroom instruction. Teachers, parents, and administrators attested to the benefits reaped by all students when explicit consent was required to support neurodiverse students in their classes as well as how some neurodiverse students might become a distraction when activated by certain language and concepts related to sexuality. Moreover, teachers recognized their need to model what they teach by engaging in clear communication with paraprofessional support staff regarding thresholds of and limits for individual student behavior and classroom community responsibilities. Collaboration amongst adults on understanding and preventing neurodiverse issues while supporting sexuality education and responding to inappropriate behaviors without marginalizing neurodiverse kids is needed. For resources that can support these efforts, see appendix C.

Self-care

Teaching is an incredibly demanding profession, so I want to recognize that engaging with this book may feel overwhelming and like a lot of additional work. It may activate a range of emotions that could include curiosity, relief, inspiration, trepidation, frustration, and/or fear. This writing is in response to the many educators I've worked with who seek guidance on how to address the organic teachable moments in schools that involve sexuality with care and affirmation versus fear and shame. My hope is that it will open up possibilities, no matter how big or small, and provide concrete language, strategies, and resources for support. As this book encourages us to cultivate empathy, care, respect, and dignity for our students, please allow for the grace, patience, and pace that will feel like that for you.

2

Building the Foundation

Kindergarten Through Grade Two

Play is the work of childhood.

~ Piaget

The focus of early elementary comprehensive sexuality education (CSE) is family, friends, feelings and fairness. The focus of CSE, anchored in those topics at this age, is about how we develop as people, people in relationships with each other, in community, as well as science, otherwise known as *sexuality* (not *sex*). In my experience, some people resist conversations about sexuality with this age group because they assume it will be intercourse education, which it is not. There is a difference between telling kids about sex and talking with kids about sexuality. In fact, research demonstrates that early exposure to good quality sexuality education has implications for improved mental and physical well-being and cultivates the ability to develop appropriate skills to avoid sexual exploitation and abuse.[1] Prosocial behaviors in kindergarten indicate key outcomes in adolescents and adults. In fact, CSE encourages these behaviors—such as effectively regulating emotions, social empathy, and positive attitudes—which lead to healthy personal development and adult well-being.[2] This chapter will demonstrate how we may use cognitively congruent language and strategies to respond to issues of sexuality with younger children.

WHY BEGIN CSE IN KINDERGARTEN?

Ideally, students' exposure to CSE starts early in life because what is learned in the younger years will have a lasting impact on how sexuality is managed later on. Social-Emotional Learning (SEL) is a primary component of this education. SEL is the anchor of CSE in the early years and has been documented in studies to promote positive youth development.[3] SEL competency in children is cited as a critical factor in social, behavioral, and academic healthy development, which promotes resilience and important life outcomes in adulthood.[4] In a contemporary meta-analysis of Universal School-Based Interventions, Christina Cipriano et al. found that SEL has a significant impact on academic, social, and emotional thriving. Evidence shows that students who receive Universal School-Based SEL interventions experienced improved self-efficacy, self-esteem, perseverance, optimism, and moral or ethical reasoning.[5] In addition to increased prosocial behaviors, SEL resulted in a reduction in emotional distress, violence/aggression, behavioral problems, and bullying.[6] Moreover, places and spaces of safety where students felt inclusion, connection, and belonging led to students flourishing.[7] CSE that starts early is a guide that aims to develop and strengthen the ability of students to make informed, conscious, healthy, and respectful choices in regards to their sexuality and relationships throughout their lives.[8] Sexuality thus becomes as much a part of their development as language learning, motor skills, communication, and self-esteem."[9]

PARENTS, FAMILIES, AND SCHOOLS AS PARTNERS IN CSE

The best approach for families and schools is to see themselves as partners who care about the well-being of young people. This requires us to keep young people at the center of educational spaces and programs.

Parents and guardians are the primary sexuality educator in a child's life. I don't know any professional sexuality educators who believe otherwise. But, parents aren't the only ones. Schools play an important role as a primary nurturing community as well. Schools can offer formal, ongoing instruction in a planned and sequenced way. They can also uphold core values—this is a mission-driven conversation after all. Look at any school's mission, guiding principles, and philosophy, and you will find consistent references to humanitarian citizenship, youth character development, and ethical community building and sustainability. Each partner has its unique offering: only parents can tell a child what they personally value around sexuality and other important issues.[10] Schools can provide a context in which children can learn shared community values, consistent language, and information together, so when they learn about *how* to have relationships with each other, they will do so in an environment that promotes prosocial skill-building behaviors and helps them develop social-emotional capacities like empathy, mutual respect, and honesty.

Socialization with students is happening all of the time. K–2 teachers are constantly bringing students together and sitting down with them and coaching to problem solve throughout the school day. Sometimes, when there are so many different energies and skill levels in a room, our guidance isn't always a well-planned lesson but in response to what's happening in a moment. Leading with mutual respect and empathy are essential. Children are observant and have a high awareness of their environment and adult behavior. What educators know is that the most effective way to teach something is to model it ourselves, which means cultivating and reflecting our own kindness, compassion, and humanity. What students see when they walk into their classroom, how they are recognized and received by their teacher and classmates, and how they experience social interactions all contribute to their sense of belonging.[11]

Developmental highlights:

- Children are starting to learn about the world through media. We want young learners to become critical consumers of media.

- Children are capable of logical ideas, independent thinking, and responsible action.
- It is essential to teach that sexuality is a broad topic that includes many aspects of our identities and experiences and that it is a natural and healthy part of life.
- It is important to emphasize that all people should be treated fairly and equitably.[12]

BODIES

Primary students explore the world through their bodies and learn best when their bodies and movement are fully integrated into their learning.[13] They have a natural curiosity about bodies and how they work, which provides an opportunity to build vocabulary, as well as foster a connection with and care for their physical development. To promote acceptance and esteem, send the message that all bodies are equally special and come in different sizes, shapes, colors, textures, and abilities. These differences make us unique. It is normal that most children are curious about their bodies and the bodies of others, and it is important for the adults in their lives to meet this curiosity without shame and encourage pride and appreciation.

Morning meeting time is effective for introducing concepts of body awareness and everyday consent. Many elementary-age classrooms include gathering together on a rug that has concrete visible circles or squares to anchor a student in their spot. When selecting the rug for your classroom, consider options. There are rugs that are very geometric and the spaces are uniform; however, this does not allow for much body size diversity. What if you have a child who is more comfortable sitting with their legs out in front of them versus cross-legged? Now, there are rugs with various sized leaves, for instance, arranged in a patterned circle. This provides structure yet allows for some flexibility based on comfort levels and provides some choice relative to what students know about how they give their attention best. So much of this early learning is about personal space, in addition to what our bodies are about, how they feel, and how to take care of them. Embrace opportunities for discussion about connecting to one's physical self.

Cognitive skills are built on a foundation of sensory integration. Encourage students to learn through playful movement and invite them to explore their feelings through their bodies. This body-mind connection encourages learning and literacy.[14] Have conversations about how our bodies do amazing things; for instance, they provide information about what we need so that we may take care of them. Normalize the idea that, our bodies and how we feel about them are a part of our well-being. For instance, you can ask, "How do you know when you're hungry? Full? Tired? That you need to move?" and provide analogous examples and embodied language for how it may feel: "When I'm hungry, I feel hollow in my brain," or "My legs feel wobbly or weak," or "I get a pain in my tummy." Encourage recognizing signals and take it further to identify needs: "If I feel hungry, what can I eat that will give me energy?" or "What kind of play or movement would make me feel energized and ready to focus?" Guiding children towards intuitive responses to what their bodies are telling them builds a foundation for informed decision-making, mind-body connection, and inspires caretaking for overall health. Consider asking students to identify a feeling they have before recess and then after. Many will notice how healthy, active play will boost mood.

In addition, planned lessons on body vocabulary and care concepts are encouraged. Research tells us that children who have medically accurate language for all parts of their bodies, including genitals, are less vulnerable to predatory adults because it is evident that there is a caring adult openly talking about bodies and bodily autonomy with that child. Sexual abuse relies on secrecy and shame to occur and persist. Not only does knowing the correct anatomical terms build children's self-confidence, but it also makes them less susceptible to those who may want to harm them. According to The National Sexual Violence Resource Center, we need all adults to be partners in teaching healthy childhood sexual development, starting with body parts. Educators and parents should communicate accurately without stigma or shame.[15] Knowing the accurate anatomical terms for genitalia is a protection factor that supports a child's confidence in setting boundaries.[16] Open dialogue is a deterrent, so include lessons that address external and internal body parts and emphasize how amazing bodies are.[17] (Specific messaging about touch, including "secret" or "bad" touch will be discussed later in this chapter.)

Visual representations and books are always helpful as modalities for instruction. There are several books that have age-appropriate visuals representing sexual reproductive anatomy that can be used to provide a body parts and systems lesson (see appendix C for references). Some of the books I recommend are banned, despite being written for elementary-school-age students, or have been taken off the shelves in certain school districts. It is imperative to recognize that there are external political realities that many teachers may have to contend with if they use some of these books in their classrooms. Think through what and how you may provide your students with what will support their knowledge and growth and maintain job security. In addition to the antisexuality education surveillance coming from some political and cultural forces, there are the possible internal associations for some teachers when considering using these age-appropriate books as well. The drawings included in these books are medically accurate representations of bodies. The meaning we give to representations of bodies within the context of education is socially constructed and rooted in sociopolitical historical contexts that shape our ideas about sexuality. If you are uncomfortable with visual depictions of human bodies, consider this is a learned association that you have been socialized to experience in that way. This is about science and protective factors, not instruction in the mechanics of sex. Normalizing conversations about whole bodies is aligned with teaching the whole child. As mentioned throughout this text, evidence-based research indicates that children who present as comfortable with their bodies and the topic of sexuality—specifically sexual reproductive anatomy—as a normal aspect of overall health are at less risk of sexual harm and exploitation.[18]

Note that we may refer to genitals as "private parts," which means they are special, just for us, and that we get to make decisions about them. All important; however, consider the wise words of Debbie Roffman: "People don't have private parts and public parts. They just have parts, and some of those parts we keep more private than others most of the time. That's a concept all children can grasp and learn to apply."[19] This nuanced approach is important so that we can build upon it as young people gain more autonomy over their bodies and when they have to make choices about their bodies for themselves. Again, we want to avoid associating certain parts of our bodies with secrecy or shame. We want children to feel comfortable and confident in their bodies and be accountable for how they experience them.

When it comes to bodies, we live in a culture that tends to value appearance above all else. Building a counter-narrative that builds body appreciation and esteem focuses on function versus aesthetics. Begin with sentence stems like, "My body can . . ." You may find that children this age are already socialized to default to appearance-based observations. Provide examples to emphasize what bodies can *do* versus how they *look*. For instance: "My body can digest food and heal from a cold" (an internal process); "My body can run during tag and climb my favorite tree" (physical capacity); "My body can smile and experience fun" (senses/sensations); "My body can draw and play musical instruments" (creative pursuits); "My body can express words and show how I'm feeling through body language" (communication); and "My body can hug a friend if they want when they're feeling sad" (supportive care).[20] You get the idea. There are other activities that promote function, like "The Best Part of Me," in which students identify a part of their body that enables them to do something positive for themselves. I remember when my own children did this assignment. One chose her "legs because they let [her] play as much as [she does]." This was part of an art project that included her statement and a picture of her running and playing. She painted a frame for it and put it up on our wall at home. The list of activities goes on and simultaneously encourages prosocial skills like appreciation, compassion, care, and empathy. Critical to these relational capacities and bodily autonomy is the concept and practice of consent.

Consent is about discovering what makes us comfortable and uncomfortable—what we want and don't want. It includes setting boundaries, talking about feelings and what we need, and paying attention to and respecting each other.

In 2015, affirmative consent legislation inspired some schools to be more intentional about teaching consent in an effort to prevent sexual harm. Any school engaged in antibullying is already doing this work. Just like all other skills we teach students, cultivating the capacity to act consensually, especially within variable contexts, takes time and practice. Starting early is imperative. Many early elementary educators are doing this; however, they may not use the concrete language and terms attached to it that will enable a clear understanding of how consent looks, sounds, and feels across time. Since society has historically stigmatized sexuality, as children get older, they may not realize how the principles of everyday consent apply to other aspects of their lives, including romantic and/or sexual relationships. Therefore, we must be intentional about slowly bridging principles of consent across contexts in concrete ways as young people grow and change so that those skills stay in constant practice.

Bodily autonomy is an important concept that has gained more traction over the years, especially since evidence-based studies reveal its importance as a protective factor against sexual abuse. Expressions such as "I'm the boss of my body," "My body belongs to me," or "My body, my choice," align with concepts of consent; however, many folks forget to include an essential component when it comes to children. In reality, there are some adults who are entrusted with the power to make decisions for kids that include their bodies but may not be what that child wants in the moment yet is important for their health and safety. Examples include: if a child is still learning toileting skills, becoming dysregulated, resisting holding hands when crossing a busy street during a field trip, unwilling to put a seatbelt on in the school bus, tantruming in a physically risky way, or refusing to wear mittens when it's freezing outside. It's important to model boundary setting with students, so if you need to appropriately state, "Some things we can talk about and some things are just the rules," in your role as care-taking adult, do so. *Context* is an important caveat to discuss, because we may undermine or confuse children with the "I choose what happens to my body" idea with our well-intentioned exceptions. Be specific and concrete about different contexts as well, because in rare cases, it may be one of these caretaking adults who harms a child.

Children need to understand that, Yes, [you] are in charge of your body, *and* there are exceptions when your health and safety or that of others is at risk, and an adult, such as a doctor (with your parenting adult present), teacher (not including your genitals or 'privates' unless you have a bathroom accident and need help getting clean), or parent (if you need help cleaning up after using the bathroom or your privates itch or hurt), needs to make a decision to keep you healthy and safe.

SCENARIO: Your kindergarten class is filing out for dismissal and carpool pickup. It's a chilly twelve degrees outside, and Alexa can't find her gloves. Your class is getting squirrely in line, and you are trying to help Alexa find her mittens in the cubby and coats area. Neither of you can find them, so you go into the extras bin and find a pair of cozy brown mittens—whew! As you go to put them on her, Alex protests, "Those are brown. Brown is a boy color. I won't wear those." Alexa hides her hands behind her back while sticking her chin out with a determined look. You need to get the kids out to the carpool line, which is typically long and arduous to get through, so you say, "Come on, we need to get to dismissal. Please put these on." You're met with an assertive "No." (Vermont Public School District, VT)

In the case of Alexa, narrate what you are doing and the reason. "I hear that you don't like the color, and we will talk about colors later. Right now, we need to go to dismissal, so we don't have time to wait, and it is really cold outside. To keep your hands from getting too cold/hurt, we are going to put these gloves on because they are the only ones we've got." Alexa may then decide to comply in that moment, and if she doesn't you may say, "So now I am going to put the gloves on your hands so they will stay warm." Put the gloves on the child. When we assume this decision-making role on behalf of the child, be sure to narrate what you are doing so the child knows what to expect and isn't surprised by your behavior. In the near future, find an opportunity to follow up with the child, and perhaps the whole classroom, and introduce a discussion about gender norms and colors. At this stage, many children are working through the right and wrong way to "do" gender—to be the right kind of boy or girl. This idea limits children, perpetuates stereotypes and norms, and narrows the possibilities of how they will evolve. You can talk about, for example, the fact that all colors are everyone colors and take them through a thinking process that highlights how different people wear all kinds of colors.

In addition to teaching about bodily autonomy, many teachers I work with field questions about bodies and birth and want to know how to validate curiosity and answer with honesty while respecting important teacher-student boundaries. Children's curiosity about sexuality is normal and part of healthy sexual development.[21] Their curiosity at this age about where they come from, how they got in there, and how they got out is really about their ever-growing awareness of themselves as separate from their larger environment and as individual human beings.[22] They seek to make meaning of the world around them.

Debbie Roffman explains this process in her book *Talk To Me First*. Between the ages of four and six, the progression goes as follows: at four, the typical question is "Where did I come from?" because children are beginning to understand themselves as separate from the world, just like every other physical thing. They now understand the concept of a beginning and an end; hence, what was my beginning? Where did I start? Five year olds typically ask, "How did I get out of there?" because they are now aware of how things move through time and place. The concepts of before, now, and later are interesting, as well as how things move from one place to another (think toy trains, buggies, cars, and carriages) or transportation. The newly discovered concept of cause and effect for six year olds inspires the question, "But how'd I get in there in the first place?" They are wondering, "What caused me?!" Debbie calls this "Existentialism 101 for six year olds,"[23] which any ECE teacher knows is cognitively congruent with this developmental stage.

GENDER AND SEXUALITY DIVERSITY

As educators, we are in a unique position and have a pedagogical responsibility to provide accurate information and facilitate thoughtful conversations about all the different aspects of self that children bring into school every single day. Seasoned clinical psychologist, author, and gender and sexuality educator and consultant, Jennifer Bryan, reminds us that "if there is a philosophical and pedagogical commitment to working with the whole child (i.e., attending to cognitive, social, and emotional development), then educators must be prepared to work with their students' gender and sexuality at every grade level."[24]

In fact, children enter "gender and sexuality school" from the time they are born. Now that there is prenatal testing and even gender reveal parties, this may start before they're born. Culturally, pregnancy, birth, and parenting can be very gendered. Gender socialization is powerful, and norms start to shape behavior from an early age.[25] In the interest of creating caring, loving, and affirming learning communities for all children, it is also important to celebrate the diverse reality of family structures and gender identities. Since gender stereotyping starts early, it is essential that we bring awareness to gender roles and how they impact behavior. We are providing implicit and explicit messages about gender and sexuality all the time in schools—and everywhere else as well. How do we respond to the boy who is being teased for wearing sparkly nail polish? How do we respond to the boys who say to a girl who wants to join their playground soccer game, "Girls run too slow—you can't play with us"? How do we respond when a child shares that their older sibling goes by they/them pronouns and other students say, "What's that mean? That's weird." How do we respond to the boy who reports that a girl often teases him, leading his friends to tease that she has a crush on him?

Working with children to grasp the concept of stereotypes, especially as they relate to gender, can sharpen their observation, categorization, and critical-thinking skills.[26] Organizing small-group work around this topic also supports effective communication, active listening, inquiry, thoughtful sharing, and verbalizing what one thinks and feels. This pedagogical approach also supports dual language learners in particular. Encouraging the capacity to identify the difference between something that is oversimplified and what, in reality, is naturally complex supports students to see themselves and their peers more accurately. Discussions about gender stereotypes should include gender roles and rules that many children are already familiar with, especially when it comes to acceptable colors, clothing choices, playground activities, and future professions.

As teachers, we all care about using age-appropriate materials and instruction, as well as language and concepts, in our conversations with our students. When it comes to the concerns that surround this subject in particular, many stem from fear and anxiety. Educators have legitimate concerns that some parents will berate them for discussing topics that are evidenced to be beneficial to all students. This may also come from colleagues, even administrators, when their politics and personal internalized stigmatized beliefs about sexuality will trump student health.

This is a real concern. "Teaching gender" has become a fraught political issue that is causing havoc in some schools. Many educators I've spoken to in this situation reveal their fears about job security and parental backlash that they and their administrators contend with. The vast majority of educators, which is supported by evidence and further affirmed through the many interviews I've conducted for this book, know that gender dynamics, norms, and stereotypes are present in classrooms every day. It is impossible not to address them and a disservice to the healthy development of students. Supporting children in understanding what's happening all the time in their classrooms is a proactive and preventative measure that promotes healthy relationships and identity formation. Educators' fears and the limitations that stem from them (1) minimizes their professional training and expertise, and (2) undermines and erodes the very factor that can make school so special for kids, an educator's magic. That is, the magic of creating learning experiences that are real, relevant, and engaging so that learning may happen for everyone in collaborative and caring ways. Every teacher in a state, community, or school that is imposing limitations on discussions of sexuality that are a part of normal development and everyday life has to navigate the inevitable tension of balancing what they know is healthy and safe for their students and their own job security. You must make those choices for yourself. Teaching is a demanding and challenging enough pursuit and profession without those added pressures. My hope is that this book provides evidence and options for how to offer information that is in the best interest of your students. As children mature, gender norms continue to influence their play, especially on the play yard.

SCENARIO: Combined grade-level recess activities have become quite gender specific and always include a soccer game. A group of boys have been playing recently, and the intensity of their play escalates so that the energy is competitive and high spirited. There is typically a male faculty member on recess duty who casually oversees the flow of the game. You're also on yard duty and notice that Gracie wants to join in and says as much the next time there's a sub from the sidelines. Finn immediately responds, "No way, we already have our teams." Gracie puts her hands on her hips and retorts, "I can play. There are extras. I'm next in line." Wyatt adds, "You're too slow. Go play with the other girls." Mr. Katz notices the contention and makes his way over. The other boys are impatient and "Oh, come ON!" can be heard from multiple kids. Mr. Katz asks, "What's going on?" Finn is quick to respond first, "We already have teams." Mr. Katz notices, "I see alternates that are being subbed in. Gracie, what's happening for you?" Gracie's mouth is turned down and her brow is furrowed, "They won't let me play. He said it's because I'm slow" and points to Wyatt, who says, "Well it's true. She's a girl, she doesn't run as fast, it's not fair." The bell rings and the students need to return to your classroom, so you offer to work through the dispute when you all get there. (Whatcom County Public School District, WA)

The majority of schools I know already have implemented peace processes—structures and exercises for talking out conflict. Many educators find it helpful to use a "talking stick" or other designated object to support taking turns, identifying feelings in ourselves and observing them in others, and creating caring and empathetic dialogue. Nonjudgemental questions to guide the discussion promote resolution and commitment. Teacher-posed questions can also guide children to discover counter narratives that dispel norms and reveal that reality is complex and that individuals often perceive it in very different ways.

As each child expresses their perspective, ask "What were you feeling at that time/in that moment?" as well as "What did you need?" and "What were you going for?" This provides a deeper understanding and encourages an empathetic dynamic. In situations where children exclude others based on gender, you may then offer something to the effect of "So, I hear that you were feeling 'x' and that you needed 'y,' so went with 'z'." You may then integrate something along the lines of, "Girls and boys play together all of the time. And it shouldn't be an insult to call a boy a girl or a girl a boy. Thinking only boys can do certain things and only girls can do certain things leaves people out and hurts feelings. Some people have the idea that boys should all be the same way, which isn't fair, because all boys are not alike and not all girls are alike. There are many people who don't want to be squeezed into those ideas, which can feel like rules. That thinking can keep people from being who they really are. Everyone should be able to do the things they like to do and be their true selves without having to worry about what other people think or to be teased about it." And then follow up with, "So how might you get your needs met in a way that doesn't exclude others?" If a child is searching, we can offer to gather and ask their peers. To avoid a child feeling put on the spot or publicly shamed, ask the children to share moments when self-regulation and listening to people's words has been challenging. Open the dialogue to be about behavior everyone has difficult moments with versus the particular behavior that was just addressed. Once you establish that we all have things we're working on, delve into a creative thought session on how to be more inclusive and the impact of gender norms as a basis for exclusion: "We are all learning about how to include each other even when it's hard or not necessarily what we want. How might we change our thinking to be more inclusive?" You may specifically recognize, too, that professional adult sports are organized by gender; however, on play yards among children (and all-gender club teams for people of all ages), the focus is fun, connection, and working together as a team, regardless of gender. This connects to the fundamental community values that are important to reinforce.

FEELINGS AND VALUES

A major focus of SEL in primary school is feelings. Identifying feelings within ourselves builds self-awareness for self-regulation, and to see them in others as a foundational aspect of character strengths, like empathy, is paramount to a future of healthy relationships and moral behavior.[27] The emotional lives of children are essential, since emotions determine whether academic content will be processed and deeply remembered.[28] This also supports and gives meaning to learning. Ultimately, Director of the Emotional Literacy Center at Yale University Marc Brackett's "message for everyone is the same: if we can learn to identify, express, and harness our feelings, even the most challenging ones, we can use those emotions to help us create positive, satisfying lives."[29]

This extends into lessons of intention versus impact and aspirations of social connection and acceptance versus the negative effect of social cruelty. Many teachers are creative with how they make these lessons concrete. I've seen purchased flashcards with children's faces showing emotion that may aid a student trying to name what they are feeling. This is a great first step for folks who are challenged for time. If you have the capacity to personalize your visual aids, consider engaging students in a feelings project that entails identifying common emotions that come up throughout the day, photographing each student modeling the expression of that emotion, printing the pictures out, making a larger laminated card of each, and putting them up on the wall. When a child needs concrete support identifying a feeling or naming what they see others expressing, they may reference the "feelings wall."

Children are also observing how we manage and express our own feelings as we navigate the day. There are moments when we may need to call upon the very language and tools we teach our students to regulate ourselves. This builds credibility with them and further reinforces that we are all evolving and will continue to do so into adulthood.

SCENARIO: Your kindergarten section this Fall feels like a roller-coaster of chaos and interventive behavior management. The majority of your students have moved into your section from the Head Start program, where you were once a lead teacher and felt you had a firm grasp on effective classroom organization and program implementation. Some students remember you and are excited to be in class with you again. You are aware that transitions are particularly hard for a few of your former students, and you plan mini lessons in feelings regulation and strategic centering of energy. You are overwhelmed after the first week, so on Friday, when several students dump the baskets of blocks on the floor and others are arguing over who gets certain art supplies and a couple of brawlers run out of the room during free-choice time, you lose your composure and raise your voice. You stand up and yell, "all of you stop!" You are typically measured and calm when addressing behavioral issues, so the children have never heard your "loud voice" before and freeze. Their eyes get wide and mouths quiet. One new student, who has also been overwhelmed by all of the energy in the room, starts to cry quietly. You gather the students into the classroom circle and say, "I apologize for raising my voice. I notice that many of you are surprised and some of you are upset. I was afraid for a moment because I didn't feel what was happening in the classroom was safe for everyone and was frustrated that people weren't listening and responding to what I was asking them to do." Immediately, Cody goes to get the "angry doll" and hands it to you and says, "Ms. Nelson, you can use the angry doll to show us how it went and what you felt." Then another student added, "Yeah, you were frustrated because you want people to listen and keep the room safe." And another, "Do you want to take some deep breaths first?" All sets of eyes are on you with expectation. (Suffolk County Public Schools, MA)

How we model self-regulation, constructive dialogue, and accepting feedback during teachable moments is the most powerful lesson. Teachers communicate in many nuanced ways through physical demeanor, what's said and not said, and with their reactions. Being consistent with what we say and do with our language and behaviors enhances our credibility.[30] Ms. Nelson does this and is affirmed by her students. She recognizes her behavior, its impact, and that she could have managed her reaction differently. She then takes the time to name and share what she was feeling and why and was open to the feedback and suggestions for how to care for herself and others going forward. Ms. Nelson's achievement is further affirmed by her students in how they were able to immediately call upon coping strategies to do this. Ms. Nelson can express pride in how her students have listened and responded with care.

Even when our students have tools to self-regulate, there are many contextual factors that can get in the way of using coping strategies, especially when energy is high. Our students benefit when we slow them down, make a shift in context, and guide them through reflection. Values education provides a foundation for that guidance.

A value is something we care about that contributes to our behavior and drives not only what we do but why we do it. Values education promotes self-awareness through genuine self-reflection that will inform future decision-making. This is particularly important when peers may be engaged in behavior that isn't aligned with family or community principles. The capacity for a young person to make values-driven decisions depends primarily on how much they have internalized a sense of morality and on their own confidence and resilience.[31] It is important to recognize that not all families and their children share individual values. This is why a combination of guidance (framing questions so that there isn't an implied right answer) towards students naming and understanding their own personal and family values, while also emphasizing shared school ideas of humanitarian citizenship and community, is ideal. Of course, there are culturally responsive implications with values education. Practicing multicultural competence stems from acknowledging the diversity of cultural perspectives present while also promoting what is shared as members of the same learning community.[32] Kindness, diversity, fairness, respect and equality tend to be character-strength values that are foundational expectations of all schools.

RELATIONSHIPS (CONSENT, COMMUNITY, DECISION-MAKING)

Primary students are starting to make decisions of consequence. They are just realizing how others exist beyond themselves and that their actions have implications. Negotiation and problem-solving skills are critical to maintaining relationships and understanding the repercussions of personal behavior on community expectations and standing.

A combination of values and emotions, as well as intuition and rational thought, drives decision-making. Elementary school is really the very beginning of developing this skill, especially since cognitive development, executive functioning in particular, takes a long time. Practicing thinking about right and wrong, enforcing and connecting to values, and maintaining focus on self-regulation will go a long way. At this age, it is mostly emotions that motivate children's decisions. It is also critical to recognize that motivation, or the process that connects emotions to action, directs the emotions. Motivation born out of an incentive in the environment guides behavior towards a goal that will fulfill our needs.[33]

At this age, many decisions are experiments in action. The goal is to learn from our decision-making so that we may make better and better ones.[34] When children make decisions, guide them to understand the feelings they are experiencing in a moment (e.g., curious, hurt, peaceful, frustrated, energetic, or happy). Welcome all emotions and enforce the idea that all behaviors in response to those emotions may not be appropriate or acceptable given the context. Inquire about the child's needs (e.g., care, help, alone time, food, or affection). Explore if their decision/action/behavior was an effective way to meet their needs. If it was, positively reinforce the choice, and if it wasn't, share ideas for more prosocial behaviors to get needs met in response to particular feelings. This process supports neurodevelopment, begins establishing patterns of behavior that will follow a student throughout their development, and aspires to develop a sense of morality or right and wrong, especially in regards to relationships and community membership and responsibility. Recognizing how others contribute to our lives in positive ways, or appreciation, is the foundation of this. In the words of Rick Weissbourd, author and human development psychologist, "The issue isn't moral literacy; it's moral motivation. There is one capacity in particular that is at the heart of such motivation—appreciation, the capacity to know and value others, including those who are different in background and perspective."[35]

As children transition from daycare or home, and/or preschool to school, finding, keeping and appreciating friends is a developmental task that spans the developmental spectrum. Healthy friendship is a protection factor for all of us, and without some friendships, children are psychologically at risk.[36] In fact, having a friend can protect a child from many traumatic childhood social situations.[37]

In their book, *Best Friends, Worst Enemies*, authors Catherine O'Neill Grace and psychologist Michael Thompson conclude that "at the end of the day, it is friendship that will nourish the soul of a child."[38] They also assert that social skills and friendship are not the same thing. Social skills will certainly make developing a friendship easier, just as poor social skills can get in the way of children finding, building, and sustaining a friendship. Prosocial skills are an important part of the capacity to have friends; however, it isn't enough. "Ultimately, friendship has to be defined by the children choosing each other, trusting each other, loving each other."[39]

All relationships, especially friendships at this time, are prime practice for developing social skills that will follow young people throughout their lives. Children this age thrive on the predictability of repeating stories, songs, and activities.[40] Many teachers I know brilliantly use stuffies and puppets to simulate interpersonal dynamics and friendship-building skills based on material that organically presents itself in the classroom.

Veteran educator, Doug Zesiger, travels the California Bay Area teaching in schools and has a website and YouTube channel called *Stinky Tales*. *Stinky Tales* is "Growing Caring and Compassionate Kids One Story at a Time."[41] Dillard the Lizard is a primary *Stinky Tales* character; he has many friends who simulate concrete interpersonal dynamics between and among students. Learners observe and actively participate as an engaged audience who provide scenario deconstruction, keen insights and observations, as well as suggestions for conflict resolution and joyful celebration. Contextual examples include differences between Dillard, who has scales/skin and no fur, and Stinky the lion, who has a lot of fur and a big mane. Topics include taking care of things, interrupting, personal space, bossy friends, and helping a friend in need—all important issues pertaining to friendship. Sometimes, characters will sit on the shoulders of others who are engaged in decision-making. Dillard (representing the amygdala or emotion/impulse) and Yoda (representing the prefrontal cortex or rational thought) will be positioned on opposite shoulders, narrating a thought process that informs decision-making. One character's superpower is kindness. The kindness superpower is amazing, because with kindness, one can instantly make two people really happy (the person who received and the person who gave), and it can happen at any time and virtually anywhere. This externalization of behavior allows children to practice critical thinking, cultivates capacities for empathy, mutual respect, and care, and allows them to be experts in their own experiences—all through play.

Play is the context in which students develop vital skills, such as decision-making, leadership, and self-regulation. It builds the foundation for abstract representational thinking and encourages children to be creative and put words to their own experiences, wrestle with challenges, and practice prosocial behaviors with peers.[42] In the words of Thompson and O'Neill-Grace, "It is the essence of childhood. It is a child's mental health. It is work. It is recreation."[43]

In K–2, the focus for consent education is on bodily autonomy, personal space, and asking permission. *Consent* is about asking for permission, specifically when it comes to things that belong to us. It is anchored in empathy (feeling with people), mutual respect (treating people how they want to be treated), and dignity (treating others and ourselves like we have value). It encompasses setting and honoring boundaries. We typically teach that asking for permission is good manners, because good manners show that we care about people.

Comfort with various greetings, especially those that include touch and space bubbles, are a cognitively congruent concept for early elementary-aged students. The ritual of morning greetings that feel comfortable is a wonderful way to come up with a plethora of expressions depending on how someone feels and offers choice. As children enter the classroom or during a meeting when learners are sitting in a circle, facilitate the myriad ways they may greet you and each other: high fives, fist bumps, a mini dance, a bow, or a foot-to-foot tap. Maybe their greeting is strictly verbal—it may be as simple as a "Hey!" or a "Good morning + (some appreciation if sincere)." This begins to establish the foundation for safety and consent. The direct teaching includes that our bodies belong to us, and we all have different comfort levels with how we feel about interactions and the space that surrounds them.

A *space bubble* is an imaginary line we draw around ourselves that expresses what our physical and personal space boundaries are. On one side of the boundary is comfort and on the other side is discomfort. Space bubbles may get bigger or smaller depending on where we are, who we're with, and how we're feeling. Some examples to support understanding may be having to give hugs when you don't want to, or tickle wars that don't feel fun or stop when you say stop, or someone taking or using a crayon you've selected while doing an art project.

During a lesson, you may have learners draw themselves and their space bubbles in different contexts, for instance, at home on the couch watching tv, in a new classroom at the beginning of the school year, in line at the grocery store, in the neighborhood with good friends. Have students post their drawings on the wall for a gallery walk. Prompt the children to notice how the bubbles expand and contract relative to different situations. Encourage students to identify how they're feeling in the pictures and verbalize the reasons the bubble size changes depending on different factors. Guide students to observe how different people have different space bubbles at different times and in different situations. Pose the question, "How would we know where someone's space bubble is if it's invisible and can change?" Provide language for how they may ask for permission and identify social cues and facial expressions that might provide clues to show how someone may feel and what they may want. Brainstorm with students how they might communicate what their needs are as well; for instance, "I don't feel like a hug, but we can play house," or "I just don't want to be touched right now and need some space," or "I'm not into wrestling right now, so I am going to find a quiet place for a while."

When I work with schools, parenting adults, and teachers, it is common in K–2 to hear about crushes, who is going to marry whom, practice kissing, and/or a child who runs around the playground springing kisses and hugs on others who don't want them. I appreciate the commitment people have towards respectful relationship dynamics when they report that they've told the child who is hugging and kissing others that "*no means no.*" However, since we are talking about children, this response represents a missed opportunity for a deeper understanding of what's happening and how touch can be an expression of affection. What's important is that affection means the same thing to both people; when we don't give people the opportunity to express whether or not it means the same thing to them or if they are comfortable with it or not, we take away their opportunity or right to tell us.

People get to decide when and with whom they want to be affectionate. They get to choose, because their bodies belong to them. When we don't respect or recognize this choice and assume they want what we want, it can make people feel all kinds of emotions that aren't part of positive friendship. It can also be hurtful. It's important to recognize all of the ways people say and show yes and no, and if we are unsure, to slow down, ask and, pay attention. When it comes to the ways people show affection or caring or loving feelings with each other, you may say, "Hugs are something for both friends and families who are comfortable with them, and kissing to show affection is usually just for families." This can be challenging for children who are simultaneously learning to self-regulate. It can take a lot for students to maintain focus and prosocial behaviors while they do school. When it's time to shift energies and for moments of release, a lot can come up for students.

These moments of release are especially common during transitions throughout the school day. Whether it's lining up to walk to the art classroom or P.E. field, go out to dismissal, or stand in line to wash hands before lunch, those pockets of time—or the in-betweens—can be when pent-up energy and feeling come out through silly or contentious behaviors.

SCENARIO: It's time for second grade art, so your students line up to walk over to the art classroom. Kevin hops up and immediately jumps in front. Benny is right behind him and scores second. Both students get wiggly and bumpy during transitions. Benny starts singing a pop song and then starts to grind up on Kevin and smacks his butt and then his own. Kevin immediately pushes Benny off and says, "Cut it out!" Kevin is laughing so hard that he loses his balance and falls out of line, so that Brianna can claim his spot. Kevin's face gets serious, "Hey, that's my spot!" Brianna responds, "No way, you got out of line. Mine now." Kevin is angry and gets in Brianna's face and shouts, "It's mine!" (Santa Clara County School District, CA)

Over my thirty years of teaching, I've heard an increasing number of scenarios in which young children exhibit sexualized behavior. This makes sense to me, because over time, our media has become increasingly more sexualized. What's important to remember in these situations is *what* motivates the behavior in children. Kids are like sponges. They are incredibly curious and neurologically programmed to learn from their environment. Most of us get the desire kids have to be first. We live in an achievement-based meritocracy after all. It's when something presents as sexual that some adults lose perspective. Benny had in fact watched the Superbowl with his family, including the half-time show the week before. He took in that the dancing garnered a lot of attention and affirmation. He has also picked up from our culture that sex is a funny word or one that is taboo, and so it holds some power that gets attention. He has observed that sexual subjects are used as humor to connect with an audience. He is most likely imitating what he's seen. If he becomes silly when you bring this up, remind him that "Sex is a serious subject, and it's important to look and sound serious when we talk about it."[44]

Benny also touched Kevin without his consent, and when Kevin became angry, Benny minimized it and compounded the situation when he laughed it off. The dynamic escalates further to involve other students when he loses his place in line, so it is time to intervene and take Benny and Kevin aside. Facilitate your talk-it-out process. Guide Kevin to hear Benny's perspective and share his own. Use language that doesn't publicly humiliate or shame. Invoke your class guidelines, because they apply wherever students are with each other, and prioritize checking in with Kevin and how he is feeling. Of course, accountability is critical and open-ended strategic questions will support your discussion. Did Benny get to say what he wanted? How does he feel at the moment? Is he up for going to class? And reassure him that you will be checking in again at the next recess or lunch. As much as we need to focus on teaching people not to disrespect and/or harm, protection skills can benefit the person who was disrespected. You might say, "Some kids like to use sexual words or gestures to make other kids feel uncomfortable or because they think it's funny. What you experienced or overheard today is a good example. Let's think about what you could say or do if someone said that to you—tell them what your boundaries are."[45]

As you turn your focus to Kevin, engage in a restorative process that gets at what Kevin was going for or what *motivated* the behavior and identify the cost to relationships and community. Specifically ask Kevin what he was feeling at the time (reference concrete examples from the feelings visuals) and what he needed. Was he feeling playful and rambunctious and so wanted to expend the energy and connect? Feeling silly and wanting attention? How did his intentions align with his impact? How did his behavior make Benny feel and are there other ways to get his wants/needs met that don't negatively affect a friendship and culture of consent? Let Kevin know what grinding is (a sexualized dance that older people do) and that it isn't appropriate for school. Be concrete about how Kevin was in Benny's bubble and touching his body in unwanted ways. Follow up with both students, and see if you can facilitate a genuine apology and commitment to changing behavior from Kevin. Model the language and communication it takes to restore a friendship.

It may take a while for Benny to accept the apology, so you might say, "Yeah, I get that, sometimes feelings stick around for a while, and it takes time to rebuild trust." How much of an impact a moment like this has will depend on Benny's resilience and protection skills, so follow up with him. If Kevin's behavior continues, consider a functional behavioral analysis, which is a documented plan for contextual information, relational skills inventory, and strategies for modifying behavior with measurable objectives. This may include outreach home to Benny's parenting adults about the media he is consuming.

CONNECTION (INTIMACY AND LOVE)

As humans, we need social connection. Love, in its many forms, is critical to a child's capacity to thrive. How do we feel and show love? Sometimes people don't use words to show love, and there are different cultural norms around expressing and demonstrating love and affection. Sometimes, children may experience closeness and feelings of affection for friends that they then associate with marriage. I hear about a lot of banter that takes place among children about crushes, dating, and marriage. Many times, these relationship structures and feeling close to someone get conflated. It is normal and healthy for a child to witness the intimacy of a marriage, but not the sexual expression of it, so when they feel positive feelings of wanting to be close to someone, they assign it a label. They are merely trying on what they see as it connects to how they feel. Elementary school is a wonderful opportunity to celebrate the many ways humans love each other and how we assign meaning and language to express the feelings we experience. Normalizing different types of love and how they relate to different types of relationships primes children for a more sophisticated understanding of this desired intimacy.

SCENARIO: Gavin and Madison have known each other since preschool and are now in kindergarten together. They enjoy each other's company, talk, and play well. Madison has been feeling close to and affection for Gavin, so has been saying, "We're going to get married." Several classmates pick up on this and will playfully tease the two about crushing and marriage. Gavin doesn't like all of the attention and shares what's happening with his parents. His parents tell him to say as much to Madison and call you to say they don't want the kids to talk about marriage. The two children stop playing together altogether. (Grafton County School District, VT)

In response to the above scenario, you may say, "I notice you talking to Gavin about marriage, which is something many adults do. It sounds like you have big feelings for Gavin and that you enjoy spending time with him. Friendship includes love too but can be different from married love. When children talk about things like marriage it can seem silly to other kids, because it is a grown-up thing. I've also noticed that Gavin might feel embarrassed with the word *married* to describe your friendship. It's possible to still play together as long as we respect what makes each other comfortable." Notice that Madison may feel rejected—guide her to recognize and name the feelings she's having in response and to understand that good friends pay attention to what feels comfortable and uncomfortable.

You may also coach Gavin in language like, "I don't want to talk about marriage. Let's play magna tiles instead." Reaffirm the idea that friends respect how someone wants to be treated and that there are and say, "so many fun ways to connect with each other that don't include talking about something that makes friends feel uncomfortable." Next steps would be to facilitate a conversation between the children and encourage empathy, understanding, and a commitment to new language and boundary setting.

SAFETY

Consent laws and policies are in place to protect people when they may not be able to themselves. How we cultivate cultures of consent in educational spaces can be tricky when we must navigate the inevitable tensions of sexual misconduct prevention and accountability, parenting constituents, administrative exposure and liability, job security, absent CSE, personal histories with stigmatized sexuality, and what is developmentally congruent behavior for children who are learning through making mistakes.

Practicing concepts of consent through effective communication enables us to authentically connect with others, which is a protection factor that promotes safety. Connection is a part of intimacy. Social connectedness is proven to benefit our well-being and mental health. It also leads to young people performing optimally in school. Strong connections make our experiences feel satisfying and secure. They affirm, reassure us, and give positive meaning to our lives—our health and happiness depend on them.[46] Feeling connected is essential for physical and emotional health at all ages. Connection is a protective factor of mental health and encourages children to thrive.[47] Sometimes children need support in understanding how to connect with others so that they may build the relationships they need to support keeping them safe.

SCENARIO: Liam and Kai are good friends who are laughing and playfully rough housing during recess on the grass. While wrestling, Liam grabs at Kai's genitals. The vibe of the play shifts, and Kai stops and says, "Cut it out!" and side-eye glares at Liam as he walks away in a huff. Liam is disheveled and sporadically giggling as he calls after Kai and says, "Awe, come'on. I'm just playing." Kai's face is distraught, and he's looking at the ground as you walk by as he's walking back to his classroom. You ask what's up and if he's okay. He shrugs and reports what happened while still walking. You ask him to stop, but he expresses needing to get to class and doesn't want to talk about it. As per policy, you relay what's happened to the Lower School Administrator, who sets a bunch of disciplinary measures in motion. (Hawai'i County Public Schools, HI)

In cases like this between Liam and Kai, which several educators have told me about in recent years, the teachers involved follow school policies and bring the incident to an administrator right away. These policies are now in place for good reason, should there be a situation that involves sexual misconduct. With good intention, administrators take such incidents very seriously and set disciplinary wheels in motion. The important increased awareness of consent and the need for schools to be accountable is necessary, *and* there hasn't been a lot of training on how to approach issues of sexuality when they arise or to determine whether the behaviors are sexually exploitative or not. In some schools, there is understandable anxiety when it comes to issues of sexuality and safety, since many adults haven't received much CSE or professional development on how to handle issues of sexuality when they come up in the school environment. In most cases, children are not engaging in predatory behaviors, rather, they are mirroring normative cultural representations of sexuality that they are, in most cases, too young to understand.

In this particular situation, Liam is feeling rambunctious and seeking out connection through play with Kai. Liam has two older brothers who wrestle at home and nut-tap (hitting or flicking the testicles) each other and Liam as a joke. This is a widely normalized behavior amongst young boys and even adult men. As Liam and Kai's rough housing escalates, Liam nut-taps Kai, who understandably doesn't like it. Kai bravely tells a caretaking adult what's bothering him. We actually don't know at this point exactly how Kai experienced the nut-tap. Is he annoyed and looking for ways to get his friend to stop that particular behavior? Is he frustrated because Kai has done this in the past and it's a potential pattern? Is he angry and feeling out of control or that the action was exploitive? In this situation, it was assumed that Kai felt victimized. Ascribing how Kai felt about the experience has the potential to compromise Kai's capacity to understand the impact and relevance for himself. How he actually experienced what happened will depend on his relationship with Liam, his own developing protection skills and resilience, as well as his understanding of consent and personal agency.

The adults who immediately applied the school's sexual misconduct policies to the situation defaulted to addressing Liam's behavior as sexually deviant. Because this was the content of the parent phone calls home, other parents immediately started talking within the community, and Liam was gossiped about as if he were a potential sexual predator. Unfortunately, I hear about these situations more and more. In other cases, the child (he is only seven after all) and his family are judged and ostracized from the class and greater community. In some situations, the family must relocate geographically because of social cruelty, the impact of which is devastating.

In the case between Liam and Kai, one may take a restorative approach and find out if predatory sexual misconduct took place at all. A greater definition of the problem and its impact is necessary to respond in a way that supports both boys. Of course, it's important to reinforce lessons about boundaries and respect for body safety and autonomy. The structure of a functional behavioral analysis for Liam would support a process that explores the social dynamics and cultural context, as well as an inventory of skills and potential learning that may restore the impact of the incident. Liam's parenting adults need to hear that nut-tapping is absolutely not okay at school, and those boundaries should be reinforced at home so that there is consistency for Liam about acceptable behavior specific to consent.

A shame-free approach by a professional/school counselor or educator who is trained in inquiry as to the impact of Kai's experience is important as well. This is an opportunity to celebrate Kai standing up for himself and his bodily autonomy as well as his courage in telling an adult. Maybe he feels brave for not tolerating the disrespect—even more so during an adult-mediated follow-up between the boys (if he is amenable of course)—and hasn't experienced what happened as traumatic. If he has, however, then a support system that involves home and school will be paramount.

Most of the time—as long as this isn't a pattern, given the context of this sort of experience—friends are able to restore their relationship and learn important lessons about consent, respect, contrition, and restoration from these situations.

If Liam continues to engage in sexualized behavior with other students and/or other sexual behaviors emerge, further inquiry may be necessary. Problematic sexual behaviors that may be warning signs of sexual abuse in the early childhood years include advanced sexual knowledge, frequently drawing pictures of people that feature genitals, patterns of sexual play that cannot be redirected, repeated sexual engagement even though boundaries have been clearly communicated, duplicating specific adult sex acts, or compulsive and aggressive forceful play or specific sexual play.[48] Ultimately, these students are children who are learning how to treat each other with respect and dignity. It matters that we take the time to approach these moments of sexuality with care, as they have lasting impacts throughout a young person's life.

As we guide children towards the practice of consent and communication that cultivates a capacity for desired connection, preventative measures through stories are helpful in applying the information we provide about relationships and the feelings that motivate behaviors in different contexts. Stories also support children in identifying skills and gaining the deeper understanding needed for how all of this comes together in everyday interactions. Stories illustrate and affirm the multitude of identities, family structures, and other forms of diversity in our classrooms, as well as those in the larger community. There is a list of suggested books in appendix C that encourages a deeper understanding of the relationship skills and capacities that lead to authentic social connectedness, the capacity for close emotional ties that lead to intimate platonic relationships (and those that are romantic down the road), and the ability to sustain those connections in healthy ways. Unfortunately, there are also scenarios in which children are survivors of sexual abuse and exploitation.

If you are an adult who has experienced sexual abuse, the following information may understandably bring up a lot of feelings for you. Please take care of yourself and your own healing first. If you are at the beginning of your healing journey, you may seek someone who is trained to help and support you—consider speaking to someone at the National Sexual Assault Hotline: 800-656-HOPE (800-656-4673) or chat online at https://hotline.rainn.org/online.

The need to teach children sexual abuse prevention safety skills is an unfortunate—but essential—reality. Child maltreatment specific to sexual abuse perpetrated by an adult,[49] in addition to peer to peer sexual contact abuse, shows that about one in ten children are sexually abused.[50] In regard to definitions of child sexual abuse, how to encourage child resilience against sexual abuse, and what to look out for should a child experience harm or cause harm, Laura Hancock PhD and Karen Rayne PhD have written an extremely helpful, comprehensive chapter in their book, *Sex Ed for the Stroller Set*.[51] Their age-appropriate, survivor- and restorative-centered approach lays out concrete language and instructions for how caretaking adults might address this challenging issue during early and middle childhood. In the spirit of prevention, SIECUS also recommends the following information be taught at this developmental stage (adapted from the National Sex Education Standards, second edition). See appendix C.

Books are a great way to teach children about sexuality and body safety. There are several recommendations in the appendixes. As noted before, it is important to screen any books first to ensure that you make an informed decision should you teach in a state or district with limitations on teaching about sexuality. Some books may have sections that are acceptable given parameters and others that aren't, so you may consider gleaning those that support what you feel you can teach, given restrictions.

Corey Silverberg's book, *Sex is a Funny Word*,[52] has an excellent section on touch, specifically our different experiences of touch and how it can change the way we feel. Silverberg writes that touch can feel like "helping" or like "hurting." Their text goes on to include consent, bodily autonomy, and questions that guide children towards connecting different experiences to the discussion: "Can you think of a time when you touched someone and it helped? When is touching okay and not okay?"[53] This prevention oriented understanding of touch includes "secret touch," and how someone "may want to keep it a secret because they know what they are doing is wrong, and they don't want other people to find out."[54] Hancock and Rayne suggest saying adults "understand that sometimes [children] have thoughts and feelings they don't want to share, but no one should ever tell them to keep a secret."[55] Acknowledge that surprises can be fun, that they are like little secrets because we hide them, but the important difference is that there is always a plan to give away the surprise. Should a situation with secret touch happen, Silverberg includes the potential feelings that may come up, how to understand them, and what to do. It's always important to ask children, "Who are trusted adults you can talk to about how you're feeling?" and encourage them to name a couple in different contexts.

Initial indicators of possible sexual abuse usually manifest as social and emotional changes, such as withdrawal, refusal, reluctance, or fear of certain people, behavioral regression, outbursts of anger or other forms of emotional distress, and/or difficulty sleeping that may be caused by a sudden increase in nightmares. Physical indicators may include discomfort with walking or sitting and/or genital discharge or unexplained genital bruising.[56]

As educators, we are all mandated reporters. Should you suspect sexual abuse, your response matters and can greatly impact the trajectory of a young person's healing. Be mindful of your interpersonal response to your student as you engage the protocols of your school in response to mandated reporting. Recognize and express to the child that they are brave for telling you and that secret touch is never their fault and that you will help them get the support they need. Leave the further conversation of the situation to a professional with trauma-informed training. Continue to be present for your student and listen for how they are feeling and provide reassurance without minimizing their experience. Consider having school counselors provide concrete language and offer suggestions for survivor-centered approaches in response to disclosures in a faculty meeting.

The nuances of what we are legally responsible to report, to which particular child protection agency, and the parameters of timing and information provided may vary from state to state and even county to county. Be clear on what your county requires. Many child advocacy agencies provide information and training for teachers. An annual update of protocols and procedures is always a good idea. Administrators can call their local agency and Zoom or have them present in person. I have found folks in these positions to be informative and open to any questions. This is helpful when there is a report to make and we find the students we care about to be in compromised situations. Administrators can also help colleagues and staff by providing resources for support should the weight of a child's abuse require self-care on the part of the reporting adult.

While interventive and support skills and resources are critical to our profession, the protective and preventive factors of CSE cannot be underestimated and must be scaffolded over time. Like the scope and sequence of all good programs, we must circle back to topics and provide next steps and learning. Revisiting these topics so that concepts are reinforced and built upon towards overarching learning objectives are the reason you will find scenarios for each category identified in this first chapter. As you read further, you will find how to support students in a moment as well as hone language and skills for building confidence and competence with addressing issues of sexuality in ways that promote student well-being.

3

Playground Games

Grades Three and Four

There can be no keener revelation of a society's soul than the way in which it treats its children.

~ Nelson Mandela

Third- and fourth-grade classrooms are wonderfully vibrant. Students are curious and eager to understand cultural and social concepts as their cognitive abilities develop in step with the world around them. This means that, perhaps for the first time, their attention is easily captured by gender and sexual messaging. As their perspective broadens, they become aware of and begin to understand the cruelty of the world as well. As their brain develops, they are primed for empathy and compassion as how people are treated becomes more meaningful to them. It's an optimal time for teachers to pose questions about that messaging and create space for making sense of all they are exposed to. This can lead to mood swings that are typical of this age and stage and generate questions like, "What does this mean for me?" and, "How does this change how I see myself?" Pondering these questions can also contribute to feelings of insecurity and uncertainty. Thus, the focus of third and fourth grade continues to be on physical changes and abilities, care and safety, gender roles and expectations, relationships with family, friends, and each other, as well as building and sharing in and sustaining community. Encouraging and supporting third and fourth grade curiosity and motivation, flexible thinking, generosity, and kindness to others, as well as the development of supportive relationships and positive self-identities all contribute to resilience building. These are protective factors in preventing harm and mitigating the effect of adverse childhood experiences and trauma.[1]

Developmental highlights:

- The well-known developmental concept that Third and Fourth graders are no longer learning to read but reading to learn is profoundly relevant. As children become literate, when they are at grade level academically, there is an onslaught of exposure through the discovery of words.
- They can now pursue and engage in different realities and narratives through stories and print media. This stokes their curiosity and wonder. It can feel empowering and also make them vulnerable to harmful aspects of culture and negative messaging inappropriate for children.
- Puberty—the body's transition from childhood to adulthood—will begin for many students. The onset begins when a protein, kisspeptin, stimulates a part of the brain, the hypothalamus, to release hormones.[2]

The lived experience of puberty (post the hormonal onset) usually starts with breast development for girls and AFAB (assigned female at birth) people between the ages of eight and thirteen years. For boys and AMAB (assigned male at birth) people, it starts between the ages of nine and fourteen with testicular enlargement.[3] Puberty that happens before these age ranges is called precocious puberty, and puberty that happens after these ranges is called delayed puberty. At present, approximately four in ten girls and those who are AFAB go through precocious puberty. That's ten to twenty times more often for girls than boys.[4] So at eight to eleven years old, a solid number of third and fourth grade students may be experiencing or are about to begin this process.

Pubertal changes are important to address within the context of education. We know that children who start puberty earlier than their peers may face social-emotional challenges because they look older than they are.[5] According to research, this is particularly true of Black and Latina girls. Whenever we adultify children, there can be harmful consequences. For Black and Brown girls, when coupled with existing stereotypes of hypersexuality, there is more risk for harm and suffering at the hands of some teachers.[6] For example, I've heard educators refer to Black girls as "fast" in their development, often said without considering the negative sexual stereotypes associated with this word, but nevertheless, has a racist and misogynist impact. The incongruity of external physical characteristics and internal cognitive development of chronological age can be challenging for all kids, and it is critical that we remember to treat them as their actual age versus how old we think they look. Just as early bloomers may experience unique challenges, late bloomers may as well. Visually, we may see a diverse representation of students along the path of puberty but depending on variables, they may be cognitively consistent. Still, keep in mind that they may be experiencing the social aspects of the lived experience of puberty differently. In many ways, puberty defines this life stage, so to feel ahead or behind can be difficult. This chapter will address how we can support students while they experience those changes and typically manifest within a context of sexuality.

BODIES

There are many wonderful books on the physical, emotional, and social changes that take place during puberty. See appendix C for recommended titles. Again, the overall approach to bodies is to promote a sense of confidence and agency through the normalization of body changes and abilities. As teachers, we are helping students build towards a sense of responsibility as it relates to the care and keeping of bodies and decision-making that will impact growth and health. Encourage students to be the boss of taking care of their bodies as they take on a new shape. Food as fuel and nutrition, physical activity, and sleep are all paramount.

Bodily autonomy requires the capacity to connect with and be attuned to one's body. The skills for this, like most, require time, knowledge, and practice. Of course, there is also how we feel about our bodies that can be a challenge, especially during puberty, because young people often feel like they wake up in a different body every day.

Reinforce individual physical rights and the importance of and right to consent, using phrases like, "Your body is yours, and you have the right to protect it and keep it private based on your comfort level." Deepen understanding of the difference between privacy and secrecy in relationships, especially when it comes to touch. Point out that, as students get older, they have more bodily autonomy and decision-making power. Elaborate on different types of touch, the emotional embodied experience of touch and how that is determined based on how old we are, the communities and families we live in, and other contextual factors.

When it comes to using accurate terms for genitals, you may ask, "Do you notice that people don't talk about their private parts as much as their other body parts?" and follow with, "They are all just body parts, it's just that people keep some parts more private than others." Recognize that "just like in families and communities like school, there are times when it's okay to talk about our more private parts and times when it isn't." Tell students that it's important to know about all body parts, including "private" ones, so that we can take care of and be in charge of them. If students get silly, to deepen understanding of bodies and consent, you might ask why they think we treat these parts so differently and why people so often use silly names for them versus medically accurate terms. Be aware of context for yourself as an educator as you consider extending the lesson further to talk about this with your students. There is a vast spectrum of what is accepted, tolerated, resisted, and attacked in schools. Think of how you may safely stretch the conversation. Doing so can provide opportunities to explore the cultural history of sexual stigmatization and make the point that we can all question those attitudes and develop more open and accepting attitudes about bodies and their natural functions. This will help keep everyone safer and more informed. You may also normalize the reproductive systems that may start to cycle within their bodies.

Remember that it's possible (although they are still in the minority) that a student at this age may get their first period while at school or be caught off guard because their menstrual cycle isn't regular yet. Taking care of these students is important, as well as those who continue developing towards menarche. This will set the tone for how others experience the beginning of these rhythms. Therefore, normalize this human process (we all come into them during puberty) by integrating body-affirming books into your classroom shelves. In addition, many students in the US can't afford period products. According to some estimates, one in five American girls miss school because they lack access to them.[7] Have period kits available if possible. Maxi pads in an envelope or discreet pouch usually do the trick. Let all students know these are available and from whom. Reassure them that the dispensing adult will be discreet. Some period product companies will provide free supplies to schools. Let students know that these are available and that there are many other menstruating people at school too. If your school and/or state won't supply period products, there are many nonprofits emerging to meet student needs. Period.org and The Alliance for Period Supplies are good places to start.

Essential questions to pose are, "How do we feel about/what's it like to be growing and changing?" Delve deeper into what makes our bodies feel certain ways and provide language for accurate expression. What does your body feel like in the present moment? How do different activities (like enjoyable movement, or listening to music, or receiving and giving consensual hugs to and from someone we care for) impact how we feel about our bodies? Have students record how they feel sitting and listening, then engage in a movement-based activity. Ask them to record how they're feeling in their bodies right after. What has shifted and changed? How is this discovery relevant and does it inform how we care for ourselves and support each other? Labeling an emotion is itself a form of regulation.[8] Encouraging a mind-body connection to how movement and other activities improve our mental and physical well-being supports self-regulation. Understanding context as it relates to bodies, touch, and feelings is important too.

Many young people have discovered that putting pressure on or touching their genitals feels good. Sometimes adults judge this behavior through an adult lens that has been socialized by a sexually-stigmatizing culture and think that there are erotic motivations behind it. This is about soothing behaviors, *not* an erotic exploration of emerging sexuality. What is critical to remember is that we are all neurologically programmed for pleasure, so the vast majority of children simply know it feels good and soothing, that's it. Yes, it's about sexuality, but it's not sexualized. The meaning we assign it is socialized. Our response to this happening in school will contribute to that socialization cycle and perpetuate negative associations or offer something different. For students, it's important to understand that touching genitals is a private behavior and when and where it is okay to do so and when it is not.

SCENARIO: Student desks in your third-grade classroom are arranged in a horseshoe. The desks are two deep, so there are two rows. Gracie's desk is in the second row on the end. Sometimes when students are expected to sit at their desks, Gracie has her hands under the desk, and it starts to move as she rocks back and forth. A couple of the students sitting close to her glance over with puzzled expressions. As you approach Gracie's desk, you notice that she is putting pressure on her pubic area over her skirt. To discreetly redirect Gracie, you give her the responsibility of distributing the materials for the next activity. Gracie stops rocking and gets up to give everyone a handout. During break, you discreetly ask Gracie to stop by your desk for a chat. (Fairfield County Public School, CT)

It's in our students' interests to respond to issues of sexuality with affirmation and care versus fear, disapproval, and shame. As readers, we don't know what Gracie's behavior is in response to, and we need to set a boundary with appropriate behavior in school. Some children touch themselves to self-soothe when something else may be causing stress or discomfort. Some children may simply experience irritation due to something like an insect bite, or they may have discovered that touching their genitals simply feels good. Gracie's teacher deftly manages redirecting Gracie by subtly interrupting her behavior with a task so that her intervention doesn't garner unnecessary attention. The behavior stops in the moment and provides an opportunity for a discreet conversation. In an ideal world, a child who has discovered self-soothing or pleasure would not be shamed for forgetting that touching their own genitals is a private versus public behavior; however, different families and social groups have different perspectives on genital self-touch, so outing Gracie's behavior could create a sense of shame or expose her to the judgment and ridicule of classmates. How you approach this conversation will also depend on the sexuality education at your school. If your school provides healthy sexuality education from kindergarten, there is a broader range and vocabulary you can reference and build upon. If your school does not, and you aren't sure of the greater family context/attitude towards bodies and sexuality, take care as you realize that you may be the first adult to directly provide information about body exploration.

As an educator, we may ask ourselves: "What is the safe conversation we need to have given context?" Due to the socialized stigmatization of sexuality in our culture, some adults are challenged to have perspective when addressing these topics with students. Imagine if, instead, Gracie had taken off her shoes and was rubbing her toes. This would be a distraction and not appropriate for when she needs to be focused on her academic learning; however, it probably wouldn't feel as charged or loaded as a kid rubbing their genitals. It is my hope that someday we can have conversations with students who behave in similar ways that recognize what feels good for them in their bodies and move forward in the same way that we would if Gracie had just taken off her shoes. The focus of this conversation, however, given her age and the context, is to focus on how Gracie needs to work on managing her body in a way that is appropriate for a learning environment.

You may start with, "How's your school day going?" and/or "How are you feeling about the assignment?" Gracie may reply that she is "fine," and "it's okay." Does Gracie need an alternative coping mechanism for what she may be feeling in response to directives? You could offer a fidget tool that allows for body movement but isn't a distraction. Or is this an inconsequential issue that is taken care of in a moment? Maybe Gracie shares that she was swimming this weekend and has a bug bite or "it's itchy." Then your response may simply be, "Oh, okay, well let's let your (parenting adult) know so it gets taken care of." If this isn't the case, the next statement might be, "Rubbing on our bodies can be a distraction from taking care of our school business. Sometimes people touch parts of their bodies that feel good to them, this includes body parts that people keep private most of the time. Just like going to the bathroom is a private behavior, touching privates is too." If Gracie's response is silence and she casts her eyes downward, this may indicate that she could be feeling "caught" or that what she was doing was wrong and that [she's] in trouble. To avoid shame, you may say something like, "I notice that you're looking down and quiet. You haven't done anything wrong, and you aren't in trouble. It's okay. Having a conversation about it is how we learn about how to be in school."

Gracie's behavior is more common in kindergarten through second grades; however, it does present sometimes in third grade and is developmentally appropriate—it is actually common for some students like those who are on the autism spectrum. As mandated reporters who care about children, be aware of additional behaviors that may signal sexual abuse. There are some differentials that may help know the difference between what is developmental and what is harmful: sudden emotional changes and/or patterns (withdrawal, refusal, reluctance, fear of certain people, emotional distress, or angry outbursts). For more on the possibility of abuse, see the safety section of chapter two. If there is concern that Gracie's behavior is the result of abuse, bring the school counselor or social worker into the conversation immediately for guidance. However, within this context, Gracie had not been harmed; if you've had this conversation with a student in similar circumstances, reach out to home, and you may want to give your administrator a heads up. This also reinforces the importance of community building with your student's families from the beginning. Establishing connection early and often goes a long way. This is a potentially challenging conversation and is hopefully not the first time you've talked to Gracie's family about her. Cultivating community among families and school creates the space to say, "I just wanted to let you know that I had this conversation with Gracie today." If this is the first outreach, it is a reason for reflecting on how you may integrate community-building practices.

Since conversations about sexuality can be uncomfortable and bring up a lot for folks, when you call home, it will be important to introduce the issue in a nonjudgmental way. You may start with, "I've noticed [x behavior] during [the specific context(s)]. The way I had this conversation is . . ." You're going for a neutral feel. You may have to provide some parent education and share that this is typically normal behavior that requires some guidance. If asked, be prepared to offer age-appropriate books about bodies and sexuality. If Gracie's behavior continues, extend the conversation, "It's happened a few times now despite redirection, so I want to make sure everything is okay, and I'm checking in to see if you've noticed this same behavior at home as well." Parent responses could range from gratitude to mortification, so be aware and reassuring while keeping Gracie's health and well-being at the center—you both want that.

GENDER AND SEXUALITY DIVERSITY

Affirmation of children's emerging identities, which includes their families, is critical for effective learning and community participation. Multiple representations of gender identities and expressions, as well as diverse sexualities in content, conversation, and pedagogy is essential. Students thrive when they see themselves within their communities, be it on the walls of the classroom, in the content they are studying, or the dialogue they engage in as colearners with caretaking adults. Continued inquiry into gender roles and expectations is essential.

Third and fourth grade is a time when there is a surge in social chatter and discourse about the concept of crushes— as well as when conversations about puberty and sexuality become especially relevant, as students are exposed to an onslaught of messaging about gender and sexuality through media and other social institutions. Sometimes crushes and how students may be physically changing is relevant to how students will start to socially sort themselves. This may be the first time popularity may have an element of sexuality and likeability, and seeing physical attributes as attractive may start to emerge based on social messaging. Be mindful of conflating gender and sexual orientation when dialoguing about various identities and their meaning. It is also important to resist taking a one-size-fits-all approach to the very wide umbrella of LGBTQ+. Note, too, that the letter T in this acronym tends to get less attention than the others and that there are more favorable attitudes towards the rights of LGBQ+ people than towards those of transgender folks.[9] In fact, transgender students face the greatest psychological, academic, and physical risks at school—transgender children have the highest rates of being verbally harassed and physically assaulted in school.[10] Therefore, we must actively engage school support for trans-identifying educators and staff, as well as students and their families, and create clear and specific policies. When drafting language to protect gender expansive and transgender youth, it's important to clearly identify both the individuals being protected and the contexts where they may face the greatest risk of discrimination. This enables educators to practice discussing potential scenarios and how the responsibilities of educators and the rights of transgender folks factor into the social dynamic.[11] There are districts that have organized formal and informal professional development, such as one-on-one coaching sessions about how to integrate LGBTQ+ issues into lesson planning.[12] Professional development in the ongoing work of equity, inclusion, and belonging is a justice measure that will ensure our schools become affirming spaces of care, love, and learning for all people.

It is not uncommon for our young students to be more comfortable with gender expansive and inclusive ideas than the adults in their lives may be. However, harassment, assault, bullying, and discrimination based on students' gender identity and sexual orientation for LGBTQ+ youth is a reality in the United States, and it starts early.[13] It is understandable, given the sociopolitical history of sexuality in the US and the historic marginalization of LGBTQ+ folks, that we may not have the language or knowledge to encourage integrated learning experiences around these issues, regardless of our own sexualities. How we educate on these topics in a way that includes joy and celebration while recognizing systems of oppression is vital. What we can all model, however, is being aware of our own reactions when something is difficult or unfamiliar for us personally and being curious about something we don't fully know or understand.

As a teacher, think about how you model ongoing learning—what do you actually say when you don't know something, need help, guidance, or someone to talk to? How might we open our hearts and aspire to be inclusive and care for others, especially since all community members (and all humans, for that matter) deserve respect and dignity.

SCENARIO: Your fourth-grade class is studying the story of Robin Hood and plans to create a puppet show for younger children. You engage the class in a discussion of who will animate which characters. In the spirit of inclusion and ensuring that every student has a role, you easily facilitate a conversation that convert's Robin's "Merry Men" into a band of "Merry Friends," so that genders other than male may participate. The class also agrees to change the gender of some of the more recognizable characters; however, there is disagreement around the star role of Robin Hood. Some of your students think it's unfair that only a boy has the option of animating the Robin Hood puppet. Could the Robin Hood puppet be a girl? None of the boys want to animate a girl puppet, and the class doesn't want to alternate Robin Hood being a boy for some performances and a girl for others. One student presents a solution, "What if Robin isn't a boy or a girl?" You pick up on this and state that you will ask the school's health educator to come in and talk about Robin Hood as nonbinary. The class is satisfied and looking forward to a visit from health teacher, Mr. Gilbert, who will discuss gender expansive identity and how the class can present this in a positive light in the puppet show. (Independent School, Montgomery County, PA)

First, I know some people worry that conversations about gender may invite issues such as gender confusion and/or advocacy for different gender identities. To feel afraid of introducing dialogue about gender that some folks believe may lead to student curiosity and potential discomfort, especially if a teacher thinks they are unprepared, is understandable. These age-appropriate curiosities emerge from students trying to make sense of the world around them. Many children this age have picked up that gender matters for many folks, especially when it comes to acceptance and negotiating social power and inclusion. They notice complex issues in simple ways. Keep the discussion simple as well.

Robin Hood is a classic story, many of which were authored by men long ago and so featured male heroes. To reimagine these classic characters outside of their traditional assigned sex or gender is an update or reinterpretation of the story. This can help kids combat stereotypes about who is active or brave or needs rescuing. Overall, expanding how somebody can look or act, even if they identify as one particular gender, allows people to be who they really are without feeling like they have to fit into a box or fear being teased. Schools are responsible for protecting the fundamental right for all children to simply be themselves. It's about community and how we can all be a part of it.

In a utopian world, all caretaking adults in educational spaces would receive ongoing professional development on human development and comprehensive sexuality education (CSE), and every school would have a dedicated CSE program and teacher. These moments highlight our growth edges and limits. What do we model when we notice ourselves at the edge, and how do we ask for support without stigmatizing the conversation? In the Robin Hood puppet show scenario, the classroom teacher is comfortable with student-centered learning initiatives, discussions of inclusion, and nonbinary thinking in regards to gender and gender roles and expectations. The teacher also embraces a valuable moment for collegial collaboration, a deeper understanding of gender identity, and integrated studies. I hear from many teachers that it's easier to overlook these CSE opportunities than to address them directly, because they lack confidence in their own knowledge, want to avoid possible negative parent reactions, and/or fear the repercussions of a politicized education system that places political ideologies over student health. This is understandable for teachers given these contexts, and it is a tremendous missed opportunity. Again, each educator has to navigate for themselves the inevitable tensions between personal beliefs and experiences with CSE, job security, and what science tells us will benefit our students. However, whatever we can manage will make some sort of a contribution, even if not enough, so keep looking for opportunities to broaden your students' understanding and your own.

It's important to find out about CSE resources in your school community. So much of the time, teachers feel as though they work in isolation, that their self-contained classrooms are a boundary to community and to connecting with others who also believe in and know how to effectively do this work. School counselors, nurses, and other folks whose experience and knowledge may surprise you could be allies and resources; I know an admissions director who has a MEd in Human Development, a science teacher who went to medical school, parents who are community clinical staff, EMTs, midwives, doctors, and psychologists. Reach out to others who may enrich what you can provide. Model reaching out, asking for help, and giving others the opportunity to provide support and express knowledge and pride in what they do.

FEELINGS AND VALUES

During this developmental stage, self-conscious emotions such as guilt, shame, and pride may be felt in response to an increased awareness of how others respond to our behavior.[14] Students have the capacity to understand the causes and consequences of emotions and how context plays a role in how someone might experience an event, as well as feeling mixed emotions versus just one.[15] Students are developing coping strategies as a part of their self-regulation. As they improve their ability to self-regulate emotions, they may develop confidence, which contributes to their capacity to develop friendships.[16] Children also begin to generate or perpetuate norms around social behaviors, the acceptability of showing certain behaviors, and offer advice and support to each other, especially within conflict. All of this affirms continued social-emotional development.[17]

As part of continued skill building with feelings recognition and self-regulation, developmental psychologist Aliza Pressman suggests language to help with this understanding: "All feelings are welcome. All behaviors are not." Students are watching how we model this. Caretaking adults need to build their capacity to identify, talk about, and regulate our own emotions before we can teach kids to do the same.[18] Ultimately, the lesson is, if we can't name our feelings, we can't express them. If we can't recognize, understand, or put into words our feelings, then we can't do anything about them. "When we ignore our feelings or suppress them, they only become stronger."[19] Sometimes our emotions can work against us, so how do we make them work for us? By naming, understanding through regulated expression, and knowing how to process and take care of ourselves and others. Media literacy is an ideal way to start.

Students enthusiastically respond to media deconstruction as a way to understand certain concepts like feelings, how they show up, and how they are managed within interpersonal relationships and community dynamics. Consider using a film like *Inside Out 2* as inspiration for an activity. Select and view relevant parts of the film with the class. Discuss how the emotions characters (Anger, Sadness, Joy, Disgust, Fear, Boredom, Anxiety, Envy, and Embarrassment) are personified and connected to behavior through memories that represent various lived experiences. Then have students create personified representations of their own feelings attached to memories and behaviors. Consider creating a template, like a venn or bubble diagram, to organize their thoughts and art. Remind them that they can draw outside the lines as well, because sometimes our feelings and behaviors breach their figurative containers.

For older students, you may create an activity that includes telling a story of their experience (memory), writing the feelings it generated on slips of colored paper (that they associate with the feeling—bigger feelings could be on larger pieces), and putting them into a container (that represents the student themself). Then have them partner and collaborate to discuss how we may express those feelings with regulated behavior so that they are processed and/or come out of the container or how aspects of them stick around and shape us. These emotional skills help young people build resilience. The American Psychological Association (APA) defines resilience as "the process and outcome of successfully adapting to challenging or difficult life experiences, especially through mental, emotional, and behavioral flexibility."[20] Resiliency skills can be cultivated and practiced and help children manage stress and feelings of anxiety and uncertainty[21] that they may be confronted with at school.

Affirming the personal values of students and their families while also reinforcing community values may generate tension and/or conflict. In the spirit of learning communities, students need to understand that disagreements are normal and, within the context of a shared community, inevitable. What we commit to is not that everyone will or should get along and like each other all of the time, but that we will work through those tensions and differences together in healthy ways. District and school mission statements are value laden and an effective tool or add-on whenever navigating ethical issues.

SCENARIO: Your fourth-grade class is coming back in from lunch recess. Since students are typically in need of some grounding after yard time, you gather for circle time before academics. This is typically a check in about how the day is going. Fidel is visibly distraught. When it is his turn to share, he expresses extreme distress over what he has just discovered. Fidel's brother, George, is in Mr. Foster's sixth-grade class, which is doing a unit on families and identity. As the class shared about their identities, students asked Mr. Foster about his family, and he revealed that he has a male partner. Since Fidel knows and admires Mr. Foster as a mentor, particularly for students of color on campus, George felt he should tell him that Mr. Foster "is going to hell." Upon hearing this, other students become silly and make inappropriate comments about homosexuality. You immediately do a call and response that gets the class's attention, and all eyes and ears are curiously waiting for what you will say. (Contra Costa County Unified School District, CA)

For context, the educator, Mr. G, who experienced this incident, knows that Fidel and George's family are very religious. Just as Mr. G was as a child, Fidel and George are very involved with their church and have been for their entire lives. Also, Mr. G and Mr. Foster participated in Teach for America together and are allied colleagues and friends. When Mr. G shared this story with me, he told me that he didn't know what he was going to say in response, especially because he didn't want to compromise the importance of Fidel and George's faith or their appreciation and care for Mr. Foster. Social justice and equity are also tenants of his teaching; however, he is aware that affirmation of families and their values may not always align with his teachings. What to do?

First, Mr. G took a deep breath and allowed for a pause before breaking the silence. He then defaulted to his class guidelines and provided an important framework for young students. "Many of us have strong beliefs that shape how we view others," he said. "Some people may be different or live differently from what you know and what feels familiar to you. You may not understand Mr. Foster, but he is a human being who deserves respect. Let's go back to our class guidelines and who you said you want to be—let's talk about whether or not our current actions align with those values." The students identified the guideline, "We are respectful and caring of others," to focus on. The conversation centered around human dignity and how all members of the community bring value to the school. Mr. G followed up with Fidel and talked through this concept as it applied to him and his rapport with Mr. Foster, which provided perspective and assurance.

Sometimes teachers ask about the student in their class who says, "My dad/mom/caretaking adult says that's wrong" about someone's identity or a whole group of people that share an identity. When this is in conflict with what a teacher believes personally, they feel compelled to "correct" information/messages their student shares. Hopefully this takes place within a school that is living up to its mission and offers credible information, anchored in social and cognitive science and values inclusivity. That scaffolding, in theory, will in and of itself create and support an inclusive community grounded in mutual respect, care, and dignity for all students. Given the power dynamic of a teacher-learner classroom community, my suggestion when addressing moral-laden judgments is to say, "Some people believe 'x' and some people believe 'y,' and there are many who believe variations and combinations of those ideas. It's important not to be quick to judge others' beliefs and decisions just because they are different from yours. Your job is to figure out what you believe through learning and reflection as you get older."

You can also offer information from medically accurate credible resources. For instance, we know that being gay or trans isn't a choice. It is also true that adults of all genders have the legal right to marry who they wish. The law recognizes that people get to choose who they want to love in a committed relationship. Again, given the current political climate, if job security and what is best for children is in conflict, you will have to weigh the costs and benefits of using specific language. You may also choose not to use particular words that trigger inflammatory responses and instead use other vocabulary to convey the same information and/or meaning, as Mr. G. did. In all classrooms, it is important to affirm gender and sexuality diversity—not just that gender and sexuality diverse folks should feel safe but also cared for and celebrated from an asset-based perspective, like everyone else in the community. If you are working in a state that limits talking and/or teaching about gender and sexuality diversity, default to a discussion or multiple discussions about our shared humanity. Talk about the respect, care, and dignity all people deserve regardless of identity. Focus on inclusivity and caring communities and affirm that all students and adults deserve to be seen and heard. *How* we do this matters.

It is time to be intentional about discussions focused on intention versus impact. As students grow towards a deeper understanding of themselves and others in communities, create opportunities to engage in decision-making discussion and practice. Use scenarios that represent social dynamics that you observe in the classroom and ask students to identify what their observations are as well. Identify any power dynamics based on third- and fourth-grade social currency, such as popularity, possessions, admired talents, and an ability to attract and hold attention. Infuse dialogue about values and how our decisions align or don't align with them. Explore options for alternative choices and their potential influence and impact on others. Discuss what is ideal and what is realistic, as well as potential obstacles and concrete language, tools, and strategies for moving through and around them. This may take the form of "finish the story." Capture the beginning of an interaction between or among students that requires making a decision at an inflection point that will determine what direction that story goes. Ask students to come up with ways the scenario might continue and what the outcomes may be. Always reinforce memorable takeaways that will be useful to remember when confronted with similar situations.

RELATIONSHIPS (CONSENT, COMMUNICATION, DECISION-MAKING)

As students develop stronger relationship skills, they will become more confident contributors to positive classroom culture and community.[22] In addition to modeling how a dependable and caring person behaves, communicate the mantra that how we treat each other matters. Depending on the level of student prosocial skills, how you approach third versus fourth grade may be different. The healthy sexuality education classroom is one of the most differentiated that you'll ever teach. Different students, for all kinds of reasons, may be further along in honing their social skills, while others will lag behind. Hopefully, your school has been consistent in providing the foundation for this journey so that you may continue guiding student development. Third grade will most likely continue with lessons expressing appreciation, the language of kindness, and the self-regulation needed to bring these pieces of connection (empathy and compassion) to their developing relationships.

In fourth grade, as our students enter the realm of adolescence, which typically starts at age eleven, they must fully embrace the developmental task of figuring out how to have healthy sustained relationships in their lives. Elementary school is the building ground for the skills students need to express themselves and get along with others. Students can now grasp that how we use words can help support a relationship or hurt it—sometimes irreparably. Catherine Newman's book, *What Can I Say?*[23] is a tremendous resource in this regard. Newman helps students understand how kindness and knowing how to handle relationships will ensure positivity in our lives. She starts with "normal is not a thing, and that everyone doesn't have to be the same kind of person."[24] Yet there are certain fundamental values for how we treat people, and that may look and feel different based on who you are, who the other person is, and your relationship with each other. Sometimes relationships include conflict and "doing and saying the right thing is not always about smoothing the rough edges, conforming to norms, and making everybody's life easier."[25] We want students to get the message that what's most important is a balance of responding to other people's needs and our own.

Appreciation is the foundation of empathy. We must recognize how others contribute to our lives in positive ways as motivation to care about and recognize their experience and feelings. Designate a space in your classroom or hallways that serves as an appreciation board. Cut stars out of construction paper and encourage students to write what they are grateful for in each other. Be aware of popularity dynamics and ensure that every student is seen and included. Post these on the appreciation board. After a while, you may have constellations of gratitude and a milky way of appreciation.

Students also have the capacity to understand that consent is not just about physical touch and asking for permission but an approach and way of thinking about relationships. A consensual orientation to relationships contributes to building trust and commitment versus uncertainty and harmful vulnerability. At the same time, honoring people's right to consent contributes positively towards building a supportive relationship.

SCENARIO: As students are entering the classroom after lunch recess, you notice that Colton looks distressed. His face is red with anger and dirty tear streaks. You discreetly pull him aside and ask if he's okay and what's happened. Tears threaten to return. You patiently wait as he takes a deep breath and reports. While he was moving across the monkey bars, Violet ran up under him and "pantsed" him—she pulled his shorts down. He immediately dropped to the ground, which hurt, and had a hard time getting up to fix his shorts, which were around his ankles. Violet, Josie, and Sasha were all pointing and laughing, so more kids circled around and joined in. Colton expresses relief that "at least [his] underwear didn't go down," but he is still clearly upset. You ask who was on recess duty, and Colton confirms that Ms. Walker was on duty and told them to stop. You inquire if Ms. Walker talked to him about how he was and is feeling. Colton reports that "she didn't ask and just told [me] that the girls probably like [me] and have crushes on [me] so not to worry about it." (Teton County School District, WY)

Pulling down someone's shorts on the playground at all, let alone when it's unexpected, is an issue of consent. Colton has most likely just experienced an onslaught of emotion—being startled can illicit alarm and fright; the physical pain of falling unprepared; the panic of feeling exposed and trying to cover up, literally; public humiliation; the dread of peer ridicule; the embarrassment of "being caught with [his] pants down"; belittled by having the impact of the experience dismissed by an adult who is responsible for child safety; the anger of having a personal and community boundary disrespected; and the isolation of having had a painful experience and (until you) no one seeming to care. There are two pieces to this: the peer-to-peer interaction and the colleague-to-colleague issue. There is also a cultural context that needs attention: the community's greater culture of consent. This is the adult work that builds a restorative community to demonstrate care for all members.

First, Colton has some immediate needs. He most likely needs to feel seen and heard for what happened, for someone to care, which is felt when we notice and ask about a student's well-being. Recognize that what's just happened sounds like a lot and that his feelings are an understandable and normal response to mean behavior (it would be bullying if it was chronic, there was a leveraged social power differential, and eroding Colton's esteem). Ask Colton how he's feeling in the moment and how you can be supportive. Either in that moment or when you can provide focused attention to have a one-on-one conversation with Colton, provide choices for how to move forward. Encourage a restorative approach to addressing the issue. This means working with the students involved to create a safe, mediated, talk-it-out. This requires some training and work with the girls and Colton. Talk to the girls separately at first and with Colton only after they have recognized what they did was wrong and have sincere intentions to apologize and repair. You may enlist a school counselor for help.

It may be optimal to talk to Violet, Josie, and Sasha separately. Sometimes students go along with mean behavior even if their intuition tells them it's wrong. In isolation, you may be more likely to have a more truthful conversation and guide each student with moral suasion. Before the end of the school day, make a phone call home to Colton's parenting adults. Colton may go home and report what's happened, and as his teacher, getting in front of a discussion about how you are offering support will go a long way. There are several potential parental responses—compassion and wanting advice on how to support Colton, outrage and a demand to have the girls disciplined, anger or embarrassment that Colton couldn't "handle it," minimization and dismissal, or gratitude and support for Colton and how the school managed the incident. Provide information and assurance while being clear about your intentions and action steps. Encourage compassion as well as letting Colton have his own response. It may make it more difficult for Colton if folks ascribe more harm to the impact than he experienced. Follow up with an email and/or check in with your administrator. Give them a heads up that this issue may be coming their way, and ask about school guidelines and policy. Ensure that whatever your response, it is consistent with that guidance.

Violet, Josie, and Sasha need a review of consent, respect, and how it relates to community values. Be clear, and include concepts such as intention versus impact, and address any tendency to minimize or veil the incident with humor. Directly address "We were just playing" or "We were just joking" responses. Playing and joking is only fun if both or all people enjoy it. Preventative restorative practices would have you ask what the girls were feeling during the incident and what need they were trying to meet. What were the girls going for? Did they end up with what they wanted? At what cost? Are there other ways they could have met their needs, whether it was for attention, recognition, or feeling empowered? Do they understand that what they did was wrong because they caused harm? The girls' parenting adults need to be called as well.

Cultivating a culture of consent is a community-wide effort—all educators need to be talking to students about the culture of the playground and how to treat people the way they want to be treated through mutual respect, care, and dignity. Adults need training on how to manage conflict in ways that encourage prosocial behaviors and about how gender and sexuality show up and should be responded to so that students feel cared for and valued (i.e., in this case *not* excusing disrespect by identifying it as a crush). Professional development on bullying is critical, especially the difference between isolated incidents of mean behavior and chronic, intentional mean behavior within an inequitable power dynamic. Consider a class meeting that focuses on raising consciousness about community dynamics and building empathy and solutions, doing so without singling out specific incidents or individual students. If some students already have social access through digital communication, be aware that interactions may migrate into cyberspace and that what happens in digital environments may fuel and interact with in-school experiences.[26]

Initiate a conversation with Ms. Walker. Share what's happened and how you are addressing while inquiring about her perspective and response—or lack of one. Use the strategic questions by Fran Peavey.[27] Nonjudgmental questions that avoid why but lead with the what and how, in addition to observations like, "I notice" and "Help me understand . . ." For instance, "How did you see the girls' behavior towards Colton?" "Was there a moment when you said their behavior was because they like or have a crush on him? What did you mean for him to do with his feelings?" You may personalize your thoughts: "I worry students will think it's normal to be mean and cause harm in response to uncomfortable feelings—feelings of attraction in particular—and I get concerned how this impacts their developing understanding of consent." Strategic questioning encourages understanding across differences to inspire change without people feeling they have to abandon their own values. Emphasize through inquiry that normalizing harm as an aspect of attraction or desired intimacy is unhealthy and not in the students' best interest. Be aware that saying the girls had a crush is a gender-based assumption and that minimizing Colton's experience supports hyper-masculine norms that consent and hurt feelings aren't important to address within the context of a crush or sexuality.

When we teach about consent, it is typically assumed that someone's body language aligns with/matches their verbal language/words. When issues of consent show up in real life, this is not always the case, so students need coaching. Humanizing the concept with different scenarios encourages critical thinking and consensual responses that clarify what two people are agreeing to or need from each other. Reading about and deconstructing what characters in a given scenario are doing broadens a student's understanding of themselves and others. It is helpful to highlight that reading social cues and figuring this out can be challenging when energy runs high and students are still learning to self-regulate. To inspire curiosity and try on different forms of communication, use question-stems like, "What would happen if . . ."; "How do we know . . .";

"What do you think they meant when . . ."; "How might we know . . ."; and "What could we do instead?" Teach technique by offering examples of closed questions and open-ended questions. Open-ended questions tend to encourage deeper dialogue and sharing. Exercising these muscles gives students ideas, language, strategies, and tools to wrestle with challenging situations and prevents them from mushrooming in dramatic ways.

CONNECTION (INTIMACY AND LOVE)

When a student feels they belong, they learn and believe that they matter and are a part of something bigger than themselves.[28] As students are seeking social connection and finding their friends, cliques may form, which can lead to exclusion. Of course, not everyone will be friends or treat each other in ideal ways. After all, recess is like a morality clinic. Part of students learning how to find friends and initiate and sustain relationships includes making mistakes; circling back, apologizing, and repairing are all part of building trust and intimacy. Facilitate activities and dialogue about friendship dynamics.

Consider representing a spectrum of healthy to unhealthy (one on either side of the white board or wall) relationship behaviors. Create cards or bigger post-it notes with various behaviors like, "Apologizes when they do something wrong or hurtful"; "Teases me about my family"; "Respects your space"; "Makes you laugh"; "Talks to you with kindness"; and "Wants to keep what you do together a secret." Distribute the cards amongst the students and have them sort and post them on the spectrum. Debrief placement and encourage students to articulate their reasons for where they posted their cards. Discuss contextual factors that would move the cards to different spots on the spectrum. Consider when a behavior can be worked on and when it becomes a pattern that warrants reconsidering the relationship. Think about what behaviors require adult support and those that are celebratory. Highlight the behaviors that lead to intimacy and caring, loving relationships, and encourage students to express what it looks, sounds, and feels like when they are a part of them. These are what ultimately lead to belonging—not necessarily a physical space of belonging, rather a belonging we carry with us, because it lives within our own hearts and relationships.

Extend the lessons with ongoing conversations that include questions like, "What are the benefits of belonging to a special group?"; "What are some reasons for forming friend groups?"; "How come a clique may not let others into their group?"; "What's the impact of being excluded?"; and "What's the impact of being included?" to shine light on behaviors inspired by a need to belong. Enrich the lesson to consider what happens when a group of students don't want to include someone because they don't share the same values, or that person's behavior isn't okay with them, or they simply don't vibe with them. Is it okay to not be friends with everyone? If that is acceptable and reflective of real life, is it okay to not be friendly with everyone? What does it look, sound, and feel like to be respectful without being exclusive? Is there a reasonable way to exclude someone and still be respectful?

We want children to understand that true friends accept us for who we are and bring out the best in us. They also challenge us to become better. If students feel they need to fit in or strategically modify how they behave to be accepted, the performance creates facades that mask their true self. It is beyond difficult to form meaningful connections when trying to hide who you really are.[29] Literature is a wonderful way to discuss this.

You may begin by organizing students into pairs based on interests or attributes. Then have students investigate what they have in common through interviews. This prompts them to come up with questions that lead to getting to know each other better by connecting through similarities and getting curious about differences. Encourage them to talk about dreams, goals, and passions. Not only may they include fun facts like, "I'm in a church group" or "My Popo is from China" but also information like, "If I could have any superpower, it would be 'x.'" Invite students to share what they learned about their partner with the larger class and have other students snap or give a thumbs up if what's said resonates. Compliments and affirmation are also part of healthy relationships. You may create a shout out board in your classroom, where students post sincere compliments and appreciations for each other. Create a lesson plan on crushes, what a crush is, how it might feel, and how we may respond through behaviors when we have a crush or someone else crushes on us.

Crushes are incredibly common at this age, and they present the opportunity to emphasize and incorporate information you've been providing students about relationships and how we treat each other within the context of an interpersonal dynamic. Normalize and define what a crush is and that it's normal to have them and normal not to. A crush is a special kind of feeling for another person—typically a longing to be close to someone you are not already in a relationship with. For some, it means wanting to be physically close and affectionate, and for others, it's more an idea about someone and something about them that feels attractive.

Present students with scenarios involving social dynamics surrounding crushes. These are prime for addressing issues of consent, communication, and proposals for connection. Normalize that people may want to be close but not touch someone else (or even talk to them in some cases) and that crushes are often not reciprocated and can be fodder for gossip and used to garner attention, belonging, and wield social power. What I find most important to emphasize early is that, when a crush isn't reciprocated or someone doesn't romantically like someone else, it's not because they "don't know what they're missing" or "it's their loss." This minimizes someone's right to choose who they want to be in a relationship with. Your crush may like you as a friend but not think it's a romantic match (healthy relationships typically mean the same thing to both people), or they're not ready (that level of public intimacy isn't what they're looking for), or it's simply not on their radar yet. When we minimize someone else's right to consent/choose who they want to be close to, we promote inequitable and coercive dynamics later on. Fast forward five-to-seven years when someone expresses a desire to be intimate and the other person doesn't reciprocate, we want the initiator to respect the self-awareness, right to choose, and agency of the person responding. Minimizing what their crush knows about what they want or have the capacity to appreciate undermines concepts of consent and can lead to a sense of entitlement because the initiator assumes they know better.

We all need intimacy and love to thrive. When I ask parents or teachers in my workshops to remember their first crush and first heartbreak, someone or some time immediately comes to mind. After we discuss the emotional embodied experience of each (and I ask if they have any recollection of what they were learning academically at the time—you can guess the answer to that), I ask what would have helped and felt supportive at the time. Audiences consistently say, "to know it was normal," "to know what it was," "to feel seen and that I wasn't alone," and "to have someone to talk to." Intimacy. Intimacy is an emotional and/or physical closeness. It's a feeling of connection and affirmation. Sometimes students will say, "yeah, 'I-in-you-see-me!'" which sounds like "intimacy" when they say it. Well, sort of, but I'm happy to give them credit for efforts at being clever. It's feeling cared for and loved (not necessarily in love). Most of my students think intimacy is exclusive to romantic relationships, which is only a fraction of what it actually includes. Guide students to recognize the many different kinds of love that are out there and how it shows up in their own lives.

SCENARIO: You are sitting at a faculty table in the lunchroom during lower-school lunch. Fourth graders Thomas and Nial are at the adjacent table, so you can overhear their conversation. They are playing the "You tell me who you have a crush on, and I'll tell you who I have a crush on" game. Thomas is quick to share, "Eloise. Cuz she is beautiful and has freckles." It's now Nial's turn. Nial says, "Okay, but you have to guess." Thomas starts running through all of the girls in their class. Nial says, "Nope" to all of them. Thomas is perplexed and says, "Wait, that's everyone. Who else is there?" Thomas responds, "Peter." Thomas pauses for a moment, wide-eyed, and then responds, "Oh, I'm so sorry I didn't guess him and I thought it must be a girl. Peter. That's cool. My mom says I can like anyone I want. Like I could marry a boy or a girl or anyone as long as we care and treat each other good." Nial is quiet, nods his head, and continues, "Who do you think Peter likes?" Thomas shrugs his shoulders. (Independent School, Fulton County, GA)

We could do nothing in response to this moment or embrace it as an opportunity to think about what went into creating and/or allowing for the moment. How can we engage that more? What is it that's working in your community that you may be proud of and highlight in appropriate ways? Many young children and their families are open, caring, and loving when it comes to understanding gender and sexuality diversity. Rejoice in these moments. Notice who these students are and what values they hold. This is all important information to tuck away. Thomas and Nial have a caring and respectful relationship that seems affirming. Thomas is thoughtful and considerate as well as unafraid to own a mistake or assumption and apologize. Depending on the social climate of your school, Nial may be vulnerable to teasing and/or bullying for having a same-gender crush. Use gender inclusive language like, "crushes can happen to and on anyone of any identity." When educating about crushes, do not make heterosexual assumptions with language and interpersonal crush dynamics. Use integrated examples and scenarios that affirm all genders and sexual orientations. Remember to recognize, too, that it is normal to have a crush and normal not to have a crush. It's how we treat people in response to our feelings about a crush that matters. Also, highlight Thomas's skills as a caring friend, without providing names or details, during your next parent-teacher conference. The more we capitalize on these caring moments and acts of love, the more they will affect broader culture.

Love is a feeling that is hard to describe. Still, we seed the blooms of love by asking students what they love about themselves, what they love about other people, how they show love to themselves and others, and thinking about how people express what they love to do and who is loveable. Encourage family, friendship, and love stories in the spirit of collectively figuring out what you can about a feeling that is so universally important and celebrated yet feels like grabbing Jell-O to understand.

Children are impressionable, and the media they consume can shape their ideas about gender and relationships.[30] Acknowledge and identify examples of relationships in media when young people may misinterpret infatuation or inequitable and unhealthy relationships as intimate or caring and loving. Disney has produced a wide range of relationships anchored in traditional gender roles that would provide material for rich discussion; for instance, when Ariel in *The Little Mermaid* gives up her voice for Eric at the coercive hand of Ursula, who exploits Ariel's infatuation with him. What about Kristoff and Anna in *Frozen*? Theirs is a relationship built over time through shared experiences. Ask students for examples of media they are exposed to so that you may deconstruct and talk through them as a class. Ask who and what isn't represented as well. Relative to the plethora of cis-heteronormative representations of intimacy, romance, and love in media, LGBTQ+ relationships for young audiences are still overlooked, omitted, or intentionally left out and neglected. There is a need for positive, authentic representations of LGBTQ+ relationships that will provide a sense of identity and self-worth for all children and their families. When the majority of what little is out there are actually harmful stereotypes, token characters, and essentialized sexual identities, we narrow possibilities and harm those children who may not identify as cis-gender and/or heterosexual. Use Disney's series *The Owl House* as a start for inclusion. Luz, a main character, is a bisexual character and Raine is nonbinary. You may also show parts of the Netflix series, *Heartstopper*, which is full of different relationships that are caring, loving, and encouraging of treating each other with dignity. Students have been exploring relationships from Disney narratives to peer-to-peer dynamics and discussing the big and little feelings that go along with that; don't forget that sexually explicit media can also come out of nowhere and threaten the healthy ideas and expectations you've been working towards.

SAFETY

Many educators provide messaging about how students may keep themselves safe in "stranger danger" situations. It's also important for students to understand and know that most adults will protect children, not harm them, but when a child is victimized, it is usually by someone they know.[31] Students need to know what harassment is and that forced and/or nonconsensual sexual touching is wrong and illegal. Discuss coercion as confusing or tricking someone into doing what they want you to do. Since young people are typically taught to be polite from a very young age, give students permission to not be polite to an adult who tries to have sexual contact with them or otherwise acts coercively. Connect lessons about instincts, intuition, and trusting and talking about feelings in these contexts. Be concrete about what kids may say and do as well as who they should go to if they feel uncomfortable with how an adult or peer is talking to or touching them. This goes for any content they may come across online that activates intuitive discomfort.

Young people this age have an appetite for PG-13 movies and mature-audience-only shows. They may want to watch the new *Top Gun* movie, but suddenly, there's a sex scene that gives them an idea of what sex is, yet it's beyond what they can understand. We also know that they may suddenly come across pornography while in digital spaces online. This can also get in the way of healthy ideas about developing healthy sexuality and relationships. There are many digital filters and walls that can assist in regulating media that is inappropriate, and in some instances illegal, that children may come across. Parents may need recommendations and guidance on how to install them. Even so, there are great differences in how screen use is regulated among students, so we must be prepared to handle how digital exposure may show up at school.

SCENARIO: You receive a phone call from a distraught parent about their fourth-grade girl, Tessa, in your class. The mom reports that she discovered Tessa watching pornography on her iPad in the bathroom. When Tessa's mom asked about how she learned about porn, Tessa shared that her friend, Axel, told her about it when she asked if he knew where babies come from. (Denton County Unified School District, TX)

In addition to talking this through with Tessa's mom, this scenario elicits a conversation with Axel and a phone call home to Axel's parents. It surprises many parents to learn that the *average* age that a young person comes across pornography is eleven to twelve.[32] I work with many schools and have heard of students watching porn and showing it to other students on school buses and other parts of school campus, students airdropping porn images into other unsuspecting students' devices, and students stating that they are exposed to images of sexuality through other media and are curious about it, so they turn to porn to learn more because it's forbidden to ask questions or talk about sexuality with adults. Today, many middle schoolers have seen a hundred images of explicit, aggressive intercourse without ever having had a first kiss.[33] What does that do to their expectations and emerging ideas of sexuality?

Validate Tessa's mom's feelings, and help her understand that it is normal for kids to be curious about sexuality at this age. Point her towards educational guidance and resources (there are many—see appendix C) about different filters and firewalls that limit children from accessing sexually explicit material. Provide links to credible materials on how to talk to kids about pornography. These materials even provide scripts for different ages to ensure that what you say is cognitively congruent. You can also recommend books that inform and inspire discussion about sexuality that lets Tessa know that her mom is an askable parent. Gently remind Tessa's mom that the goal is to avoid shame and to remain composed and curious. Communicate that this is an opportunity to steer Tessa away from pornography and to offer alternative ideas of what intimacy and love looks, sounds, and feels like. She might say something like some or all of this, "As you grow older, I am so excited for you to discover who you are and what you want out of relationships, especially if you want to have a romantic partner. The most positive and fulfilling relationships include equal care, mutual respect, and intimacy. Caring and loving expressions of intimacy include talking and getting to know each other's wants and needs. People should bring out the best in each other and enjoy their shared experiences and be able to handle when things get difficult." Encourage Tessa's mom to point out that pornography does not reflect most people's healthy relationship practices and could shape ideas about sexuality that might get in the way of the stuff she has to look forward to when she grows up.

Have a one-on-one conversation with Axel. You might say something like, "I understand that Tessa was curious about where babies come from and you suggested pornography. You are right that most babies are the result of something called sexual intercourse, which is what pornography focuses on, but pornography is for grown-ups and doesn't show how most people have healthy sexual relationships. It's only for adult entertainment, not education. When it comes to questions about sex and sexuality, there are better kid-appropriate answers." Now if you are in a district that allows for CSE, you may offer that "we will continue to learn about that during Health class," and follow with, "and your parent(s) have information to share with you about it, too." You may conclude with, "We all want you to have caring, loving, and enjoyable romantic relationships in your life when the time is right. Watching porn can impact your developing brain and get in the way of that. So, let's talk to your parents about other places you can ask your questions about sex." Let Axel know that you'll be following up with his parent(s) and do so. It's important to let Axel and his parents know that your intention is not to shame or punish him and that he's not in trouble; you just want to make sure he has good sources for age-appropriate information. Because porn and other forms of sexually explicit imagery are so ubiquitous, we must create counter narratives of what we hope they aspire to: relationships that are anchored in care, mutual respect, and dignity. Read on into the next chapter for how we may build upon these counter-narratives and convey more age-appropriate, positive examples of sexuality.

4

Body Changes

Grades Five and Six

Love is as love does, and it is our responsibility to give children love. When we love children, we acknowledge by every action that . . . they have rights—that we respect and uphold their rights. Without justice there can be no love.

~ bell hooks

Cultivating a culture of love and care in middle school takes thoughtful strategy, creativity, and patience. Most fifth and sixth graders are experiencing the onset of puberty, if they aren't already completely immersed in it. As referenced in chapter three, the onset of modern puberty starts earlier; however, certain indicators like menarche and spermarche are still holding strong at an average of twelve to fourteen years old, depending on certain factors.

Based on how your school district organizes the middle school grades, students may no longer be in self-contained classrooms. Ideally, there is a designated Health Education period and a qualified teacher to support overall well-being and comprehensive sexuality education (CSE). In some schools that have this in place, the Health teachers are part of a larger department that centers on student life and well-being. The focus of Health classes is in-depth puberty education as well as continued instruction on identity formation, values, community, communication, healthy relationships, media literacy, and love.

Developmental highlights:

- Teachers describe middle schoolers at this age as creative, caring, private, quiet, energetic, messy, disorganized, sassy, considerate, responsible, ornery, joyful, moody, bright, self-conscious, fun-loving, earnest, and so on.
- Students are on a journey to discover and cultivate their passions, self-advocacy, negotiation, fitting in versus belonging, and what it means to act responsibly.
- They experience emotions in big ways. This intensity may include anxiety, sadness, embarrassment, anger, satisfaction, joy and love.
- Neuroplasticity means that students are vulnerable to poor judgement and making mistakes.

What's most important is that lessons be integrated across all subjects and in every educational space. The goal is to support students in understanding how CSE applies to life—not only inside a contained classroom as a part of learning and practice but across a spectrum of different contexts. If we want to encourage the development of personal integrity and the skills of treating ourselves and others with care and dignity, it matters how we show up in every area of life, and students are capable of learning and understanding this at a very young age.

BODIES

Bodies are changing! You may not only see it happening before your eyes in the shape of widening hips and lanky legs but smell it in the pungent presence of body odor and greasy hair. Reinforce and normalize lessons on pubertal body changes and reproductive systems. Differentiate between andrenarche (body odor, pubic hair, and oilier skin) and puberty (growth spurts, voices changing, breast buds, and testicular growth, to name a few examples). Keep students together in all-gender groups. When it comes to sexual reproductive anatomy, the rock star sexuality educator and author, Emily Nagoski, says, "We all have the same stuff, it's just organized differently."[1] In the spirit of understanding how all bodies work, not just half of the population with whom we happen to share similar parts, all students must learn about all humans. This normalizes all body parts, is inclusive of all people, and will help students now and in the future to be compassionate and supportive of what others might be going through specific to their different bodies. It also moves away from binaries and is more inclusive of what is naturally diverse. Biological or genetic sex includes a whole host of factors: chromosomes, hormones, and body parts. Nagoski's language helps young people understand that there are tremendous variations when it comes to bodies, including intersex folks. For intersex people, "stuff" got "organized" in a unique way. Nearly 2 percent of the population is intersex; this represents a similar percentage of people who have red hair.[2]

SCENARIO: You're teaching a sixth-grade health class on sexual reproductive anatomy, specifically the slang/language students are exposed to and use in reference to it. Students are in small groups listing all of the terms they regularly hear in reference to sexual reproductive body parts and writing them on post-it easel pads. You check in with each group. You notice that under 'penis' someone has written something in big letters and crossed it out. You ask, "What did this say?" Morgan replies, "Oh I didn't want to write that." You ask, "How come?" Morgan shares that they think it's probably inappropriate. You offer, "If you think it's something people hear a lot, you can add it. That's the point of the activity—to bring up the ways people are talking about sexuality and discuss how it shapes our ideas about it." Morgan nods and writes "BBC" on the paper but in much smaller letters. (Poweshiek County School District, IA)

This activity is excellent for revealing what information students have actually been exposed to and what they may be trying to make sense of themselves. You will find that young people are exposed to much more information than most people think, and sometimes you will be surprised by the things they don't know. I like to facilitate these discussions early on because it allows me to demonstrate that I can handle what students see and hear without shame (assuming this is the case) and guide them to meaningful dialogue about it. Critical thinking skills about what's real for students builds credibility with them. Afterall, they have a power that we don't, and that's to know what's happening for young people when adults aren't around. Trends in cyberspace change quickly too, so it's useful to keep up with what's "in" and "out." This is essential information for cocreating relevant curricula that is cognitively congruent. It is imperative that we create counter-narratives to what is not in the student's best interest, especially if it reinforces harmful stereotypes.

I hear students reference BBC when it's trending on certain social media platforms quite often. *BBC* stands for big Black cock. There are layers to these racist sexual stereotypes, and how you talk about them in a classroom truly matters. You must set the tone for mutual respect and safety for all students, especially for those who identify with the racial groups being discussed. This is true of any identity that is historically and/or currently marginalized. Prior to addressing BBC or the hypersexualization of any race or other group, focus student attention on anatomy-specific and sexual-behavior specific critique. This is how you will set expectations for these conversations and model what those expectations look, sound, and feel like in action.

When talking about the language they're exposed to and use about sexuality, I find students typically either get quiet, because they can't believe an adult has outed the language that's so normalized amongst them, or they start laughing and may make inappropriate comments, because they are uncomfortable, have only heard these words in a humorous context, or don't want others to know they have only a little or a lot of exposure to what their peers are talking about. What seems to be universal is that young people don't usually have adults in their lives talking to them on a regular basis in positive and constructive ways about sexuality, even though they are exposed to it constantly. My friend, student advocate and educator, Charis Dennison, likes to say to her classes, "sex is everywhere and nowhere all at once."

In general, if students laugh, you may respond in a casual tone with, "Okay I get it, this is either uncomfortable and embarrassing because adults don't talk about it much or you've only talked about sexuality in a joking way. I'm all for having fun in class together, but I want to remind us that sex is also a serious subject, so we need to call on our maturity to make sure we are respectful in class while we talk about it." (I always open my middle school puberty units with a definition of maturity and will remind students of it often). Then I may follow with, "So I will wait until you're done with the giggles so we can call upon our maturity and get to what we're going to discuss."

Start with a broad overview: "What do you notice about the wall and all of the words we have for these body parts and sexual behaviors?" Students will notice that "there's a lot" or "there's so many." You may respond with, "Yes! Typically, an elbow is just called an elbow, or a leg is just a leg. We may get detailed with calf, knee, or thigh, but when it comes to sex, we have many more names, names that are loaded with different kinds of meaning for all of these things. What do you think makes these body parts different?"; "How would you characterize the language? When do you typically hear these words?"; and "What meaning do we give them? If you were an alien who came down to earth and saw the language, what would you think our society values and/or devalues about sexuality?" Have students talk in small groups and share out. This yields a diverse set of answers to consider and supports multilingual, neurodiverse, and quiet students.

Once students engage with the lesson with maturity (an important skill to build: the capacity to have challenging conversations with grace despite feeling uncomfortable), move on to deconstructing gendered language. Ask, "How is some of the language gendered?"; "Is there some that is usually associated with a particular gender? Do you notice any double standards?"; "What does this reveal about societal messages about sexuality and sex/gender?"; "Who does the language benefit? Who does it compromise or hurt?"; and "What does it do to people's capacity to have healthy romantic and/or sexual relationships?"

When you get to language that includes racialized stereotypes and expectations, like BBC, (as students get older, you may introduce concepts of fetishized and exoticized races), you may start with, "I notice students frequently bring language like this up. Let's talk about this one. First, I want to recognize the racialized aspect of it, and remember that we are committed to respectful dialogue." This is an opportunity to recall your previous conversations about stereotypes and how people may use them to harm people. Because of hypermasculine expectations that "bigger is better," (and yes, many students this age, in boyhood in particular, have heard that it is ideal for boys to have big penises, which is about performative masculinity and is reinforced amongst peers, on social media platforms, and sexually explicit media), some students may think this is a positive stereotype of Black men. Sexualized, seemingly "positive" stereotypes are actually harmful.[3] And when students use this language, they are invoking stereotypes that may harm their peers (and themselves) without knowing what they're actually talking about. "Positive" stereotypes (which aren't compliments) are still harmful, because they aren't accurate—they are ideas about people that aren't anchored in actual people and are reductive, objectifying, and dehumanizing; they don't take into account individual, unique human experience.

As educators, it is our responsibility to be antiracist in our approach to education. There are several questions you may ask that will get at the intersectionality of this language. You may ask questions like, "What are the situations or contexts when this word (or acronym in the case of BBC) comes up? And by context, I mean what else is happening in people's minds and in their surrounding environment when they use it. How do people use the word? Who is saying it? For what reason? What do you think they're going for?" This is a big line of questioning, so chunk it up and be selective. You may extend the lesson and also ask, "How might stereotypes like this harm people?" and "What do we know about the history of racism in this country?" Depending on how much time you take with the language, consider assigning one question to each group and then having a larger full class discussion. Remind students to avoid sweeping generalizations that enforce or create stereotypes, and encourage them to take on the role of social scientists who are making observations about what they see and hear when it comes to sexuality.

Talk about how harmful racialized stereotypes are and dismantle any notion that any stereotype is "positive," "passes," or is okay in certain situations. This is an important and natural transition into talking about the *issue* versus the very specific *word.* Bring up how people justify negative behavior with humor. Ask the class if anyone has been the focus of joking around that didn't feel funny, rather uncomfortable or hurtful, and be clear about how this doesn't align with community values. Students say to me that pausing like this to think about the language they use, in and of itself, discourages their use of it. It puts it in front of them so that they cannot deny how harmful it can be. It is also critical to be aware of spending too much time on specific language, as students whose identities may align with what's being discussed could feel there is a spotlight on them, so be brief.

There are interesting turning points that take place in fifth and sixth grades. Students become aware of each other and make comments and judgements in ways they haven't in the past. People may be sizing each other up and making positive and negative comparisons. This reality, at a time when children are already becoming more self-conscious because of adolescence, can influence how students make meaning of the comments and judgments that are inspired by cultural messages they are exposed to but don't often understand. Peers start talking about other peers—gossip is common during this developmental stage. Stereotypes can play into who you are in a community—especially in regard to identity—and, in turn, how you want to be seen and feel about yourself. Older students may make sexualized comments that can confuse younger students, because they don't have much experiential context to make sense of them.

Sometimes students will deploy inflammatory language they could get in trouble for but don't really understand.[4] Whether seeking attention, negotiating power, or trying to level up to older, more mature kids, the racial and gender implications of this kind of language are complex and insidious. Fifth and sixth graders need to be able to identify when they hear or use a stereotype that perpetuates historical and current forms of inequity and dehumanization related to race, gender, or gender identity.

GENDER AND SEXUALITY DIVERSITY

Due to the sociopolitical historical context of sex negativity and stigmatization in the US (and some other countries), issues of gender and sexuality may incite conflict. We are currently navigating this, as some people in positions of power remove students from the center of their education and put their own political ideologies above student health. This thinking is also present in some parents. So, what do we, as educators, do—particularly in situations when we aren't trusted as professionals to know what's important for student growth.

Most parents don't like surprises. Ensure that you have a regular form of transparent communication in place that welcomes parent-teacher communication. This goes a long way in preventing contention. Educators frequently ask me how to respond when there are students who bring values from home into class that are exclusive or not affirming of other identities, especially those that represent people who have been systematically marginalized and oppressed. For instance, while gender expansive identities and concepts come up, a student raises their hand and says, "I'm a Christian and not comfortable with what you're saying. My parents say that's unnatural and wrong."

I suggest several approaches to these moments, and how you handle it will depend on many factors, including what you know about the student and their family, the greater culture of the school, your own training and comfort levels with this topic, and whatever comes up for you personally. I encourage transparency and direct communication whenever approaching controversial topics—I try to get in front of a problem before it happens. You may say, "We're going to discuss 'x.' I want to recognize that what I say or what we discuss may be different than what you hear at home. Sometimes mixed messages can feel confusing or uncomfortable. My intention is not to disrespect or devalue the messages you get from home, which may be different from the ones we uphold here at school. If this brings up anything for you, please check in with me after class. I really want to hear from you." If you need to respond to a public expression of conflicting messages, you may respond with "some and some." For instance, "Ah, yes, I hear you.

Some people believe 'x' and some people believe 'y,' and there's a whole in-between and variations on those beliefs. At school, we value 'x,' so that's what we're talking about now. Your job, as you get older, is to take all of those perspectives into consideration and figure out what you believe. Let's check in to talk about 'y' by the end of the day."

When you talk to the student, reiterate that, as a community of individuals, it's inevitable that there will be conflict and that healthy communities work through those conflicts in healthy ways. Focus on the feelings that are coming up for them as well. "What's coming up for you in class when we have these conversations? How does that make you feel?" and/or "How can I support you when that happens?" Your student has already gotten the information you've provided in class and is sitting with the tension of the conflict. Now you know what may come back to you from home—you'll want to prepare. You can always default by pointing out that your role is to meet the needs of *all* students and that navigating differences in family and personal values is a valuable skill that is a part of education.

Provide young people with the language and skills to honor people's identities, including gender, and ensure that they have a clear understanding of how to accurately express and discuss gender and sexuality diversity. This enables students to align with the community value of mutual respect. Students' family structures have become ever more diverse. Continue to include this variety in your lessons, not only through instructed personal sharing, like family oral histories or literature that provides an array of representation, but also include authentic representations of different family structures and identities that don't exist in your classrooms. Students are exposed to a myriad of family structures and identities through media and will eventually interact with folks from different backgrounds as they move beyond the immediate community.

When it comes to gender diverse families, remember not to make assumptions about how this directly relates to student behavior. Just because a student comes from a family that represents different social identities doesn't mean that all members of the family are aligned with how that is experienced and how they respond. There are also internalized forms of oppressive thinking that may be present. For instance, just because someone is a person of color doesn't mean that they may not be behave in racist ways. Or just because someone identifies as a woman doesn't mean that they believe they are entitled to sharing resources and/ or housework equitably within a male–female marriage. How a student feels about their family and how their family is perceived in the community matters to them.

SCENARIO: Your class is working in small groups on a long-term assignment. As you circulate, you overhear Finn say to Darius, "Dude, that's so gay." You approach and say, "Finn, we don't use words like gay as an insult or to mean something negative." Finn nonchalantly responds, "Oh, thanks Mr. 'X'. I didn't mean anything by it. My dad's gay." Darius is nodding his head in affirmation as if to say, "Yeah, it's true." The boys go back to their work after the redirection. (Hennepin County School District, MN)

"That's so gay" starts to show up in third grade and continues with frequency through middle school and high school; although, homophobic language in the later years can be far more demeaning—the term *fag* for instance. Many students respond to reprimand with, "Oh I'm just joking," or "I didn't mean anything by it," or "That's not how I'm using it." Our culture frequently minimizes behaviors that are considered offensive by justifying them as humor or focusing on intention over impact. Any language that equates people's sexuality with negativity creates a platform for more intense and demeaning language and behavior in the future.

It's important to nip this kind of behavior in the bud; however, this scenario is a bit tricky. Some teachers feel thrown off by this—the child using disparaging language has a parent who identifies with the group being insulted, so the student doesn't think they should be held to the same standards as others. The implication is that somehow the student's relationship to a gay father excuses his use of the derogatory term and that, because of his family, the teacher should not hear the term as homophobic. On the contrary, in this case, the teacher has an important responsibility to demonstrate to the student that homophobic language is *never* okay. As readers, we don't know if the student was motivated to use the word *gay* as a put-down so that he would fit in, as a means of differentiating from his family, or something entirely different. Regardless, it's critical for the teacher to recognize their role in helping the child navigate the tension between wanting to fit in with what is socially normalized for ten-to-twelve year olds and an aspect of a parent's and family's identity.

In this particular scenario, Mr. 'X' knows that Finn is proud of his family, and it is most likely true that Finn doesn't mean anything by what he said; he isn't equating a term that identifies sexual orientation with something negative. Most kids understand that open homophobia is uncool. More often, the types of homophobia that are allowed to *pass* are these subtle conversations; interrupting this nuanced homophobia is critical for real change. Allowing the use of language that some may minimize as being no big deal contributes to unsafe spaces for LGBTQ+ youth (which ultimately compromises all of us in the community, especially folks who identify with groups that have been and/or are historically marginalized) and could contribute to the escalation of behavior that is even more harmful.

Find a discreet time to talk to Finn. Initiate conversations with nonjudgmental language. "Finn, remember when I brought up that we don't use *gay* as something negative and you said 'you didn't mean anything by it?'" Finn says, "Yeah. I didn't." You ask, "Okay, what is it that you 'didn't mean'? What do students usually mean when they say, 'that's so gay?'" Finn will most likely articulate what you're getting at, that something is negative or bad, or in the words of some students, "It just means 'stupid' or 'dumb.'" Add that you've also heard it used as an insult or a "put-down." You may then ask, "How does being called a name feel, especially if someone is targeting an important part of who you are?" or "How do you think someone who may identify as gay, is wondering if they're gay, or cares about someone who's gay feels when they hear that, especially in such a normalized way?" Focus on the feeling so that this isn't just an intellectual exercise but something we connect with on an emotional level. "What do you think people may associate with being gay then?" "What will people think of when they hear the word *gay*?"

Some folks may suggest connecting the situation to Finn's dad, but I think that if you can have the discussion without making it personal, Finn will be less likely to experience shame for what he's said and done (i.e., using language that is "normal" among his age group without critical thought or justifying language that may be othering of his family). Show Finn that you appreciate his willingness to discuss the issue, while making the point that *gay*, when used negatively, continues to be a word that people use to tease and bully, so "It hurts gay people directly and ultimately everyone. And we want everyone to be able to be themselves."

FEELINGS AND VALUES

Middle school is *a lot*—an exciting time of growth and transformation. Change is a constant in life, and it is valuable for our students to be flexible thinkers, which is essential to building resilience and protective factors that will support navigating the ups and downs of life. Flexible thinking deepens our self-awareness and our social relationships with others.[5] Most of the time, flexible thinking promotes getting along with others, because it encourages us to consider other points of view and situations from different perspectives. It enables us to be empathetic and better understand other people's intentions and how they want to be treated.

The capacity to adapt to change helps students maintain their emotional health. Students who fail to adapt to change may experience emotional overwhelm and/or meltdown at events that seem small and inconsequential. Behaviors associated with flexible thinking include emotional self-regulation, the ability to improvise in unexpected situations, multitasking with ease, thinking creatively when problem-solving, and seeing a situation from different perspectives.[6] When faced with challenging situations, validate student feelings. When children feel understood, they are less likely to resist and dig into negativity and more inclined to seek what's constructive.[7]

Partner with students to solve problems and let them know you have their backs. When I talk about relationship dynamics with students (of all ages, adults included), folks focus on telling a story that revolves around the chronology of events and typically leave out the emotional embodied experience—the element that may resonate with and connect us more deeply. As students move up the grade ladder and school becomes increasingly academic, we tend to intellectualize our stories, especially as they relate to our human connections. As teachers, we may need to remind students to tap into their emotions. The ability to name feelings helps us understand our experiences and share them with others, express our needs and get them met, do the same for others, communicate, support social connection, and allows for empathy (feeling with someone).[8] This practice will more likely lead to compassion, empathy, and getting our needs met. In the words of Marc Brackett, "How students feel is what gives meaning to what they are learning. The research is clear: emotions determine whether academic content will be processed deeply and remembered."[9]

SCENARIO: After you dismiss your sixth-grade class to recess, you notice a few girls lingering. They are talking in hushed whispers. You ask, "Is something up?" Ariana responds, "Well there's this game the boys are playing, and we don't like it. It's not a big deal—we don't want to make a big deal out of it but want it to stop." You become curious and inquire about the game. The girls (Ariana, Monique, and Jasmine) have a hangout spot during breaks, which is a bench in the yard. Jet and Robbie have recently started to come over and initiate a game where Jet softly tickles Jasmine up and down her arm and sometimes on her side towards her armpit and breast. Jasmine is supposed to have her eyes closed and say "stop" when she doesn't want him to continue. Monique adds that it's like a game of chicken and that Robbie is always elbowing Jet with a smile like he's daring him to go further. Ariana comments that she guesses "it's kinda fun but doesn't feel right. Like kinda creepy." (Santa Clara County Unified School District, CA)

There is a lot to unpack here, and focusing on what students have the capacity to understand and will contribute to their continued growth and safety is the priority. Games like this at this age are typically innocent in nature; however, there is also a lot of gendered socialization that is evident and that we can address. Elements for us as educators to highlight (and that provide insight into the interpersonal social power dynamics of the situation) include the fact that the boys initiate the game and the girls go along with it. In my experience, girls in similar situations typically engage in the game and present as enjoying it. It feels a bit risky; it also provides attention, so they express mild thrill, which is potentially mistaken for having fun. I always keep in mind the gendered cultural expectations that girls are valued for their appearance, which is for others' consumption.[10] There's perceived agency, because the girls get to say "stop," but the daring, how-far-can-you-go aspect of it compromises expressing a genuine boundary anchored in comfort and mutual understanding. The game is really about pushing boundaries and how someone may or may not assert them, despite potential judgment or admiration, which detracts from or contributes to social currency.

There's also a lot of opportunity in this scenario to educate and reinforce important feelings, values, and skills. I always like to start with an appreciation for what has been shared, especially within the adolescent context of "snitches get stitches." Hopefully these students receive CSE that includes scenarios like these that bring up these kinds of issues in more neutral safe spaces. When it comes to us one on one, we have to prioritize. Exploring sensuality, boundaries, and interpersonal dynamics is all age appropriate; however, *how* we do that has the potential to shape behavior over time. Ariana, Monique, and Jasmine are sharing a pivotal moment in solidarity. Their intuition is telling them that their boundaries are in play, and they are looking for guidance on how to stay true to their autonomy, make sense of the push and pull of playground politics, and exercise agency without losing face.

Start with mirroring language and getting curious. We want the girls to affirm their own intuition and discover a solution for themselves. You may support this process by helping them hear and, in turn, develop their own voice and plan through strategic questions. Start with something like, "I hear that you don't like the game and want it to stop. What about it feels uncomfortable to you?" Listen and mirror back what the girls say. You may choose to affirm by saying something like, "I get that, especially because we all know that we don't touch the parts of people's bodies that they usually keep private without permission and definitely not at school." Consider continuing with, "That part inside you that tells you what is uncomfortable is really important to listen to and take care of—it's called your intuition. It is the voice inside you that tells you what feels comfortable and welcome and what doesn't. Sometimes there are in-betweens, but it sounds to me like you are sure about this one."

Once you've validated the girls' feelings, continue with, "What is getting in the way of saying no to the game?" They will most likely reference the possibility of judgment, minimization of their assertion, or ridicule, which will be encapsulated in "we just don't want to make a big deal out of it." (Which sounds to me like these girls are already being socialized to protect masculinity by thinking of their boundaries as permeable or unimportant and thus reducing their agency). You may say, "Okay, I get that, so what's a way you could say and show no but then distract them with something else so it doesn't become a big deal?" Collaborate to come up with a couple of options and identify roles to be played. Be concrete with language and have them say it back to you and share how it feels. For example, one girl says, "Nah, we're done with that," and the same or another says, "Yeah, we want to play on the rings instead." You may want to add, "About not wanting to make it a big deal, I understand where you're coming from, and sometimes our society tells girls to ignore their feelings in situations like this. I want you to know you have every right to take them seriously." Follow up with the girls to ensure their boundaries are being respected. Since you didn't witness the game in action, the girls don't want to "make a big deal" of it, and the game is indicative of wider community learning opportunities when it comes to boundaries and consent; be intentional about a class lesson. Make sure there's a class scenario as a part of your health lessons that you all go over with similar dynamics; present a collection of very short stories/case studies that students deconstruct and discuss to raise critical consciousness and explore decision-making intentions and consequences. As a part of the discussion, you may even say, "Another example of this kind of dynamic is a tickle game I've heard of on the yard." Teach about the role gender plays in an interpersonal dynamic that feels flirty but pushes the boundaries of consent.

As educators, it's important that we facilitate activities that recognize all students and reinforce that their beliefs and ideas are important. It is inevitable that conflicting personal values will emerge within communities. It's important to recognize this when we talk to students about the value of social connectedness and community. Part of the value is that we learn how to be in community with each other and resolve conflict in healthy ways. Everyone isn't going to agree or get along all the time. And not everyone in the community will be friends with each other all the time either. Sometimes schools' community values also conflict with students' home values. What we can expect, however, is that all members of a school community embrace the values of humanity (mutual respect, care, and dignity, to name a few) despite holding other different opinions and values.

RELATIONSHIPS (CONSENT, COMMUNICATION, DECISION-MAKING)

The adolescent brain is still under construction, which can lead to poor decision-making—despite really good intentions. The adolescent brain grows from the back, forward. As a child enters adolescence, the limbic system in the amygdala, the part that is needed for survival, is pretty well developed. In humans, mother nature has determined that, in the interest of survival, the primal reward center of the brain be developed sooner rather than later. This part of the brain also has to do with emotions and impulsive behavior. However, the prefrontal cortex—the part of the brain that has to do with executive functioning (i.e., rational decision-making)—is still very much under construction. The prefrontal cortex is needed to govern the amygdala. The processes of neurological pruning and myelination are the primary ways by which the brain develops.[11] A simpler way to describe neurological pruning is summarized in the phrase "use it or lose it." If kids don't use certain neurons, they will literally disappear. Myelination is a process by which the brain insulates neurological pathways that are stimulated through a child's activity—the brain organizes itself based on what the child or adolescent does. This is why we encourage skills and drills during sports and go over scales in music: this practice literally shapes the brain. The issue is that this essential part of the brain won't actually be fully developed until a person reaches their mid to late twenties or even early thirties. Hence, our children and students will make some really silly and sometimes even very scary mistakes and decisions.[12]

As educators, we can help our students understand the science about their own developing brains. It's important to recognize that this isn't an excuse for poor decision-making but rather an explanation. Understanding the basics of brain development can empower young people and help them be mindful and thoughtful about their actions and support them doing better and living their amends when they mess up.

Take the time to explain this science to your students. Kids are curious, and it can be a relief for them to know the reasons they may have the best intentions and still act in ways that yield unwelcome behavior and difficult consequences. This also gives them a sense of ownership when it comes to behavior, because there are actually steps they can take to help themselves make good choices. Cara Natterson and Vanessa Kroll-Bennett offer this language in their excellent book, *This Is So Awkward: Modern Puberty Explained:* "At your age, your brain has a super highway to your limbic system (the area that controls pleasure-seeking and risk-taking behavior), but the road to your prefrontal cortex (which controls thoughtful decision-making) is under construction, so traffic heading there moves slowly. That's why sometimes you do some pretty silly stuff or you make choices you kinda know you shouldn't. Understanding this can help you make better decisions."[13]

Natterson and Bennett suggest taking a pause when faced with a decision so that the prefrontal cortex has the opportunity to catch up to the amygdala. This can look like slowing down and taking a deep breath or two or counting to ten before reacting to a situation. Ask students, "What can you do to remind yourself to pause for a minute?"; "What would it take to slow down to check in with yourself?"; or "How can we help each other to take a pause, especially when you're in a group of friends making a decision?" These are all great questions to add whenever going through scenario deconstruction.

Work with your students to cocreate scenarios—structured like the ones in this book for educators—that feel relevant and are an accurate representation of the social landscape they are navigating in middle school. At this age, it's a good idea to keep the scenarios relatively simple and to ask approximately three questions per scenario. Depending on the scenario, there's typically a lot to unpack, and it's possible that the questions will inspire a meaningful dialogue that riffs in many directions. However, I find it's best to provide multiple scenarios with less questions versus one scenario that is overdone. Keep the questions concrete and focused on the feelings, motivations, and decision-making of the characters. Emphasize intention versus impact and how we may optimize decision-making so our intentions align with our impact. Always balance scenarios that feature prosocial behaviors and decision-making, as well as those that provide opportunities for growth. Practice nonjudgmental dialogue by using, "I notice . . ."; "It seems as if . . ."; or "I'm wondering . . ." Lead inquiry with, "How would it feel . . ."; "What if . . ."; "What would it take . . ."; or "What would that actually look, sound, and feel like?"

This kind of exercise may feel futile at times, and it may be hard to tell how much students are absorbing, but I assure you that they have an impact. Students have told me that externalizing their behaviors onto paper or through discussions in class give them greater perspective on those behaviors. Given what we know about neuroplasticity, practicing decision-making supports a higher probability of students making better decisions in the future. Like all schooling practice, this contributes to scaffolding in that direction. We must also educate students that discussion in a "cold" cognitive environment is different than in a "hot" environment. Young people are neurologically programmed to seek the acceptance of their peers, so a friend's presence can influence decision-making when outside of the classroom and in a context that includes peers. In some ways, this approach is like teaching math. We guide kids through practice in classrooms in preparation for when they transition to using those skills in the real world, like leaving a tip at a restaurant or budgeting for groceries at the market.

As students mature, they continue on the developmental task of finding and sustaining healthy relationships. *What Can I Say?* by Catherine Newman is a relevant text for fifth and sixth grade. In sixth grade, you may need to teach up to a slightly more sophisticated audience; however, I find students this age always benefit from review and practice of what may seem basic or elementary. You can guide the reflection in more sophisticated directions by asking questions like, "What has been a challenging moment in your relationship?"; "How did you handle it?"; "What did you learn from it?"; "What's a favorite memory you share with your friend—would they recall the same one?"; "How have you treated them in a way that made you proud?"; "How have they treated you in a way that made you feel cared for?"; or "What do you wonder about this person now?" Newman's language and strategies for mutual respect when navigating conflict within relationships is particularly useful. Proactively teaching how to stick up for someone, report bullying, be a courageous ally, and disrupt prejudice and offensive behavior is applicable to the following scenarios regarding consent as well.[14]

SCENARIO: Your class is on a field trip to a local museum. The docent is leading all of you up a stairwell to another floor. Cora slides up next to you and whispers, "Ms. Garcia, I saw something inappropriate. Freddy did the 'clamper' to Gabriel." That is, as the students were going up the stairs, Freddy was walking behind Gabriel and stuck a finger in between his butt cheeks (what the students in your class call a *clamper*). You can see that Freddy is still walking behind Gabriel, who is frequently turning around in anticipation of it happening again. (Marin County School District, CA)

This nonconsensual behavior needs to be immediately addressed. *How* you respond to a student's reporting behavior—that is clearly making them feel insecure—will determine whether students perceive you as a responsive caretaking adult who models and upholds ideas of consent and bodily autonomy or someone who minimizes and discounts nonconsensual behaviors with harmful societal messaging like, "boys will be boys"; "they're just crushing on you"; or "they're just playing—ignore them." Appreciate Cora for her report and affirm her courage in coming forward. Hopefully you've had class conversations about the difference between snitching (telling on someone to purposefully get them in trouble) and reporting (reporting information to right a wrong).

Go to Freddy and discreetly take him to the side, which removes him from any audience. Tell him what you've observed, "it's been reported that you did the 'clamper,' you poked someone in the butt with your finger." I've also heard this referred to as "fish in the creek." I'm sure there are other euphemisms (which make it easier for the student to justify the behavior) for it in different locations. Start with, "What's going on?" and become genuinely curious as you get to, "What were you feeling in the moment, and what did you mean by/or get from doing it?" Mirror back what Freddy shares—"so I hear you saying . . ."—which may include minimizing and justifying, and continue with, "Touching someone without their permission, especially parts of their body that are considered 'private,' is nonconsensual. It's never okay. It disrespects their right to choose what happens to their body and can make people feel scared, and/or disrespected, and/or insecure. If you're feeling 'x' or the need for 'y,' there are other ways to do that without disrespecting someone. Let's talk about that."

Depending on what kind of consent education has or has not been scaffolded across Freddy's education so far at your school, you may need to review and/or teach Freddy the values of consent and the importance of cultivating cultures of consent in school and other communities. You will then need to explain to Freddy that there are consequences for disrespecting and inflicting harm on others. Talk to Freddy about the classroom norms of respecting others and the school's policies that include unwanted touching, which can be experienced as aggressive. Parents need to be contacted—as a general rule, anytime you talk to a student about unwanted touching of another student, it's a phone call home—and, potentially, one to your school administrator as well. You'll need to collaborate so that you provide a consistent message to Freddy.

After thanking Cora and swiftly addressing Freddy's behavior, check in with Gabriel. Since Gabriel didn't tell you about Freddy's behavior, start broad—avoid an abrupt check in and ease into it. You may casually say something like, "Hey Gabriel, how's the field trip going?" or ask how it was for him. After his response, if he doesn't bring up Freddy, you may continue with, "I heard there was some inappropriate behavior in the stairwell. Everything okay? I'm just checking in to see if you want to talk about anything or need any support." Go from there.

How we communicate with our students about relationship skills when addressing inappropriate behavior, especially nonconsensual behavior, is critical. So much of the time, middle school students will say to me, "My parents tell me I'm supposed to respect everybody, but what does that mean exactly?" Interestingly enough, I get this same question from older kids in high school. At that point, it's usually in reference to sexual expression and activity. How we approach these conversations can elicit respect and care or shame and shut down. What we're going for is a receptivity to information, understanding, and the capacity to put these values into practice.

CONNECTION (INTIMACY AND LOVE)

As humans, we thrive on connection. Social connectedness is critical to our healthy development and sustained well-being. Young people are neurologically programmed to seek the acceptance of their peers so they can feel connected. Peer influence is powerful in shaping *how* they do this. Bids for acceptance may be maladaptive due to external and internal factors. So we want to guide students towards prosocial behaviors that establish positive relationships, compatibility, and social inclusion.[15]

At this age, crushes have peaked and are a potentially powerful distraction, fodder for gossip, source of uncomfortable feelings, and/or reason to explore flirting. They are rich ground for discussing feelings and how we may or may not express or act on them, as well as how our behavior may impact those with whom we desire connection.

SCENARIO: Miguel is attracted to/crushing on Alexa, but she does not reciprocate his feelings. While in the lunchroom, Alexa is waiting in line drinking a bottle of water. Miguel quietly comes around her back to her front, where he then swiftly hits the bottom of the bottle and says, "Pop!" The water gets all over Alexa, who then retaliates with what's left in her bottle and another so that Miguel ends up soaked. A water fight is about to ensue when you intervene. (St. Louis County Public Schools, MO)

The first priority in this situation is to calm the chaos. There are several ways to do this. Hopefully, you have colleagues and students who will quickly come together to bring down the energy and redirect the crowd so that a water fight is avoided and everyone can get on with their day. Interrupting the dramatic, escalating dynamic between Alexa and Miguel is an effective first step. Removing the audience is always a helpful strategy. In this case, leave the audience and remove the source of the "entertainment." Find a quiet space in the moment, if you can, to avoid inflammatory gossip, or else give Alexa and Miguel a time to find you again as time permits, and speak to each individually. Ask the students to provide context. Lead with a curious tone and be firm about boundaries.

There are a lot of possibilities. Alexa may not reciprocate Miguel's feelings but the attention feels validating. She may also feel like the water situation was no big deal and be okay blowing it off, at least for now; still, if unresolved, there is the risk that it could happen again, which is what we want to prevent. Miguel may be feeling frustrated and hurt that his crush is unrequited, which provoked his actions. Despite knowing Alexa doesn't reciprocate his feelings, he may still desire connection, and this is his way of engaging. Afterall, silly pranky behavior is a middle school norm, and male expectations of what clinical psychologist William Pollack calls "Boy Code" dictate that Miguel deny his feelings of disappointment or sadness that leave him vulnerable and instead "clown around" for attention.[16] Whatever the reason, the debrief is an opportunity to reinforce the fact that crushes are normal, but that they don't justify invading another person's space or pranking them.

In addition, if someone is crushing on someone else and the feelings aren't reciprocated, it's not kind to gossip, aggravate, or magnify the vulnerability of the person who is crushing. Alexa should hear that she isn't obligated to reciprocate or justify her feelings/decision about the crush and that she deserves to be treated with respect in response. Ideally, you can affirm Miguel's feelings (if he acknowledges them) without affirming his behavior. If Miguel is willing to share (which can take some time), he may express feeling rejected and/or disappointed and/or sad. You may ask, "What do you do with those feelings?" and then talk together about more prosocial ways to process them. It can be helpful to let students know that an unrequited crush simply means that it's not a match. This can hurt, and it may feel personal (who wants to be rejected?), and it might make you feel angry and disappointed. All these feelings are understandable, but how Miguel expressed them is not okay. This situation presents an opportunity to discuss consent, ways to cultivate connection without becoming aggressive, or to seek connection somewhere else if your crush doesn't return your feelings.

Fifth and sixth grade is prime time for addressing what makes healthy versus unhealthy relationships and exploring how to create authentic connections with peers. There are many available lesson plans that address this important topic (see appendix C for curricula suggestions). Unfortunately, in these materials, healthy and unhealthy behaviors are typically siloed in binary lists. I have rarely seen materials that recognize and address instances when a relationship has qualities of both. Lists of healthy and unhealthy relationships need to be made relevant and translated into fifth- and sixth-grade speak. Relevance is important, so anchor the relationship qualities and behaviors in cognitively and socially congruent ways. For instance, instead of only identifying a healthy relationship quality with an abstract term like *independence*, add a concrete example like, "Your friend is cool when you have plans with your family and can't hang out." Or instead of simply identifying manipulation as an unhealthy quality/behavior, show what that looks like with an example: "If I say I don't like what they're doing, they make fun of me or say they were joking."

Have students brainstorm qualities/behaviors in relationships that feel pleasant and bring us up—you can use a feelings wheel to select more nuanced emotions, like fun, joyful, fulfilling, optimistic, playful, or comfortable—and qualities/behaviors that feel displeasing, distressing, or bring us down—use a feelings wheel to get more nuanced, like discouraged, drained, worried, frightened, or annoyed. Be specific by naming behaviors, for example: You both put an equal amount of energy into your relationship; your friend will sometimes wreck your stuff; your friend wants to keep what you do together a secret; they pay attention if you're uncomfortable; they make you laugh; they respect your space; they tease you about your changing body; they aren't nice to you when "cool" kids are around.

Working with slightly older students to generate examples for younger students is a great way to coconstruct curricula that feels relevant to them. Put the qualities and behaviors on individual post-its. Distribute the post-its to your students. On the wall or board, identify a spectrum, with healthy relationship qualities and the feelings associated with them on one end and unhealthy qualities and the feelings associated with them on the other. Have students place the post-its where they belong on the spectrum and discuss the placement. Get curious about their thought process when they're making the placements, and discuss what it would take to move a characteristic or behavior from one side to the other on the spectrum. What are the in-betweens? Put characteristics and behaviors from each side in the middle and ask students what can be worked on, when one should reconsider a relationship, and when one needs to get out of a relationship altogether.

Discuss what people can do to work on certain aspects of relationships. Remind students to personalize their knowledge with "I statements" and to use language for nonjudgmental questions. Encourage students to avoid "why," as they've already made a judgment, and practice using "what," "how," "where," and "when" to lead their inquiry. What are the clear it's-time-to-end the relationship behaviors? What is the difference between a couple of mistakes and a pattern? Who is a trusted adult someone may reach out to if they need help with a challenging situation? Recognize that different people have different standards, needs, and boundaries when it comes to relationships and that there are some things that make them feel unhealthy and unsafe. Name those things, like physical aggression (if someone pushes, pinches or smacks) or verbal aggression (teases, does mean things that hurt your feelings, or makes you feel like you don't know what's going on or makes you feel insecure on a regular basis so that your world starts to feel small). Discuss language to end a relationship that is clear, direct, and noninflammatory. I sometimes have students "try on" the language through scenario work and then process with students how it feels to use assertive language, as well as be on the receiving end of it.

Always recognize that students may learn through this exercise that they have caused harm in relationships, and identify trusted adults who they may talk to about it. I always like to extend these lessons with appreciation circles or shout out/appreciation boards that recognize people who enact healthy relationship behaviors.

SAFETY

Students today are exposed to aspects of adult sexuality at younger and younger ages. Currently, the average age by which a young person comes across pornography is twelve.[17] In a 2022 study conducted by Common Sense Media, 15 percent of teen respondents said they first saw pornography before the age of ten.[18] Mainstream media is also evermore sexually explicit. This exposure can shape students' ideas about what sex is and/or should be.

SCENARIO: Malcolm Ford is the principal of a middle school. He receives a phone call from a father on Monday, who reports that his sixth-grade daughter, Evelyn, has been sexually assaulted by another sixth-grade student. The father states that sixth-grade boy, Mark, forced Evelyn to give him oral sex in the school bathroom after school on Friday. Malcolm brings Evelyn into his office and asks if the assault happened as her dad reported. Evelyn confirms what her dad said. Malcolm gently tells Evelyn to stop relating what happened so he doesn't inadvertently cause harm by asking questions that may compound trauma or impact her memory of the event. When addressing an alleged sexual assault, California state laws (where this takes place) require the case automatically be handed over to a law enforcement official to conduct the interviews, including the forensic interview at a trauma center as a part of the SVU investigation. Malcolm calls the police to report the offense and then calls his superintendent as well. A criminal investigation is set in motion. According to penal code, the parents of the offender cannot be notified when there is a legal investigation set in motion to prevent evidence tampering. The school must give the police forty-eight hours to conduct their investigation, after which a school investigation is launched. Evelyn has been interviewed by detectives and received the appropriate forensic exams. Mark and his parents have also been interviewed. Malcolm follows the progress of the investigation and is proactively collecting all of the information he needs but experiences some external pressures to swiftly suspend Mark. As Malcolm is preparing to do so, a concerned friend of Evelyn's approaches him to report, "Boy, Mr. Ford, Evelyn is really getting it from both sides." Malcolm learns that both Evelyn and Mark's friends are tormenting her for lying about the incident and insist that Mark didn't force her to have oral sex. Malcolm realizes he needs more information, especially because Evelyn's friends, who typically stand by each other, are giving her a hard time as well.

Malcolm interviews Evelyn again and frames his inquiry this way: "I want to make sure you're okay. I want to be sure you're protected, so I need to ask you an important question. Did Mark force you into oral sex?" Evelyn hesitates and responds with, "Weeellllll, he asked me to?" There is an emphasis on the query; it isn't a statement. Malcolm wants to assess for coercion and says, "When he asked you to do it, did he make you?" Evelyn says, "Well, I asked him if he wanted to go into the bathroom and do it and he said yes." Malcolm says, "Okay, and when you were in the bathroom, did he hold your head down or did he say that if you don't do this he was going to do something else?" Evelyn responds with, "No, he didn't do that. I started, and then he said he didn't want to anymore, so we stopped." Malcolm says, "So you asked to do it, and he said yes?" Evelyn agrees, "Yes." Malcolm submits his second statement, Mark is not suspended, and Malcolm turns his attention to the support and education of Evelyn, Mark, and their families. Evelyn shares that she got the idea from an adult reel on Instagram called "How to Take Care of Your Boyfriend." When Mark almost immediately decided that he didn't want to engage in the behavior, Evelyn was afraid her father would find out and react, so she got in front of it and told him she was made to. (Marin County Public Schools, CA)

This scenario reveals the disciplinary procedures activated whenever there is a report of sexual harassment or sexual assault. The penal education code for disciplinary proceedings in schools in regards to sexual violence varies from state to state, and Title IX—which is a federal 1972 civil-rights gender-equity law—ensures that all students in schools that receive federal funding have the right to access an education free of discrimination based on gender identity, expression, or sex.[19] This protection is essential, and schools—specifically administrators who interpret and implement the policies related to it—need training in survivor-centered proceedings, nonshaming sexuality education and counseling, as well as restorative practices for repairing harm that has impacted individuals and the community. For more information on Title IX and how to assure youth civil rights, see appendix C for resources.

The focus here will be on how we support young people who have engaged in harmful sexual behaviors towards one another. Understandably, administrators mobilize quickly with policy and protocols. Any student-administrator and/or adults supporting the process of communication must ensure the dialogue be student- and victim-centered and equitable. We all have biases, and charged situations tend to reveal them. It is to the benefit of our communities and the children we care for to have done our own work to raise our critical consciousness with regard to bias, especially when it comes to those who have been historically marginalized. In this case, the lack of CSE that most of us have been exposed to and the sociopolitical history of stigmatization when it comes to issues having to do with sexuality have the potential to impact the process.

There are four primary dimensions to this: (1) the individual students (Evelyn and Mark), (2) their interpersonal relationship, (3) their friends/greater community, and (4) their parents. Malcolm's support as an administrator is critical, and it should be recognized that he represents and may wield authority and power. Who, then, are the best people within the community to assume responsibility for supporting the education and facilitation that will lead to learning and restoration? This may be one or two individuals, or it could be a team. Ideally, all caretaking adults in the community have received training on how to effectively address issues of sexuality, and the boundaries around student confidentiality and privacy have been made clear. The school counselor, a health teacher, an advisor, a homeroom teacher, or a campus social worker are all possibilities if they are comfortable with the circumstances and have training. What matters is who Evelyn and Mark will be most receptive to, and most schools will understandably select a school social worker or counselor; however, if they are not available, people the students trust who have the competencies to do so may talk to them.

It is critical that the adults talk to Evelyn and Mark separately and privately and that they understand oral sex is an adult sexual behavior. When talking to Evelyn, make sure to recognize that the reel may have sounded like a good idea, but the intended audience is grown-ups. Consider avoiding "you're not ready," because some kids may hear this as a challenge, especially if they want to assert independence or are interested in growing up quickly. You may say, "It sounds like you were hoping to help your connection move along; grown-up sexual behaviors can actually hurt a kid's relationship, not help it. There are a lot of other ways to care for a romantic partner, including many ways to show affection that don't have to be explicitly sexual." Come up with some of those together—getting them a snack, listening to music in split headphones, sharing about fun things that make you laugh, etc. Invoke empathy as well. Ask, "How come you lied about what happened?"; "How do you think Mark felt?"; and/or "What happens when people are dishonest about their relationships?" Hopefully these questions lead you to a discussion about honesty, trust, and what happens when trust is eroded and what that feels like. There isn't a California education code to cover a false allegation by a student against another student; however, it is imperative that Evelyn understand how her dishonesty impacted Mark and his family.

Mark will need to process his feelings and what's happened as well. As readers, we don't know Mark's reason for saying yes. He could have been clueless and just going along with it, he has probably heard reference to oral sex and may have been curious because he probably has no idea what it actually is; he may know what oral sex is and think he wanted it based on banter but quickly realized he didn't when he told Evelyn to stop. You may ask, "How are you feeling about what's happened and going on?" He may default to facts and chronology of events, so guide him to feelings. Feelings cards, charts, posters, or wheels can really support a student talking within this context. Mark may disclose that he didn't like the oral when it started, which is an opportunity to affirm his intuition and that he had the courage to say no/stop and leave the bathroom. Reinforce the ideas above about grown-up sexual behaviors, and include that, when kids try out adult sexual behaviors, they are risky and can be harmful; be concrete about what expressions of affection and romantic gestures are appropriate for middle schoolers.

The tenants of consent should be communicated in concrete terms and without judgment. Hopefully this has been a part of their education; if that is not the case, this situation will highlight how valuable that scaffolding is. If the students have the vocabulary and previous learning, a teacher may draw upon that and help the students understand how it applies in this situation. If there hasn't been any explicit education regarding consent, invoke any bodily autonomy, asking permission, values instruction, or relationship/conflict-mediation lessons that they've received.

Consider mediating a meeting between Mark and Evelyn. Both students will need important guidance and commitment to repair, which doesn't necessarily mean to fix. Since Mark was wrongly accused, default to his comfort levels and readiness for a meeting. It may take time working with both sides before you come together to facilitate an apology and/or expression of need and boundaries for restoration. Through your conversations, take note of what's happening in Mark and Evelyn's social circles. The harm that's happened within the community as the result of the premature sexual activity, dishonesty, and accusation is sure to be fodder for gossip, contention, exclusion, and teasing. Adults may need to address the additional talk and repercussions in one-to-one conversations and/or pairs or groups. True restorative justice programs require training and an established program. See appendix C for references.

As students move deeper into adolescence and strive for individuality and independence, their need for credible information, support, and guidance rapidly increases. Students are primed to make mistakes of increasing consequence; how we cultivate their learning as a result will make all the difference. Due to neuroplasticity, there is tremendous opportunity and possibility to inspire patterns of behavior that will contribute to a solid foundation for relational and physical health.

5

Puberty Positive

Grades Seven and Eight

Resiliency is something you do, more than something you have. You become highly resilient by continuously learning your best way of being yourself in your circumstance.

~ Al Siebert

Middle school is notorious for its intense and tumultuous social dynamics. American culture tends to consider middle school a gauntlet to endure, which it certainly can be. It is a time when students are deeply engaged in their identity formation, looking for meaning, building a capacity for moral reasoning and ethical quandary, as well as beginning to think abstractly. There is a large academic shift for students at this age, because they are no longer in self-contained classrooms. They are learning how to understand and balance different classrooms, subjects, teaching styles, and workloads. Many teachers are "turning it up" when it comes to academic demands in preparation for the high school years ahead. Adolescents are hyper aware of themselves and their peers, as well as the surrounding popular culture. Layer in a global pandemic that resulted in a decrease in social skills, and the result is that students are struggling to catch up after a period of arrested development, while also navigating normal adolescent growth.[1]

Developmental highlights:

- The majority of seventh and eighth graders are well into puberty.
- Currently, the latest Surgeon General Advisory, *Social Media and Youth Mental Health*, reports that "up to 95% of youth ages 13–17 report using a social media platform, with more than a third saying they use social media 'almost constantly.'"[2] The average eight to eighteen year old is on a digital device about seven and a half hours a day.[3]
- Social media platforms, gaming chat rooms, and messaging in all forms present risks and promises. What is essential to remember is that this is how students now connect and communicate.
- Common Sense Media reported that, in 2022, 73 percent of teenagers have consumed pornography, 54 percent reported first seeing online pornography when they were 13 or younger, that 41 percent reported seeing it during the school day, and 31 percent during the school day while present in the physical classroom (i.e., versus during online learning).[4]
- Students are wired for novelty and sensory stimulation.

Seventh and eighth graders are eager, and many are earnest, in their curiosity and quest for information and guidance. At the same time, they may present as detached, indifferent, obstinate, prickly, and complacent. I find that the qualities we appeal to are the characteristics that tend to show up. This further affirms the importance of asset-based and culturally responsive approaches to our practice. Enlisting students in the cocreation of our work invites ownership, accountability, and engagement with what feels real and relevant. This can also hold us accountable as we move through our teaching days pulled in various directions and occupied by competing needs. Earning student trust and credibility, especially in the realm of comprehensive sexuality education (CSE), happens when we walk our talk and avoid hypocrisy by reflecting upon our own behavior.[5] We must model what we aspire to teach. How do you express sadness? Anger? Joy? Care? Disappointment? What are your conscious and unconscious biases? We have to recognize, too, that this stage can be unique in its demands on us as educators. A day in the life of a middle school teacher, teaching, guiding, and caring for middle schoolers, is certainly challenging. It is heart work and it is hard work.

BODIES

People get to choose how they touch and get touched, because their bodies belong to them. This is fundamental to understanding consent. Find specific, designated times to teach about consent and how it relates to healthy relationships with ourselves, each other, and within our communities. Consent is educating people on how to treat us and listening for how other people want to be treated.

SCENARIO: You excuse your class for lunch. Students are expected to line up and wash their hands at the classroom sink first. As kids are moving towards the line, Bradley and Josh move towards each other and go for a high five. As it happens, Josh pulls a "psych," misses Bradley's high hand, and brings his own around to smack Bradley's butt. Bradley whips around and says, "Fuck you," and falls in line. (Marin County School District, CA)

This is a common middle school behavior that disrespects people's boundaries and right to consent. Moments like these typically happen during transitions. Students are working to self-regulate so that they may have focused attention in class. When there is a break in the structured time, sometimes everything takes a break, including a student's capacity to manage impulsive and inappropriate behavior. When I talk to students about these kinds of behaviors, they may say they were "just joking" or "letting loose." The problem is that, their feelings—which may range from energetic (they were sitting quietly for a long time), to frustrated (because what they were working on was hard to get or understand), to insecure or anxious (because they may not have someone to sit with at lunch)—are being expressed by angering someone else and then justified by masking or minimizing what they did with humor. The impact on Bradley is anger (expressed by his profanity) and possibly more (because his boundaries were crossed and then justified).

Upon witnessing this behavior, you call Josh over and tell him you "just noticed what happened over at the sink with Bradley. What were you going for?" Josh may say, "I was just messing around. I didn't mean anything by it." Again, Josh focuses on intention versus impact to avoid accountability. You might continue with, "It looked like Bradley didn't think it was funny. It seemed you set expectations for a high five and then dissed him by pulling your hand away and instead smacking his butt. I noticed the look on his face and what he said sounded angry." Ask Josh how the lesson was for him and what he was feeling at that moment. Feelings cards, charts, or wheels can help. Ask what his need was. To connect? To see his feelings in someone else? To be acknowledged? Again, needs-cards or charts are helpful and concrete. Continue by asking Josh to name what he saw in Bradley's reaction and what he thinks it may have come from. Review the concept of consent—that is, that it's not okay to touch people where they don't want to be touched, especially when they are set up to expect one thing and then are surprised by another. Work with Josh towards genuine remorse and accountability by apologizing to Bradley somehow and committing to not doing it again.

Check in with Bradley. You may start with, "I noticed that . . . and you reacted with . . . it sounded like you were angry, is that accurate? How are you feeling about it now?" Support Bradley in putting language to how he feels, and if he's up for it, talk about what he may say to Josh when something like that happens. For instance, "Hey, uncool. You can't smack me there," or "That's not what I was expecting—don't change it up like that." Or he could get really explicit like, "That totally crosses a boundary and makes me mad (realistically a middle school kid would say, 'it pisses [him] off.')" Ask Bradley if he's up for a conversation with Josh and offer to mediate and/or give him a heads up that you talked to Josh and that he may apologize.

Sometimes, in situations when someone's right to bodily autonomy is disrespected, the person whose boundaries are crossed doesn't express discomfort or know how to assert themselves and become suspicious or anxious about it happening again. They also may not seek the support of a teacher, so you may hear about it from other students. When students are witness to or the target of this kind of behavior and it's not addressed, the overall safety of the classroom and learning is compromised for all students.

GENDER AND SEXUALITY DIVERSITY

Continuing to nurture the healthy development of gender and sexuality diversity, a developmental process that is at the heart of adolescence, is critical at this age.[6]

All of us have a gender identity, and all of us have pronouns. This is an essential facet of people's larger identity. A developmental task of adolescence is figuring out one's identity and how we may express and give meaning to it. This is the beginning of a lifelong process that is shaped by the information we gather, the experiences we have, and the people we know. Students need models of gender that are broad and inclusive. Part of normalizing and understanding this as a human process is supporting our students by using concrete terms that their developing brains can understand and hold on to. Recently, in a class at The Harvard Graduate School of Education on Gender and Sexuality, colearners came up with a wonderful analogy that exemplifies how we can effectively make this accessible in the classroom (shout out to Group 3). Gender is a spectrum, and for many, there is fluidity to it. The analogy they came up with was, "Power Rangers! Time to Morph!"

Using popular cultural examples that meet students where they are garners interest and engagement and helps make learning about charged topics fun. A dash of popular lore is a bonus! Find visual representations of the Power Rangers to present in class. Power Rangers are different colors, which can be representative of different identities and expressions. When Power Rangers combine in an infinite number of ways, they form what is called a *MegaZord*. In the same way, identity is multifaceted and may fluctuate in different contexts. Each Power Ranger, or identity/expression, can be presented in whatever way fits the context they're in best. There are multitudes of variations depending on what the Power Rangers are navigating. These variations represent the contextual identities we present to the world—what we show to others about who we are through different personal expressions. This allows for fluidity and intersectionality, too. The labels and identities are not permanent, and MegaZords can rearrange or represent the pieces the individual wants to showcase at any particular time. Sometimes the Power Rangers are up against what feels insurmountable. How they come together as a MegaZord to navigate the precarious social landscape can be challenging, particularly in potentially threatening situations.

Middle school is notorious for its social cruelty. LGBTQ+ students are at higher risk than their straight peers when it comes to bullying and cyberbullying.[7] This is also a time when students engage in enthusiastic use of offensive and disrespectful language, although they will adamantly defend it as benign. If you've overheard middle school dialogue when the participants didn't know you were listening, you know exactly what I mean. It is peppered with profanity and punctuated with sexualized slights. As students negotiate power through popularity and carelessly hurl insults at each other, they often hone in on personal attributes and identities. Most students are seeking to fit in (different from belonging, which would actually serve them far better) and are developmentally self-conscious and vulnerable to judgment and potential exclusion. Homophobic language is included in the arsenal and can create a hostile environment for LGBTQ+ young people and their families.[8]

SCENARIO: One of your students, Stella, is home sick. Her older sibling is going to come by to pick up the books she needs for her assignments, so you go to her cubby to gather them and organize the make-up work. You come across a folded piece of paper. It's a note about Malia, a girl in the class, who recently came out as bisexual, and her performance in the school play last week. It refers to Malia as a "fat-lipped faggot bitch." This is affirmed in someone else's writing with, "Yeah total hoe." When Stella returns, you meet to go over her work and present the note. You ask if she recognizes the handwriting, and she denies it is hers at first. You pause and point out that it looks like it could be hers based on the work you're looking at together. Stella admits that she wrote it but won't reveal who the other handwriting belongs to. She explains that Malia was bullying people and that's why she wrote the note. (Geauga County School District, OH)

It's important to address this with Stella right away. After welcoming her back from being sick and appreciating that she is well again, show her the note that is in her handwriting and point out the language as homophobic and misogynist. You may have to define those words for her—she no doubt knows what they mean and that they are powerful; however, she may not realize the impact of this language on others and the cost to herself. You may ask, "What was going on for you? What were you going for when you wrote this?" and "What were you feeling at that moment?" A lot of relational aggression among girls is about displaced anger, an emotion girls are socialized to suppress. Girls often perform "nice" on the surface and take their "unbecoming" feelings underground.[9]

In my experience, students tend to focus on the chronology of events, which can amplify their emotional response and is often unproductive. Stick to a brief synopsis of the situation and then guide the student to their feelings. "When you feel (mirror her language), what do you usually fall back on? How do you express it verbally or through your behavior?" You may then ask, "How does writing something like this serve you? How might it impact the community?" As readers, we don't know what Stella might say in response. Writing the note could have felt like a moment of connection with a friend, albeit by demeaning someone else to feel superior. Maybe she felt confused (she may get strong negative messages about LGBTQ+ identities at home, for example), or hurt and/or sad, or angry if Malia really is causing harm to other kids, perhaps in response to experiencing bullying herself.[10] In general, it's important to teach girls to be assertive and encourage them to stand up for themselves while respecting the rights of others. However Stella responds, mirror the language, be genuinely curious, and be ready to affirm school values. "How come you chose these words to express how you were feeling?"

This scenario is complex, and it will be important to hear Stella out, talk to the other person who responded to the note (if Stella will reveal who it is, which is unlikely), and Malia. It's essential to acquire a better understanding of the problem. It's possible that this was an isolated incident; it could also be evidence of homophobia and mean behavior that Malia may be contending with and potentially projecting into her relationships with others as well. And, with the changing face of bullying and prevalence of cyberbullying, it's possible that there is a digital aspect to the dynamic that is also playing out at school. Cyberbullying tends to be more common in the higher grades; however, the mental-health vulnerabilities and antisocial behaviors and outcomes associated with bullying and cyberbullying are serious, so it's important to ask.[11] Verbal vandalism can follow a student beyond a moment and invite more teasing. Biased-based bullying is also on the rise. The attack of someone's personal attributes, "you look like a fat ass," or kids who are targeted because of bias or prejudice, in this case, sexuality, can be significantly more traumatized by an incident.[12]

Encourage Stella—and her associate, if possible—to name what they were feeling and identify what underlying need motivated the mean behavior. Sometimes shame can motivate girls' relational violence. In *Girlfighting*, psychologist and educator Lyn Mikel Brown explains, "When conflicts or disagreements arise, how better to avoid them than to pick on someone else all together; how better to shore up one's self-pride and reestablish shaky group solidarity than through violent targeting of an outsider."[13] Explore what other contextual factors might be at work. Your curiosity will let the girls know that you care and are interested. I often hear girls call each other bitches and minimize the demeaning nature of the word by claiming that "it's different now" and "normal to do." This reclaiming falls short in my mind, because its use is still pervasive within a context of aggression and abuse. Appropriating misogynistic language that is still used to limit, restrain, and oppress women is using the tools of patriarchy against other girls.[14] This kind of internalized sexist thinking must be interrupted and redirected. Mean behavior, casual cruelty, and bullying typically involve power dynamics and anger. Coming across this note is an opportunity to address this in a meaningful way.

When speaking with the girls, listen for feelings—the girls need to feel seen and heard. Consider talking to the girls about societal socialization that spurs competition among girls and women versus sisterhood and solidarity. Describe historical examples of women coming together to demand equality, and help them recognize the intersectionality of sexuality with gender and bias-based slurs they use. It is also essential to invoke community values and recognize that not everyone is going to like each other and be friends; however, community expectations value mutual respect and healthy methods for resolving conflict.

It is important to determine if the contents of the note were kept between Stella and her friend. We don't know if Malia saw or heard about it; however, we want to make sure that Malia isn't facing discrimination for her sexuality. Remember that, as students enter puberty, heteronormative expectations of sexuality become more intense, and even though students don't all mature at the same rate, social expectations demand that students proclaim their identities on many levels.[15] It's also possible that Malia is also engaged in mean behavior. An intentional, casual check-in that conveys care and curiosity about how she's doing is important. Pay attention to social dynamics that may be taking place under your radar (they always are), and make sure that inclusive and celebratory resources for LGBTQ+ students are present, on display, and integrated across curricula. Teaching all students to be respectful of gender and sexuality development and diversity supports everyone.[16] Is there a Gender and Sexuality Alliance (GSA) at your school? Are the meeting times and places clearly posted? If you work in a district that does not allow these important affinity spaces, there are still ways to signal that you are an ally (assuming you are or aspire to be) and see, hear, and support all of your students.

Homophobic language in middle school is common.[17] In the GLSEN 2021 National School Climate Survey, 89.9 percent of LGBTQ+ students heard homophobic remarks like dyke or faggot, and 44.2 percent heard this type of language frequently or often.[18] Students of all genders and sexualities are exposed, and it is particularly common among adolescent boys. Fag talk and fag imitations serve as a discourse with which boys discipline themselves and each other through joking relationships. Being a fag is associated with failing at the masculine tasks of competence, heterosexual prowess, and strength, or in any way revealing weakness or femininity.[19] Of course, these attitudes also enforce sexist ideas about girls and women. Demeaning anyone is unacceptable and should be directly addressed in ways that promote equity and dignity for everyone in the community. Since gender-related disrespect and harassment is experienced by students of all sexual orientations, (e.g., being misgendered and called homophobic slurs regardless of one's orientation, sexist portrayals of femininity, leveraging normalized homophobia as a means to negotiate social power dynamics, etc.), teaching students about respect for gender and sexual diversity supports everyone.[20]

FEELINGS AND VALUES

Upholding class guidelines and reinforcing community values are critical to learning environments. These apply to all educational spaces, even the hallways, outdoor spaces, and other areas of the community. Rosalind Wiseman, acclaimed author and expert on children, writes, "We all want to feel a sense of belonging . . . it's fundamental to the human experience . . . but it's also true that our need to belong can be the cause of our greatest inhumanity."[21] It is our responsibility as educators to make sure young people understand community values and that we hold them accountable for doing so.

SCENARIO: During your last class, students worked in pairs. Davis, a boy, and Harper, who presents as gender nonconforming, worked together. Class is over, and as students file out, Harper walks past a trio of boys that includes Davis. With a little distance, although potentially within earshot of Harper, one of the boys, William, says, "I saw you were working with that weirdo," and Davis snickers and says, "I identify as an Apache helicopter." The other boys start laughing and high five him. (Grand Forks County Public Schools, ND)

Many educators report to me that inappropriate behavior and social cruelty usually happens during unstructured and transition times. We don't stop being teachers or shed the accountability of our influence with students when we step across the threshold of our classroom doors. Davis, as far as you have observed, worked respectfully with Harper during class time. It was when he got to his buddies that he felt he could or should demean Harper with disrespectful comments. In the words of C. J. Pascoe, "Homophobia is indeed a central mechanism in the making of contemporary American adolescent masculinity."[22] In my experience, anything that is within the realm of queer, such as someone presenting as trans, is a target in situations that are a perceived threat to hypermasculinity. By targeting someone else, they shield themselves from peer punishment. Wiseman observes that "what's so frustrating and ironic is that homophobia represses boy's courage—not the courage to fight someone if challenged, but the moral courage to raise one's voice when someone is being degraded."[23] This is the change we must see: boys affirming their masculinity as courageous when they stand for human dignity, not taking it from someone else.

In response to the scenario above, you could start by asking Davis and the other boys something like, "I want to talk about the pronoun comments you were just laughing about—entertained by." When you have their attention, add, "We don't disrespect people's identities. It's hurtful and unkind. William, please stay, and Davis, please wait in the hallway." You may let the other couple of boys go, but make sure to add, "Even if you didn't directly contribute to what was said, your laughter supports it and that's not okay." Address Davis and William separately.

There are typically hierarchies in Boy World, and we don't want to make assumptions about where each boy stands and how that may influence our ability to accurately understand and connect with each of them.[24] When you speak to each of them separately, you may start with, "I heard you guys making fun of Harper. What was going on for you at that moment?" They are likely to say something along the lines of, "Nothing, we were just messing around," or "We didn't mean anything by it." There are many options for how to approach these conversations. What is essential is that the behavior is identified as hurtful; even if Harper didn't hear it, other kids may have. Make it clear that disrespectful behavior based on people's identity is never okay and that put-downs based on individuality and not conforming to standards that some think is normal or cool is exclusive, mean, and unacceptable. We want Davis and William to understand that their use of slurs violates their responsibility to maintain a safe space for everyone in the community. How we communicate these messages is important. Guiding Davis and William with empathy and respect, versus scolding or shaming or talking down to them, could make the difference in affecting change. This typically takes a "Let's think about this together" tone, which will hopefully inspire empathy and illicit curiosity versus defensiveness and anger, which could result in more anger and derision directed at Harper.

If you're talking to William, you may clarify and say, "I heard that, and I'm asking about how you felt going into that moment. I'm interested in understanding what was going on for you and what you were going for or got by saying what you did. I know that sometimes guys tease as a way to connect with each other, but this was at the expense of someone else. And everyone here gets to be treated with dignity (or like we all have worth/value)." Addressing homophobic and transphobic teasing, aggression, and bullying is critical for establishing and maintaining respectful environments in which everyone can learn. If this type of behavior persists, it will require a call home and/or a meeting with the family and the administration. Hopefully this isn't the first point of contact you've had with the boys' families.

Building community requires meaningful touch points and dialogue. An introductory letter home at the beginning of the school year, as well as a regular (brief and friendly) newsletter, helps foster communication. Translated materials are inclusive and communicate that you're paying attention and value family origins. I know teachers who make a point to quickly write an email to a student's family or make a quick call home to highlight positive work and/or citizenship they witness in their classrooms. Caretaking adults absolutely appreciate this. I make a point to include caretaking adults in homework assignments in the form of interviews, prompted dialogue about case studies, or oral histories. Be sure not to assume literacy and provide options to ensure different oral traditions are honored. Time is also precious and may be difficult to come by, so ensure enough time to get the assignments done. However, if you can invite and include families in their many structures and configurations, do so.

In middle school, when students transition to individual classrooms per academic subject, this kind of connection and communication can get lost, but I would argue that it's more important than ever. Generating good will and creating open lines of connection during a time when students are developmentally vulnerable to making all kinds of mistakes is worthwhile and can prevent having to navigate hostility later. The key is to ensure the outreach is from a place of genuine curiosity, respect, and without assumptions. The vast majority of parenting adults have wisdom to share about their child. In the words of Paulo Freire, "Dialogue cannot exist without humility."[25] I think it's safe to say that any seasoned teacher has engaged with a vast range of parenting adult behavior, so it goes without saying that our respectful outreach should be reciprocated if we are to cultivate the community I suggest. If a student's parents or guardians are not respectful and open to communication in return, then we must adjust to assert boundaries, seek administrative support, and respond accordingly.

These lessons and this practice for self-regulation, kindness, and citizenship must be included—formal instruction on feelings is paramount in middle school. As students mature, their cognitive capacity for naming and understanding emotion becomes more sophisticated. Provide a feelings wheel and feature it prominently in your classroom to support students in making the connection with what they're feeling, how and where feelings show up in their bodies, and shape and influence their behaviors. Encouraging students to explore their feelings beyond just mad, sad, and happy increases their emotional literacy—that is, the capacity to recognize and understand the feelings and needs of oneself and others.[26]

Teach that feelings are information and help us to understand ourselves and others more deeply. Teach students to ask, "What is the feeling telling me, and how can I deal with it in a healthy way?" Reference the feelings wheel and colors associated with specific feelings to promote somatic awareness. Which feelings resonate when, and where do they show up? Make it concrete by providing a worksheet with an outline of a body. Have students fill in parts of the body with corresponding colors that represent different feelings. Facilitate discussion about how different contexts (internal and external) may activate more feelings in us and how we may manage those feelings to contain the colors.

Other visuals may be helpful. For instance, expressing anger in healthy ways can be represented with a volcano. We typically focus on the behavior of an eruption, but what dynamics are happening underground that may not be visible but may be building up to create the eruption? What underground shifts lead to eruptions, and how might we anticipate and manage them in ways that strengthen who we are versus spewing our feelings onto others in compromising ways? Part of managing difficult feelings includes reaching out to trusted adults and friends. Ask students to identify several people they may go to when they face difficult challenges. "Who can you turn to when you're experiencing different emotions?" This is helpful, since middle school can feel like a minefield at times for many students.

Schools expose students to values all of the time. Whether intentional or not, implicit or explicit, how we treat each other and *what* we give time and attention to, as well as *how* we do that, matters. Many educators do this with intention, especially folks who are cultivating care and dignity in the community through class guidelines and conversations about family, district, and cultural values. As students age into middle school, we may assume that they understand basic community values and will automatically manifest them. But with the many changes that accompany adolescence, including brain development, it is more important than ever that we be explicit in how we talk about and reinforce values. The gauntlet to adulthood can be tricky—there are sure to be obstacles ahead. As students establish patterns of behavior they will carry into adulthood, we want to make sure that values play an important role.

Sexuality educator and author, Al Vernacchio teaches students to distinguish between a value (our deepest set of principles that guide our decisions—not just what but why we do what we do), an opinion (how we think about something—a view or judgment), and a fact (something indisputable). I like to be specific about values that are personal and societal. I will introduce concepts of morality (individual values) and ethics (values typically shared within a society).[27] It is also important to introduce concepts of accountability—in particular, personal integrity and what it means to live by one's values despite external influences. This requires us to be actively honest about who we are, what we say and do, and how we manifest and express that honesty. Highlight that it is common to experience conflicting values and to face ethical quandaries. It is also common for there to be tension between our individual morals and community ethics and responsibilities. Cultivating empathy will help us adhere to our values in situations that impact others.

The value of empathy cannot be underestimated. Human contact and deep relationships are essential to overall health and well-being, and empathy is foundational to those relationships. Educational psychologist, Michelle Borba, author of *Unselfie*, defines it as follows: "Empathy is what lays the foundation for helping children live one essential truth: We are all humans who share the same fears and concerns, and deserve to be treated with dignity."[28] Borba contends that empathy can be taught. In my mind, it is our ethical responsibility to teach kids empathy, but there are many practical arguments too. For starters, research tells us that empathy promotes kindness, prosocial behaviors, and moral courage. It is correlated with higher academic scores, keen critical-thinking skills, and helps minimize bullying, aggression, prejudice, and racism.[29] It is the transformational human capacity that cultivates cross-generational and cross-cultural connections.[30] Any of us who teach kids know the inherent value of these skills and capacities. Students are more likely to embrace a value that isn't dictated to them by an adult but rather cultivated through their own judgment, experience, and sense of right and wrong.

Psychologist and author, Brené Brown—in her Royal Society for the Encouragement of Arts, Manufactures, and Commerce (RSA) short about the difference between empathy and sympathy—states that empathy "drives connection." She invokes nursing scholar Theresa Wiseman and her four attributes of empathy: (1) taking on someone else's perspective, which recognizes someone else's perspective as truth; (2) being nonjudgmental so we don't discount their experience; (3) recognizing someone else's emotions or understanding their feelings, which puts your feelings aside so that you can focus on the other person; and (4) communicating your understanding of a person's feelings, validation that demonstrates that you accept, acknowledge, and understand them. As Brown puts it, "empathy is feeling with people." Empathy is a vulnerable choice by which we authentically connect with others.[31] Integrate empathetic questions into classrooms and one-on-one discussions with students. Include questions like, "How do you think that makes them feel?" or "What do you need from me right now?" Infuse dialogue with empathetic observations like, "I notice you have a disappointed expression on your face. Is that accurate? Please help me understand how you feel" and encourage students to do the same in all aspects of their school life. The capacity to be empathetic is the foundation for scaffolding relational learning and creating communities that are safe places for all students.

RELATIONSHIPS (CONSENT, COMMUNICATION, DECISION-MAKING)

Remind students of the opportunities embedded in mindful decision-making. Teach them about their brain's neuroplasticity and how their experiences literally shape their brains and, in turn, their reality. This organization and construction process also means that the limbic system and prefrontal cortex responsible for rational thought are out of whack at this age. In fact, if two messages were sent via neurological pathways to both of these parts of the tween or teen brain, the one going to the limbic center will get to its destination three thousand times faster than the message going to the frontal lobe.[32] Pausing is one of the most powerful tools in the face of incomplete myelination.[33] Affirm that students can make decisions that are in their best interest as they practice independence; they just need to find ways to slow down and allow their brain to catch up with itself when making decisions. This is challenging when the part of your brain that has to do with impulse is so well developed in contrast to the part that is supposed to govern it.

We deepen these lessons when we take a concept and encourage students to break it down in meaningful ways. This is where case study/scenario work supports a deeper understanding. When we contextualize social dynamics and break them down into manageable parts that they can see and understand, students will typically readily engage in this process to make sense of the information, which leads to understanding for themselves and each other instead of us doing it *for* them.[34] Students aren't empowered when they are fed advice; it comes when they are inspired to stretch their critical thinking and imagination and tap into their felt experiences through inquiry and facilitated dialogue. It's important to recognize that this constructivist approach supports the student's search for understanding, but in a cold cognitive environment. When context becomes "hot" with peer presence, students will have to call upon their patience to allow their developing brain (prefrontal cortex) to catch up with their mostly developed brain (limbic system) to make decisions that will support them.

Cocreate scenarios with students that accurately reflect the daily decisions they are confronted with. To help students organize their thoughts, create a worksheet with a grid that students fill out according to the different facets of a scenario. Identify feelings, motivations, values, and possible outcomes/consequences to their actions, as well as what moves they can make that will make them proud. Recognize that there are many ways to approach a decision and that practice is a way to develop the capacity to listen to their intuition, think ethically about who they are as people, and recognize what might get in the way of acting in alignment with those values. Get concrete with strategies for managing obstacles and how they may mitigate situations that feel rushed or pressured. How can they slow down and pause to let their brain come together to make a decision that feels right to them? Include a concrete identification of the trusted adults they may go to in different situations.

Middle School is a time when students are reckoning with all of the cultural scripts they've received, read from, and are enacting. This includes romantic and/or sexual relationships. If your students have learned about asking permission, mutual respect, empathy, and caretaking, along with effective communication and conflict mediation, you'll be able to bridge these concepts to contextualize them within a romantic and/or sexual context. At this point in middle school, students are exposed to many representations of sexuality. Some of this is healthy, inclusive, and equitable, but most is not. Common Sense Media's 2017 study, *Watching Gender,* found that young people who watch television and movies learn the following: to value masculine traits over feminine traits, that girls and women are valued for appearance and their bodies as sexual objects for other people's consumption, more tolerant views of sexual harassment, and support for the belief that women are at least partially responsible for their own sexual assault. The report also found that young peoples' expectations for romantic and sexual situations are shaped by the media they consume and that these expectations are therefore deeply gendered.[35]

It's critical that we teach media literacy skills and give students opportunities to practice them. We want our students to be filters, not sponges. Students this age have a keen sense of justice and are sociologists in the making. They are annoyed, and sometimes downright offended, when they learn that many of those producing online content are attempting to manipulate them. Provide information about media and its impact on adolescents. Highlight how they may take charge and be selective or, at the very least, informed about the media they choose. Cocreate counter narratives to emphasize alternatives.

When it comes to romantic and/or sexual relationships, open with short clips, such as Aurora's awakening kiss (*Sleeping Beauty*); Anna and Kristoff's first kiss (*Frozen*); *In a Heartbeat*, the animated short film by Pixar studios about same-gender attraction and how to communicate that; and *Drawn to You* by Seneca, a short film about two girls finding their way to each other despite heterosexism. Have students consider the following questions in small groups with a larger class share out:

- Who (what identities) and what ideas are being represented?
- How might *how* the identities are depicted impact our ideas?
- What is being said about gender and sexuality?
- What are the implicit and explicit interpersonal dynamics saying about the relationship between or among the people represented?

Extend the lesson by asking how consent, communication, and connection are represented and if those images and messages align, don't align or seem unclear based on what students know about these foundational concepts of healthy relationships. Take the lessons further with future conversations about cocreated scenarios that represent the social culture of your school, and see if they can identify those ideas (supportive and not supportive) in their current relationships. Practice critical-thinking skills to explore what patterns of behavior will be beneficial as they move into later adolescence and then adulthood, as well as those that are antisocial and detrimental to making positive choices.

While the media examples above can feel rather innocent, it is true that many young people are exposed to explicit media that isn't, especially if they and their friends have phones. When I consult with schools, many educators recognize that their middle school students have come across sexually explicit media (even mainstream media is increasingly explicit) or have already come across and/or are already watching pornography. They wonder how to bring this up in a cognitively congruent way with appropriate boundaries.

Given the greater school culture's understanding of CSE, you may use other media deconstruction and reflection as a way to help students understand how sexually explicit media may shape their ideas and expectations of sexuality. As I have worked in many schools across the country and talked to thousands of kids, it seems internet pornography has become the default sex education in our country. This is deeply concerning. What does it mean when you have a middle school student who has seen over a hundred explicit images of aggressive sexual intercourse without ever having had a first kiss? Not only do we need to safely address this in a structured classroom, we need to be conscious of the CSE counter-narratives we create in educational spaces and outside of the classroom as well. This is how we will affect change and keep kids on track for positive, healthy romantic and/or sexual relationships as they get older and mature.

Always open this conversation with, "It is normal and natural to be curious about sexual relationships and sex." Given how accessible pornography is online, it is possible that students may come across it even if they aren't seeking it out. There are also some adolescents who watch it to learn about sex. Help students understand that there is nothing educational about porn and it is not representative of most people's healthy relationship behaviors and practices. It's often about making money, it's contractual versus consensual, and it typically masks aggression with directed, exaggerated pleasure responses. I tell my students that learning about sex from porn is like learning how to drive by watching the *Fast and the Furious*. There are lesson plans and scripts that address this conversation in classroom-appropriate ways. Consider participating in professional development that provides coaching on how to discuss sexually explicit media within a classroom setting and ensures appropriate teacher–student boundaries.

Much of the media adolescents consume does not exhibit effective relationship communication either. Relationship negotiation is rarely equitable and typically flawed so that it will incite drama. In response, be deliberate with teaching effective communication skills, which are fundamental to the practice of consent. Different contexts require different levels of communication. Transactional communication is different from relationship-building communication. Using metaphors that students can relate to and use to understand an abstract concept in concrete terms is helpful. For instance, I'll say, "When it comes to communication in relationships, especially romantic and/or sexual relationships, it's important to think of a bear."

I instruct students to think of a bear. Give them a minute and continue with, "think of what the bear looks like—what color, how furry, what size—where they are, what they're doing." Then I ask students to share their bears. As they start to share, some students will simply say, "a brown bear." So, I model clarifying and curious questions like, "Is it alone?" and "Where is it? A zoo? A forest?" Some follow with, "it's fishing for salmon in a river," and I'll come back with, "Oh, what time of year is it then, is it fattening up for winter hibernation?" and so on. Kids come up with a whole host of bears. Polar bears, Winnie the Pooh, their childhood teddy bear, koala bears (marsupials), or a Panda bear (sometimes classified as closer to raccoons than bears). You get the point. Then say, "We all could have had a superficial conversation about bears, that they have fur, two ears that stand up, walk on all fours, etc. But when we started to share about our bears and got curious about them, what did we discover?" Kids understand this immediately, "They're all different!" Yes! Everyone's image of a bear is distinctive and personal.

In the same way, if we are going to treat people the way they want to be treated and approach our relationships with respect and a vibe of consent, what happens if we have very different images of what that looks like? In the same way that the bear in my mind is a polar bear in the Arctic and yours is a childhood stuffed toy on your shelf at home, we're likely to see things differently. Students get this: there could be miscommunication. If we assume our bears are the same when they're not, then we aren't talking about or agreeing to the same thing.

Support students in understanding that context is *everything* in relationships and how we make meaning of what we share and say. Continue by asking, "What determined the bear you thought of? What contributed to what your imagination came up with?" They can get this too, "Who we are. Our experiences." Yes! "Is that frame of mind stagnant?" Students know that "It's changing all the time. If you thought of a brown bear at a campsite trying to get into a trash can today, but the next time I asked you to think of a bear, you had just watched a documentary film on polar bears and the disappearing ice of the North Pole, might you think of a different one?" Yes!

To bring it back to the everyday, affirm that context is variable, and proceed to invoke whatever hangout spot or area they chill at off campus. You might say, "So when you are walking up to the corner store with your good friends to chill, after a tough week of homework and tests, how might you feel?" Affirm that their time together is playful and fun—that students are decompressing by laughing with each other and may be clowning, horseplaying, and a bit rowdy. Ultimately, it feels positive and affirming, because there is a connection among them. Ask, "But what if a random person on the street joined in and mirrored your behavior? What would the emotional embodied experience of that be?" Your students will all have some sort of a response and/or reaction. Help them put words to the feelings. Typically, it's scared, surprised, confused, uncomfortable, or defensive, and many will say they'd want to physically push the person away. Draw attention to the fact that the stranger was simply mirroring what they saw happening in the group, yet in a moment, the emotional embodied experience of those same things changed. The shift was quick and almost the opposite. Why? Context. Context is variable and shifted so the experience of what was happening changed. This affirms why we must pay attention when communicating (a part of practicing consent) and have the right to change our minds about what we're discussing or experiencing—because context is variable, so our comfort levels are too. This is why we need to communicate and ask curious questions in our relationships—so that our understanding of each other is ongoing and evolves in real time.

As in all learning, lessons take time to take hold and for students to apply them into their everyday lives and behavior, especially within the context of sexuality and relationships. Sometimes it may feel easier to avoid, dismiss or, disregard students' behavior, because society provides us with escape routes, one of which is silence—particularly when it comes to sexuality, specifically sexual violence. Silence leads to isolation, and unhealthy, dysfunctional, harmful, and violent behaviors thrive in isolation. Our silence speaks louder than words in these contexts and communicates that it's okay to minimize, disrespect, and abuse someone. For the person being abused, silence communicates that it's a problem they should keep to themselves or deal with alone. Harmful and inequitable histories and systems normalize and condone sexual violence.[36] The socialization of these norms starts early, and we see that socialization among our students, often veiled in humor and/or minimized and excused.[37] Important note: If you have experienced sexual violence yourself, and a student's experience triggers difficult memories and feelings, protect yourself by enlisting other adults to handle the situation.

SCENARIO: Students are standing in line outside the gym, ready to file in for P.E. As you round the corner, you come across two boys, Luke and Gio, who are messing with each other physically. It looks like wrestling but is against the wall of the gym. Suddenly, Luke slams Gio up against the wall, and Gio blurts out while laughing, "You're raping me." (Washington County School District, OR)

Gio has probably not considered the implications of joking about rape and why it's wrong. As an educator, it's important to intervene without using language that serves to shame and shut down (e.g., don't say, "What's going on here?" or "How could you say something like that?"). I've had many boys say to me with sincerity, "How come everyone thinks I'm doing the Patriarchy. What even is that?" The vast majority of boys are simply reading from cultural scripts that promote sexual aggression and sometimes rewards harmful behavior. Boys may not know what the Patriarchy is, but that doesn't mean they aren't socialized by it. Humor is a powerful force in Boy World, and it can complicate interactions. Often, boys connect through action[38] and humor. If they want to communicate a boundary without coming off as weak (and risk being ridiculed, shamed[39] or iced out of a friendship or social group), they may use humor to shield themselves from that risk and confirm their masculinity.[40]

Interrupt what's happening and calmly pull Gio aside. Deep down, he may know that what he said is wrong, and there may be cultural factors at work that cause him to minimize and dismiss the incident as no big deal or to insist that he was just joking without being aware of potential impact. Get curious about what's happening behind the behavior. There may be an underlying need for guidance towards different behavior if a boy feels his only way to save face and stay connected to his friends is through dehumanizing expressions of unhealthy masculinity. You may ask, "Hey, is there anything going on with you and Luke?" Gio may minimize with, "Nah, we were just messing around" or "What do you mean?" Either way, consider continuing with, "I heard you say that he was raping you, while laughing, and I'm wondering why that happened. Were you okay with the wrestling?" Again, potential responses may include, "Yeah, I'm sorry, I know that was wrong. We were just joking; I won't do it again," or "Oh I was just saying that, it's no big deal, we mess around all the time," or "Kinda, yeah, I shouldn't have said that." You might follow up with, "Do you feel like you could say no to what was happening if you wanted to?" He will probably say yes. In which case, you can say, "Alright, I just wanted to check, because sometimes it can be hard to assert a boundary, and I know that disrespectful joking can happen between people when they feel uncomfortable. It doesn't excuse it, but I want to understand it."

As you explore what happened with Gio, how much time you invest will communicate that you take what's happened seriously and he should too. Finding the balance of how deep you go is contextual and will depend on his response and your comfort level with that response. The situation is likely to feel super awkward and uncomfortable for him. It should, and that's okay. That's evidence of his conscience emerging. But pushing too hard or shaming him may cause him to shut down just to get away from the situation. That is unproductive. Let him know that "joking about rape or sexual violence is *never* okay. Minimizing rape justifies behaviors that dehumanize people and makes those behaviors seem 'normal.' It also contributes to an unsafe environment for all of us. Even if it isn't your intention, you may make people feel scared that others don't take something that harmful seriously, or it can bring up feelings of sadness, anger, fear, and shame for people who have experienced sexual harm." This statement is important, and it's heavy, so follow up with, "What's coming up for you? How are you thinking and feeling about this?" Mirror Gio's language as you create closure, and let him know you are available to talk about it further should he have questions.

CONNECTION (LOVE AND INTIMACY)

We need connections that are heartfelt and matter to us. They are what protect us and make life feel satisfied and secure—our health and happiness depend on it.[41] That social connectedness begins to feel ever more important, as much of middle school is navigating friendship dynamics. These can be joyful and fulfilling as well as painful and challenging. They are an opportunity for students to learn important relationship skills and evolve in ways that lead to authentic connections and resilience. Many students need support in finding friends and figuring out how to engage with them to build connections. Phyllis Fagell suggests that cultivating good matches in middle school should focus on connecting, not impressing. She coaches students on how to join a conversation and "look for hooks" in a potential friend.[42] For instance, notice a music group on someone's shirt or ask if they watched a sports event. Create space for their responses and build from there. Sometimes these conversations are brief, other times they may blossom into a shared interest. Either way, patience is important.

Much of student interaction in middle school is characterized by sarcasm and humor, which are obstacles to real social connection, so engage students in dialogue about positive friendship matches. When young people veil their actions and interactions with sarcasm and humor, a hallmark of middle school banter, they distance themselves from others by evading the healthy vulnerability required for authentic representation and connection. If everything is a joke, students risk nothing, so they deflect vulnerability, which is what's actually needed to connect with others in an honest and meaningful way.[43] Other barriers include popularity, specifically who has social currency and how that affects inclusive environments.

Ask students to define popularity. Make distinctions between what earns recognition for being well liked and fun and being ascribed social status and influence. Ask, "What does it take to be popular? What are the costs and benefits?" Continue with, "How do popular people get that status?" and "What kind of influence do popular people have? How does someone lose popularity?" and "Once lost, can status be restored?"

Connect well-liked popularity and popularity status ascribed due to material possessions or being feared to how students want to be thought of and their reasons for this. Hone in on the actions of negotiating interactions, like whispering, eye rolls, under-the-breath digs, sarcastic remarks, and basically all small and subtle-yet-impactful acts of exclusion and degradation. Guide students to a more in-depth critical-thinking process with questions like

- What is baseline human dignity, and how do popular/power social dynamics influence dignity (treating ourselves and others like we have value)?

- What's your responsibility given the group (popular, neutral, unpopular) you are a part of to be a member of this community?
- How does your awareness of power change the way you will behave towards your peers, especially those who are in a different group?

Popularity is really about negotiating power and influence. Social identities within the greater culture of the school (which is informed by greater society) certainly plays a role in this. Many times, relational aggression is gendered based on gender roles and expectations. *Mean Girls* is a movie notorious for how accurately it captures the ways gender plays a role in negotiating adolescent power. I have students create their own "cafeteria tribe map" as a mode for discussion and use clips from the movie in my teaching about popularity and social power dynamics. Girl aggression is often about power and finding ways to feel powerful.[44] "Mean girl behavior" provides ample opportunity to discuss the complexities of how this may manifest.

The onslaught of gendered messages girls receive pulls and pushes them in different directions of never being enough. For example, don't be so smart that you're a threat, but be smart enough so you aren't labeled a ditz; or have *some* sexual experience so you aren't labeled a prude but not so much that you're slut shamed. Getting the balance just right is tough, and girls turn on each other as they attempt to navigate these tricky waters. As Brown observes, "Girls take their feelings and frustrations out primarily on girls; they blame and turn away from girls as the source of their problems. The power that girls gain comes at the expense of other girls (and ultimately themselves) because it draws on and thus perpetuates stereotypical arguments."[45]

SCENARIO: You notice that your student, Ava, is no longer sitting with her usual girl posse. In fact, she's become quiet and doesn't actively participate much during class discussions anymore. You discreetly ask her to check in after class. You tell her that you noticed that she hasn't been as engaged and wonder if there's anything on her mind that she may need some support with. Ava forces a smile and says, "Oh, there's just some friend drama." She shares that her friend group of eight started dissing her. She would see them all together on Snap Map and 360, but she wasn't invited. She reached out to the group and to girls individually, looking for clarification, and they would blow her off. So, she dropped a message into their group chat and directly texted that she could see and feel that they weren't including her and asked what happened. One of the girls called her and said that "it's nothing you did so don't feel bad. You just don't fit into the vibe of the group anymore." (Hennepin County School District, MN)

You may start with, "Thank you for telling me. That sounds rough. How are you feeling about it?" It's likely that Ava feels devastated but possible that she will minimize her feelings. As girls get older, they learn to hide their anger and feelings of aggression and consider bullying a boy thing; they tend to dismiss harmful gossip, note passing, and eye rolling, and not acknowledge them as bullying behaviors.[46] Affirm Ava's courage in asking the girls what was going on and in sharing the situation with you. Betrayal and exclusion can really hurt, and a situation like this may eventually help Ava understand the meaning of true friendship. While the effects of these situations may be psychological, the roots of them are social. Guide Ava to connect what she's feeling with what's happened, and make it clear that she has some options for how she wants to act and maintain her own sense of dignity.

Explore with Ava what she wants from the situation and what may help. Talking productively about feelings and mistreatment can sound cringey to an adolescent and even to some adults. But given how girls are socialized to deal with anger (cat fights, revenge campaigns, brutal gossip, yelling misogynist accusations and labels, or just hiding and not acknowledging feelings), this provides a different perspective on confrontation when treated ethically. Not everyone is going to like each other, and sometimes friendships fade or end; it's *how* we handle these situations that matter and contribute to or whittle away at our own sense of self-worth. Help Ava to see that the power differentials in a group chat were uneven and to think about the individual people in the group. Does she want to say something to any of them? There are seven after all. Was she friends with all of them in the same way? Are there some who may not feel the way the "spokesgirl" of the group represented? Seven can feel overwhelming, and we can't underestimate the social currency of such a large alliance. Break it down and consider the following strategy should Ava want to talk it out with someone.

Rosalind Wiseman uses the acronym SEAL to use whenever a student is in a situation where there is conflict, worry, or anxiety:

- *Stop and Strategize.* Breathe, listen, and think about where you want to talk to the person. Do you want to do it now or later—or maybe a little of both?
- *Explain.* Explain what happened that you didn't like and what you want.
- *Affirm.* Admit (*recognize*) anything you did that contributed to the conflict but affirm your right to be treated with dignity by the other person and vice versa.
- *Lock.* Lock in the friendship, take a vacation, or lock the friendship out.[47]

If Ava considers SEAL, offer to practice what she might say. Be realistic about the possibility of a disappointing response. Point out that the only person she can control is herself, and if saying what she needs to say helps her, then it can be worth it. In the spirit of resilience, you can also inquire about Ava's other friends and acquaintances at school who might provide support, as well as her community outside of school. Does she have family friends or extended family that she enjoys? Is she part of a youth group or organization that provides service to the greater community? What does she enjoy doing on her own, and what other connections are there in her life? Without minimizing Ava's feelings, help her realize that the world is bigger than the social dynamics at school and that she may find love in other dimensions of her life should these friendships be lost. Edward Hallowell, in *Connect*, writes that "to oppose the pain of loss, we use a human glue, the force of love."[48]

It is possible that this disruption in the social organization of Ava's class becomes gossip. Again, in addition to supporting students in naming and processing their feelings, they need tools to shore themselves up when adults aren't around. There will also be moments when students could and should handle situations for themselves. Whenever teaching about friendship dynamics, which is a fundamental aspect of middle school culture, provide concrete language for communication. Positive "clapbacks" or "comebacks" are essential for building confidence and protection skills. Have students collaborate on comebacks that don't feed into negative behaviors by demeaning someone else but rather affirm the person saying it in a way that shuts down the interaction.

Provide assertiveness education, which includes direct eye contact, setting one's weight in a brave body stance, and speaking with a clear and firm voice. Introduce the concept of affirmations that counter internal negative talk. Have students identify the negative talk they typically engage in and collaborate to come up with personalized affirmations that they may write on sticky notes to post on their mirror or tuck away in their backpack. Create one in the notes app on a phone that they may look at when they need to remember what they want to say to themselves. Break down and provide ways to understand the limiting and harmful social constructions of gender, race, class, and sexual identity so that students may see how these can get in the way of mutual respect, connection, and care. Highlight the importance of allyship among students against societal norms that limit their capacity to express themselves authentically. Recognize that not everyone should like or be friends with everyone. This isn't reality and discredits us with kids—they know this isn't true for adults. Instead, reiterate that despite this fact, a connected and caring community in which people appreciate the right to dignity for all benefits everyone. Remind students that conflict and disagreement is healthy and a normal part of every community—there will be rifts among us, but we can commit to resolving and repairing them in healthy ways.

A lot of my students draw a line between platonic relationships with family and friends and romantic relationships. When I explore this with them, many notice that in the media, there seem to be different standards for how people treat each other in a romantic and/or sexual relationship versus friendship. Middle school is a time when students are figuring out the power dynamics and ethical aspects of friendship. Build a concrete bridge into the realm of romantic relationships as well. Remember to be inclusive of all the ways people may pair with someone else, and be sure to make the distinction that for some students, asexuality best reflects their experience so far and for others, romantic and/or sexual attraction isn't close to being on their radar. Everyone, however, is exposed to ideas of how romantic attraction is expressed and explored. It's critical to point out that all relationships matter and that intimacy and social connectedness are something all humans need to thrive.

Finding this in our American achievement-based perfectionist culture where everyone is trying to get everything right all of the time can be challenging. Intimacy is based on trust. Expand students' understanding of what it means to trust someone and what that looks, sounds, and feels like in different contexts. Discuss what it means to pace a relationship with trust and how it develops through shared experiences, which typically take time and patience. It also requires managing uncomfortable emotions, since conflict in relationships is inevitable and we usually care a lot when we are in an intimate relationship with someone. In other words, it's important to get comfy with the uncomfy.

SAFETY

In my experience, the vast majority of educators care about kids. Even though they do, this doesn't mean that we are creating safe spaces for all students. Cultivating safe spaces for all students is an intentional process that requires an up-to-date understanding of how bullying and cyberbullying are related. It is critical that schools provide digital literacy education for all students and their caretaking adults. Many parenting adults need information, education, and demonstration on how to install filters and manage settings on phones. Folks need to know how to limit apps, which are to a student's benefit or detriment, and the reasons, time locks, and types of accounts. Although a bit late, policy makers can no longer ignore the current data on the often harmful impact of social media and digital devices on young people, their developing brains, and well-being. Teen accounts, limited algorithms, and publicized warnings are starting to emerge on state and federal levels. These kinds of guardrails are a positive development, but it's also important that adults help our young people learn to safely navigate this tech landscape, because it isn't going anywhere. As my students tell me, "social media is life." They are digital natives who use devices to communicate and connect. Phones, for many students, have simply become another aspect of how they interact with each other in person and online. This normalization requires adults to include digital education as a part of discipline and counseling support.

SCENARIO: You are an administrator at a school with uniforms. Girls are required to wear skirts. Many girls opt to wear shorts under their skirts, some do not. After school, three girls come to your office and report to the front desk receptionist that there are several boys running after girls, trying to take pictures under their skirts. One of the girls, Danika, is upset because she believes one of them snapped a photo of her and has it in his phone. Danika states that she and her friends were laying in the grass hanging out when Michael snuck up on her and tried to take a photo under her skirt. When she got up to run away, Michael's two friends started to run too and blocked her. Danika's friends got up and tried to get the phone away from Michael, but he and his friends ran away cracking up. (Santa Clara County Independent School, CA)

Reports like this trigger certain policies and/or penal codes. Those may vary depending on what kind of institution you operate in (public, independent, or faith-based). In a California public school, this incident would fall under California Ed Code 48900.2, which addresses "committed sexual harassment, inappropriate touching as defined by Education Code Section 212.5."[49] The burden of proof required for an administrator to take action is to have clear testimony from the student who made the complaint and witness statements that support the claim. The education code in California recognizes that the threat of harm is enough for school leaders to take action.

In this scenario, the receptionist would promptly inform school leadership. The principal (or vice principal or dean) would mobilize an additional dean, campus supervisor, or school resource officer to find and bring Danika and her friends to the office, as well as Michael and his associates. Michael would need to wait in a supervised room and have his phone confiscated. In a separate space, the principal would ask Danika to write a signed statement describing what took place. If she is unable to write, the principal may transcribe it, check its accuracy with Danika, and ask for her signature. Right after receiving the statement, it is important to notify Danika's parents of the incident. Under confidentiality of the law (FERPA), educators may not talk to anyone about another person's child.[50] If Danika's parents want to know how Michael's behavior will be addressed, you can tell them of your legal responsibilities concerning confidentiality and lay out the school's policies and steps taken with incidents of this nature. Assure them that you will follow up with details of your investigation that involves their child.

The principal will interview Michael and may look in his phone for the photo or other evidence. If Danika was not wearing shorts and Michael has a picture of her genitals, this could be considered possession of child pornography. Some states have reduced penalties for teen sexting (which includes the possession of and sharing of sexually explicit photos); California does not. The disciplinary process for Michael should be clear, straight forward, and consistent. For kids to learn from their mistakes, we must be direct and tell them exactly what they've done. What happens to Michael will contribute to the moral groundwork for his future behavior, so approaching the situation with genuine guidance and empathy will help Michael learn from the experience versus resisting authority and shutting down in shame.

In this particular case, the picture Michael took was of the inside of Danika's skirt, so it was just a navy-blue screen. This incident took place in an independent school. Within that context, a similar response/investigation would be set in motion, and a sexual harassment and/or digital safety policy would be applied. No matter what the type of school, policies need to be continuously reviewed for consistency in terms of how they are applied. Are they equitable, or do they perpetuate harm against some students and adults of specific identities and not others? Ideally, school policies and protocols are created to protect people during moments when they may not be able to protect themselves. In addition to creating safety for individuals, the school community must be considered as well. Policies also communicate school values for how we should treat each other.

For our purposes, let's focus on the counseling, education opportunities, and restoration that needs to take place for the students involved in the above scenario.

Many school dress and uniform codes are born out of tradition, not aligned with how education is evolving, so they tend to be sexist and reinforce gender binaries and norms. A skirts-for-girls-only policy does just that. Again, has the school provided any CSE, specifically including consent as well as digital citizenship? If they have, the adults entrusted with counseling the students will be able to use familiar language and concepts to discuss what happened. The conversation will reinforce information, deepen understanding, be applied to context, and stretch to include values education regarding agency, autonomy, mutual respect, and dignity. If there isn't that background and grounding, the adults involved will have to work from very little and may have to dispel misinformation and assumptions about this important facet of sexuality.

It's important to recognize that many of us, certainly young people, shield and armor ourselves when we fear something. This is understandable and may be the result of experiences, including an abuse of power by adults or a power imbalance because of race and/or gender, ability, or religious faith. And it is that need for personal "protection" that gets in the way of openness and our ability to reach students and authentically connect, so as to genuinely support and understand them. Students have a keen sense of when adults are disciplining them fairly. One way to be fair-minded is to remember that shame is typically lurking when a young person has made a mistake or messed up. Pollack observes that student behaviors in response to shame may be gendered, that girls are shame-sensitive and boys are shame-phobic, which means they will do just about anything to avoid it.[51]

Consider what is known about Michael and the other boys involved. As much as they operate as a friend group, they are also individuals and may have felt conflicted about participating in and complying with Michael's plan. Engage another adult, like the school counselor, to collaborate. Talk to the boys separately so that power differentials don't influence the conversation. Ask, "Help me understand how this happened.

What was going on that led to chasing the girls and taking pictures?" You are looking for underlying reasons (usually feelings and needs) and what caused them. Ask, "What happened?" and "Was there something else going on?" This nonjudgmental inquiry or detective work communicates that you are interested in how a student was feeling and recognizes the greater context of culture and social dynamics. It communicates that you care. Sometimes a teacher is one of the few trusting adults who will see a child for who they are and what they may be struggling with; oftentimes, it is our students with the most difficult academic and behavioral challenges who need our support the most. These are middle school students. They most likely know that what they did was wrong and already see it as a stupid mistake. However, these are the moments when meaningful conversation balanced with appropriate consequences can shift a trajectory.

True accountability requires a young person to understand what they were feeling, how they managed those feelings or didn't, what need they were trying to meet, their impact on others and the community, as well as what they can do to restore the trust eroded and aspire to do better. This is critical practice as young people establish patterns of behavior. It directly serves them as well as the communities they will be a part of moving forward.

It's possible that there are other social dynamics going on among these friend groups and/or the individuals within them. Hopefully your detective work contextualized the situation. When interviewing the girls, affirm their appropriate response as well as how they supported each other. Focus on the moment, and appreciate that they didn't tolerate the boys' behavior. Be direct and honest: "Sexual harassment (unwanted sexual attention—photos under skirts) and taking pictures of someone without their consent is never okay." Ask how they are feeling and mirror what they share. The nuance of next steps is critical. You don't want to ask questions and use language that is victim blaming; this is also an opportunity to give the girls tools should something like this happen again. You may also explore what they could do in a similar situation if adults were not accessible or if they weren't on campus but rather hanging out at someone's house. Suggest language like, "Stop—I'm not down with that," or "Hey, that's harassment. Uncool."

Convene with other adults who are involved in supporting the students to assess how you might mediate a conversation between Michael and Danika and/or their friends involved. Michael would need to process what happened and the impact so that he gets to a place where he could express a sincere apology, and Danika would have to feel okay hearing it. This will take several conversations and only happen if Michael is genuinely contrite. Danika has the right to support and decide if she is open to Michael's apology. It will be important for the school to separate them, should Danika wish, from shared classes and/or other meeting times, etc. In addition, address the potential repercussions that may follow the incident, including gossip, overt or covert retaliation, judgment, or/and public shaming. This kind of backlash erodes community as well. Explicitly explain this, and if feelings keep coming up, provide resources for where the students may go to take care of them in healthy ways.

It is possible that there has been ongoing teasing between Danika and Michael's friend groups, and the boys saw this as an extension of that. This is when community education and health classes are essential. Students need clear communication about certain behaviors and relationship dynamics. They need to understand how context plays a role in people's experiences, how to self-regulate, and where the boundaries are. When does behavior go too far, and what can we do about it? Provide critical-thinking practice by using scenarios that represent these dynamics between students. Inform students about sexual harassment, it's short- and long-term impact on individuals and the community, as well as how to prevent these incidents. In *The Talk* by the Making Caring Common Project, it was found that 76 percent of the adolescent respondents surveyed had never had a parent talk to them about how to avoid sexually harassing others.[52] Reinforce what it means to be an active bystander who stands up to those who demean and disrespect others. Young people need this education, and school is one of the few places where they may get it. These are essential conversations needed to promote real honor, courage, and dignity within a community, because "there is, of course, no honor or courage in degrading or sexualizing others . . . But there can be honor in standing up to your peers . . . to protect peers in one's midst who are vulnerable to harassment or assault."[53]

Middle School can feel like a tumultuous time. Even so, most middle schoolers will at least understand the daily schedule and expectations of their school, be familiar with the campus, know their teachers, have some friendships of varying depth, and be the oldest with the most relative experience in their schools. However, as students transition into high school, most of them will be the youngest and most inexperienced, not know about school operations and/or the campus, be clueless about who their teachers are and what class content and the homework load will be like, and not have as many points of contact through friendships. This can cause kids to be off balance. CSE, specifically the information and skills it offers, can be an anchor to steady a ninth grader. As students enter into the realm of high school, the opportunities, stakes, and exposure increase exponentially. Continued CSE will be essential for young people as they navigate this gauntlet to adulthood.

6

Big Transitions

Grades Nine and Ten

"Stories matter. Many stories matter. Stories have been used to dispossess and to malign, but stories can also be used to empower and to humanize. Stories can break the dignity of a people, but stories can also repair that broken dignity."

~ Chimamanda Adichie

Through adolescence, students start to reflect upon, write, and narrate their own stories. One of education's critical goals is to support the evolution of how those stories unfold, helping young people find their voices and acquire the language and tools to accurately express their lived experiences.

Developmental highlights:

- Students are navigating modern puberty, which starts earlier than previous generations.
- Cognitive development continues. The brain grows from the back forward, so the amygdala (emotions, impulse, reward center) is well formed, but the prefrontal cortex (rational thought, decision making) is still in process.

- Due to neuroplasticity and myelination, students' behavior and experiences shape their brains.
- There is an increased capacity for abstract thought. This growth means that your student will more often (but not consistently) demonstrate the capacity to grasp more abstract concepts.
- Adolescents are neurologically programmed to seek the acceptance of their friends and peers. They care deeply about belonging.
- Teen brains are responsive to what's novel, yet they need clear boundaries and structure.
- The process of individuation (establishing a sense of personal and communal identity, as well as exploring and asserting independence) is taking place.
- There is a focus on morality, meaning, and a deeper sense of identity as well.

BODIES

Adolescent bodies continue to change at varied rates. In nine and tenth grade, you may see a majority of teenagers, especially those assigned female at birth (AFAB), catching up with those students who started puberty on the earlier side of the spectrum. Sex characteristics such as breasts, penis, and testicular growth continues. For some, hips will widen, hair continues to show up, acne may surface, voices may change, and there will be an increase in muscle and/or fat growth. Some teenagers will seem to grow a few inches a week, while others seem like they'll stay at their tween height. Menarche and spermarche has happened for the majority, while some may be waiting for or dreading the moment. Periods and spontaneous erections can happen at school, too. Students may feel like they really get a challenging concept one day and then find themselves feeling lost the next. Kids may have the intention of doing one thing and then impulsively do something instead that makes them think "Ugh, really?!? I *knew* I shouldn't have done that." Students may feel like they are waking up in a new body every day. It's a state of being and a set of changes that can feel like *a lot*!

Adolescents are also increasingly self-conscious and figuring out how to authentically connect with others, sustain relationships, and be a positive contributing member of a community. As they negotiate power, feeling it within themselves or not, and as a member of social groups, they may make decisions that serve them and their social connectedness and esteem and/or make decisions that isolate them and leave them feeling lonely. There is a range of ability within student populations. In addition, many young people may be managing mental and physical health issues.[1] How these show up and are met at school can contribute to the development and maintenance of a teenager's esteem—positive or negative.

SCENARIO: It's the beginning of the school year. Jason is a somewhat quiet student who livens up around a couple of kids he knows. He is polite and respectful towards his peers and teachers. He participated in and enjoyed the icebreakers you facilitated. As class starts one day, you notice that he hasn't removed his baseball cap. The school's dress code states that heads may not be covered—a teacher must be able to see a student's face—so you ask Jason to remove his cap. He hesitates and softly asks if he can please keep it on. You respond, "It's a community rule that we all abide by, please take it off." Jason tries to discreetly take off his cap. When he does, it becomes obvious that he has alopecia. Trey, the student behind him, says, "Dude, what's up with your head?" And, Marcus, to the side, sucks through his teeth while shaking his head and adds, "Damn, you should cover that up." (St. Louis County Public Schools, MO)

As teachers, we weigh decisions all the time about rules—what they are, how we interpret them, and how we apply them. A student who typically complies with school rules and teacher requests deserves special consideration when they are hesitant and ask for an exception, especially if they have a health issue. Adolescence is a time of heightened self-consciousness, and bias-based mean behavior and/or bullying has an increased impact on the recipient.[2] Despite our best intentions, we may expose a student to this kind of social cruelty. Jason's teacher may have been caught off guard or distracted by something else and defaulted to the habit of rote rule enforcement. Maybe it's the beginning of the school year and they aren't aware of Jason's health issue. Maybe they have a "the rules are the rules, no matter what the cost" attitude. Maybe they simply didn't think of it. Whatever the reason, Jason has been "outed," and a couple of kids have drawn negative attention to his vulnerability.

As teachers, we all know the most effective way to teach something is to do or model it ourselves. Prosocial behaviors (e.g., accountability, kindness, compassion, empathy, helping behaviors) are crucial for positive adolescent socialization. Cultivating prosocial behaviors supports students to learn and adapt well—they can also protect from and reduce the negative consequences of daily stress, aggression, and perceived peer rejection.[3] This psychological resilience and perceived social support is invaluable.

Respond with a sincere apology, "I apologize Jason. I didn't realize you have a legit reason. You may keep it on." Then request that Trey and Marcus see you after class, and move on with the lesson. Some educators wonder if they shouldn't make more of a public example of Trey and Marcus and how their responses were unnecessary and unkind—as a community, we don't criticize someone's disability or compromised health. Jason already feels self-conscious. We know this because he wanted to keep his hat on (most likely in anticipation of negative comments and/or teasing) and was hesitant to take it off (despite a history of compliance). It's important to center Jason's needs at this moment. Continued attention on what Trey and Marcus said will keep the focus on Jason's alopecia. The simple public request that they see you after class communicates that you take what they said seriously, it isn't okay, and they will be held accountable in some way. To make a public example of Marcus and Trey would most likely be experienced as shaming (especially because they are adolescents), which typically shuts kids down and gets in the way of learning. It is also important to be aware of other social identities (your own and the students') that may compound the interpersonal dynamics and your student's experience of how you reprimand them.

When you talk to Jason, see what's going on with his haircut and hat. Be empathetic and support him in navigating the tricky social landscape of adolescence when managing a visible health issue. Would Jason be okay with his teachers knowing so that the incident isn't repeated? Does there need to be an accommodation? In this particular scenario, Jason typically keeps his hair close to his head so that the alopecia isn't noticeable. His mom wasn't able to get him to the barber that week so there was the temporary need for a hat. Use nonjudgmental language to ask about it and determine whether or not Jason's alopecia is a source of bullying (behavior that is chronic, intentional, and includes a leveraged power dynamic). If Jason is being bullied, address it swiftly with responsibility and compassion. Be sure to include Jason in how it is addressed. Sometimes formal interventions can make bullying worse. Work with Jason, and/or an administrator, and his family to figure out what will be most supportive. If it's an isolated incident because the condition isn't typically evident or the remarks are uncharacteristic of Marcus and Trey, ensure that Jason has emotional support and tools, and language and strategies for handling it at times when adults aren't around.

Go over clapbacks/comebacks that he may say that aren't at the expense of anyone or perceived as a challenge but rather affirm him and empower him to walk away with dignity. The goal is for Jason to shut down the aggressor who is looking for a negative response. It will need to feel realistic and doable. Using humor, naming the behavior and the intended impact, showing vulnerability instead of defensiveness, or engaging in a power struggle are all possibilities. Suggest that his comeback isn't something that fuels the incident or mirrors negativity. For instance, say, "Well now you're making this awkward," and then pivot to something else; or say, "That's just mean," and walk away; or say, "Just pointed out my biggest insecurity—cool move." Jason might simply agree with them so that he takes away the aggressor's satisfaction at making someone else feel bad—turning it back onto the aggressor. "You're right Marcus. What are you doing right now, you okay? Because what you said is pretty uncool."

Initiate larger class discussions about commenting on people's appearance or attributes and the fact that such comments aren't aligned with community values. Encourage students to pause and ask themselves, "Is this necessary? Is it kind?" Criticizing someone's physical health or attributes is hurtful behavior. Use scenarios that surface these interpersonal dynamics, and explore the ethics of behavior. Engage students in dialogue about hurtful behavior, where the boundaries lie, and how such behavior aligns with the people they wish to be and become. Some students may be resigned to mean behavior because they gain popularity through intimidation or are performing an "I'm too cool to care" demeanor. Rosalind Wiseman, author of *Queen Bees and Wannabes*, suggests posing the critical question: "What is the difference between what you do and who you are? If you repeat certain types of disrespectful or dishonest actions, at what point do you become a disrespectful or dishonest person?"[4] Deepen the lesson to include owning mistakes versus making excuses and justifying actions. Demanding an insincere apology teaches students to be dishonest and can feel worse than the action that required it. In the spirit of restorative practices, evoke empathy and discuss what it would take to mediate and mitigate what happened. What would true accountability look, sound, and feel like? Create closure by crafting genuine apologies that account for ownership of the mistake, a sincere brief explanation, and an expression of remorse that is tied to a specific commitment to do better and live the amends. The criteria can be one that makes them and the people they care about feel proud.

Practice decision-making in context through scenario/case study work so that students can recognize how complex situations may be and distinguish between healthy risks (taking a chance that may be uncomfortable but lead to growth) and unsafe risks (putting their own or someone else's well-being at risk with no benefit). As students transition into high school, they will be confronted with a variety of situations that will include a cascade of decisions. It is through the practice of critical thinking and consideration that they will develop an individual and community ethical framework for expanding their capacity to make informed and positive decisions. This is critical skill development; however, current societal trends indicate that there is diminished risk taking on the part of young people, which may impact their capacity to be empathetic. Empathy is essential for healthy relationships anchored in authentic connection. When students evade healthy risk taking because of the inherent discomfort that accompanies it, they withhold the healthy vulnerability that is needed for authentic connection. And if we don't truly connect with others, we cannot take their perspective.[5] This is foundational to how we cultivate care.

GENDER AND SEXUALITY DIVERSITY

It is to everyone's benefit that we are all able to bring our full, authentic selves to our work with young people. This is true in at least two ways. More broadly, it benefits all of us in a community to know and understand folks who are both different and similar to us. More specifically, this is inherently true for students who share identities with teachers that have been historically marginalized.

Jennifer Bryan, the author of *From the Dress-Up Corner to the Senior Prom*, encourages us to "recognize how heteronormativity in schools allows heterosexual preadolescents and adolescents to develop gradually. This privilege of pace provides patience so they may 'come in' to a more public expression of their sexuality as it develops. They may wait, flirt, meander, or jump in. For LGBTQ youth, 'coming out' provides the possibility for participating in the personal exploration and interpersonal process of sexual development, but pushes them to make declarations about their identity that may not be congruent with the natural course of their individual development."[6] Adolescents are also neurologically programmed to seek the acceptance of their peers, to be on par with each other in many ways, to fit in, or better yet, to belong. There are many societal messages and experiences that may shape how a young person begins to connect with and understand their sexuality as a part of their greater identity and well-being. Many LGBTQ+ youth share how the added layers of queer-specific stigmatization, minoritization, and focus on victimhood versus the resilience and joy of the LGBTQ+ experience can create pressure to claim an identity and serve to make that process particularly fraught.

SCENARIO: As an appreciated teacher on campus, many students seek out Mr. Davis's support to talk about personal social issues they are managing. Mr. Davis receives an email from a student, Logan, who would like to schedule some time to talk. Logan shows up during a tutorial period and takes a seat on the small couch in Mr. Davis's office. His head is in his hands, with his elbows on his knees, as he looks at the ground and takes a deep breath. Mr. Davis is present and patient. Logan sits up, looks at him, and shares, "I think I'm gay." Mr. Davis doesn't immediately react, gently smiles with an empathetic expression, and says, "I appreciate your courage," so Logan continues. He explains that, since middle school, he has had several girlfriends, but that "it never felt 100% right." He did, however, have a couple of crushes on guys but would never act on them—the risk was way too high to be labeled a "fag" or "homo" and ostracized, especially because he's a celebrated athlete. Then Logan asks, "Mr. Davis, how did you know you were gay?" Mr. Davis hasn't explicitly come out in the school community; however, he has a picture of himself with his husband and two kids on his desk. His teaching is known to be inclusive of many identities, including different genders and sexualities. There is also a rainbow flag sticker on his bulletin board. Mr. Davis is also aware that administrators are fielding some resistance from parents in the community about the book, *The Perks of Being a Wallflower*, especially how it depicts sexuality, which has been on display in the school library. (New York City Department of Education, NY)

The cultural context of your school and whether or not comprehensive sexuality education (CSE) is valued and supported will determine how you may respond to student questions about sexuality and relationships, especially if there is a personal aspect to them. Unfortunately, this is particularly sensitive for teachers who identify as LGBTQ+. There is still a tremendous amount of trans and homophobia in greater society, as well as in most schools, which creates a hostile environment for some folks. Currently, there is increasing anti-LGBTQ+ surveillance in schools, which can jeopardize job security and dignity for LGBTQ+ individuals and their allies. Due to this continued marginalization and homophobic culture, which has been amplified by leading political and media figures, many LGBTQ+ teachers express feeling that they could be at risk if they were to respond to queer youth requests to be allies and affirming role models.

Many of the teachers I've spoken with in these situations are empathetic towards their students. They know how challenging it can be for LGBTQ+ youth to be immersed in cis-heteronormative contexts without affirming role models, curricula, or activities that honor this exploration and/or aspect of their identity. LGBTQ+ educators express how critical and helpful to their mental health it would have been to have had someone in whom they could see themselves and understand them for who they are with care and value. And many have to navigate the homophobic assumptions and accusations that, if an LGBTQ+ teacher provides a safe space for a student to "see" and learn about the positive possibilities for themselves as a gay person in their school and other environments, their intention would be to "groom" or "indoctrinate" the student into being gay.[7] This inaccurate and fallacious assumption is rooted in and fueled by increasing abhorrent and disgraceful bigotry and discrimination. Sexual orientation is a complex interplay of genetic, hormonal, and environmental factors. It is polygenic with epigenetic effects. It is not something someone chooses or is brainwashed into that makes them into a felon. Every student deserves positive role models and to learn about themselves, their histories, and prospects for a bright future. We must all find a way to ensure this right.

When speaking to students about issues of sexuality, there are some practical steps you can take to prevent any kind of misunderstanding or misinterpretation of your intentions. For one thing, it is important to be aware of the psychology of space and the social power dynamic between you as a teacher and your student as a minor. Position yourself with some distance between yourself and your student, and make sure you are sitting at the same level. Face each other but slightly askew to avoid creating intense intimacy. Make sure that the student sees a clear path to the door so that they don't feel trapped and they have a clear direction if they feel they want to leave. Make sure the door is slightly ajar, and if you have blinds or shades, modify them so there is privacy but not an atmosphere of perceived secrecy. If you think a student may be about to disclose information that is reportable, make sure to be upfront that you are a mandated reporter, and explain what that means before they begin their disclosure. You may say, "I appreciate you coming by, and before we start, I like to remind students that I'm a mandated reporter. In this county, that means that if you share 'x' then 'y' may happen. I just want to make sure you know so you feel you have the agency to share what you want without starting something that you aren't ready for yet."

As readers, we know that Mr. Davis is discreetly out in the community. We also know that there is some parental resistance to integrating issues of sexuality into curriculum. As readers, we don't know how administrators are handling the resistance from parents. Is the administration supportive of LGBTQ+ faculty, students, and their allies? Will they manage the resistance effectively so Mr. Davis may be reassured of his position at the school? I have worked in schools that are proactive and initiate the integration of all identities into all aspects of school life with enthusiastic family support, and I have worked in schools where I have been told that I "may not teach gender or talk about LGBTQ+ in any positive light." There are schools where administration is supportive; however, some parents are not, and still others where the majority of students are inclusive and embracing of LGBTQ+ identities and many of the teachers are not and vice versa. In communities that have an undercurrent of homophobia, some teachers may fear bringing up LGBTQ+ issues up will cause people to question their sexuality, no matter how they identify.

What's important for all educators to remember when talking to youth about sexuality is that they may ask about us personally, but in most cases, they are really just wondering about themselves. It is also our responsibility to empower them with skills to discover what is true for them and how they may make decisions that support them, versus enabling a situation where they become dependent on our advice. Therefore, affirm their fortitude: "It takes a lot of courage to figure out one's identity and what it means. For many that's a lifelong process."

Mr. Davis may continue with, "I hear you asking about my identity, and it sounds like you're really wondering about yours." Ask questions that (1) are open ended and inspire reflection and personal action and (2) stick to feelings versus chronologies of events. When students come to us with questions about their sexuality, guide them towards a healthy balance of agency and vulnerability. Engage them in an exploration of risk and benefits: "What's your experience of LGBTQ+ rights and issues here at school?"; "How are things at home?"; "Have you shared this with any of your friends? Is there one friend you trust who you could share this with?"; "What might that conversation sound like?"; "What would need to happen for you to feel like you could trust them?"; and/or "When you think about your responses, how does it make you feel? What comes up for you?"

More often than not, our students need adults to listen and be present. Mr. Davis may also suggest resources. As educators of tweens and teens, it is a good idea to have prepared references of medically accurate, gender and sexuality inclusive resources and advocacy programs and organizations on hand that students may access for further information. LGBTQ+–affirming literature can be helpful as well. If Mr. Davis feels the need to be even more discreet, he may suggest stories that aren't necessarily LGBTQ+ focused but also include other aspects of history or stories and poetry that have LGBTQ+ undercurrents, as well as other aspects of learning that align with district standards and core curricula and competencies.

It is critical to be attuned to your students' intersecting identities, especially those associated with race, ethnicity, and religion. Intersectionality is a way to think about social categorizations such as gender, race, religion, ethnicity, or social class, and the ways an individual or group may identify as part of more than one such group or identity and thus experience dual or multiple forms of oppression simultaneously. It is possible that your student's multiple identities may compound their experience of marginalization and minoritization.[8] In the context of sexuality, bias, marginalization, stereotypical tropes in media that fetishize and eroticize identities, as well potential messages of spiritual condemnation may be at work and affect your student's understanding of themselves and how they feel about their social connectedness and acceptance.[9] Pay attention to their mental health in general and how you may be supportive and work within the school, community-based organizations, their families, and/or chosen families (accepting caretaking adults and peers who the student is connected with) to ensure student support and safety.

On February 13, 2023, the CDC released an alarming study, *The Youth Risk Behavior Survey*, that documents record levels of sadness and anxiety in teen girls. Adolescent girls reported high rates of depression, suicidal thoughts, and sexual violence, as did LGBTQ+ youth. The increase in sadness and hopelessness, measured over the last ten years, was present across girls of all races. Reporting focused on the experience of girls specifically, as well as LGBTQ+ youth; however, it is suspected that gender differences may mask the aggressive and violent behavior in boys that can signal depression as well.[10] According to the Journal of Adolescent Health, the mental health of young adult males is also at risk. Young men are experiencing elevated rates of suicide, conduct disorder, substance use, and interpersonal violence relative to young women.[11]

In response, the CDC recommends "implementing quality health education that is medically accurate, developmentally appropriate, culturally and LGBTQ+ inclusive, and grounded in science [because it] can help prevent violence and reduce mental health challenges by equipping teens with essential knowledge and skills such as negotiating sexual consent, managing emotions, and recognizing and asking for the help they need."[12] This sexuality education needs to not only be happening through direct teaching in classrooms but throughout educational spaces where students reach out and seek information, understanding, and affirmation.

FEELINGS AND VALUES

At this age and stage, emotional literacy is an important tool that you can help your students practice and develop. It's important to help students expand their vocabulary to accurately express emotional embodied experiences. Many students default to storytelling with a focus on chronology and articulating narratives that intellectualize lived experiences instead of the emotional impact of those experiences. Encourage the use of feeling words and speaking from the heart. It is through shared experiences, how we feel about and give them meaning, that strengthens authentic connections. Encourage the personal writing process as a way to explore, express, and further define what students care about and value. Have students revisit personal reflections and infuse them with emotional vocabulary that encourages an empathetic response on the part of the reader (you). Help students define different values and express them; this will support students in discussing challenging topics and learning from each other. These skills and practices are essential to active participation in and sustaining the health of communities. As community members, it is unrealistic to expect that everyone will get along, and to think that people cannot learn and be inspired to care for each other across differences underestimates peoples' capacity for empathy and growth. Conflict is inevitable in any relationship. It is also reasonable to expect that we may address those issues in a healthy way. How we care across differences is an essential capacity and skill that builds resilience and benefits us all.

SCENARIO: Mr. Asghar teaches at a racially diverse school that has a dominant liberal culture. Many students speak a native language other than English, which seems to be the basis for segregated social groups. The school prides itself on inclusivity, and Mr. Asghar, who is a first-generation Muslim-identifying straight man, has been asked to conduct a focus group of Muslim students from the Middle East to better understand how the school may support cross-cultural connections between students. The students express feeling pressure from the larger community to "be for gay rights" and to "say it's okay to be gay," when it conflicts with their religious beliefs. Some students share that they don't know what to believe and that the school culture isn't accepting of politically conservative viewpoints. When their teachers publicly prompt perspectives on LGBTQ+ issues in class, students feel like they can't say what is true for them, and if they do, it will further marginalize them. (Middlesex County Public School District, MA)

Identity development—how we integrate our past, present, and future experiences into a self-concept—is a primary and complex developmental task that starts in adolescence and continues for a lifetime.[13] This process is an interplay of forces based on how we see ourselves, how others see us, and the influences of the cultural contexts we navigate. Today's youth, more than ever, are steeped in a plethora of cultural messages (digital and otherwise)—norms and expectations that tell them who they are and who they should be. Trying on, filtering, and working through all of these aspects of identity in a quest to make meaning for themselves can feel arduous, confusing, exciting, and challenging. Students may be vulnerable to the traps of stereotypes and minoritizing narratives, and since they are neurologically programmed to seek the acceptance of their peers and friends, these influences may compromise a student's capacity to realize their full potential.[14]

Educators can support students by providing spaces for them to gather and explore what they think and feel about themselves with adult guidance, especially within a context of contradictory cultural messaging. Some schools support students with affinity spaces. Some feel these may serve to reinforce ethnic and/or racial segregation. Contradictory cultural values can be tricky for students to navigate. Young people need information, skills, guidance, and practice to respectfully engage in dialogue with others in a classroom about different points of view. In the scenario above, Middle Eastern Muslim students whose native language is not English and whose religious values are in the minority could benefit from adult-guided dialogue about sexuality within a context of shared identity and assumed cultural understanding.

Be aware that there may be Middle Eastern Muslim LGBTQ+ students who may identify with and feel included based on their ethnic and/or racial identity, while struggling because of their diverse sexuality, which is perceived as negative within their community in and out of school. This possibility affirms the value of affinity-group guidelines and additional instruction on how to effectively communicate with others through conflict and disagreement.

If students feel more comfortable in a smaller group, they may be more receptive to learning about LGBTQ+ science and social issues. It is an opportunity to reinforce the values of inclusion at the school and to recognize that, sometimes we receive messaging about conflicting values, but the school is committed to affirming every student's dignity, even when not everyone agrees. Students need to hear and have modeled for them how we may care for others, lean into understanding, and practice empathy without having to abandon values that may not align. The adult advisor will need to create and cultivate an environment of learning, discovery, and growth versus a place where students come together to compound exclusive thoughts and denigrate others. It is also an opportunity to discuss how an affinity group may model and assume a leadership role in bringing people of differing backgrounds and ideas together and recognize how various forms of oppression are connected, which may also generate empathy for LGBTQ+ students. To prevent further racial separation, the affinity group may reach out to other groups and collaborate to encourage dialogue about difficult issues, as well as hold open meetings that encourage students of different identities to attend.

RELATIONSHIPS (CONSENT, COMMUNICATION, DECISION-MAKING)

Teenagers are notorious for their developing prefrontal cortex and how it impacts their capacity to make sound decisions. This neuroplasticity also provides opportunity. With mindful practice, adolescents can be agents in shaping their own brains and behavior. A young person's activities and choices will influence their brain development through a neural process called myelination. This means that their choices and behavior will serve to insulate and organize the neural pathways of a young person's brain and establish patterns of behavior that will follow them into adulthood. This is true of the relationships they are in as well. The decisions young people make about the foundational characteristics of a healthy relationship are critical to their development.

At the beginning of the #MeToo movement, whenever I would visit a school to provide sexual consent education, students would refer to me as "the consent lady." They were eager to learn what consent is and why it's a legal responsibility. Today, I find most students know what the definition of consent is but are searching for a deeper understanding of what it actually means. That meaning typically comes from how we contextualize relationship dynamics, and what that looks, sounds, and feels like leads to the meaning it has for us. As educators, we are modeling what it means to be in relationships with individuals and community all of the time. How we talk about, handle, and process issues of sexuality contributes to our students' ideas about them.

SCENARIO: You forget your laptop on the Spirit Bus that went to the away soccer game that afternoon. You take a walk across campus to find it before heading home. As you step up to the aisle, you surprise two students, Dylan and Jordan, who are partially clothed and obviously engaged in sexual activity. They acknowledge you and start scrambling to put their clothes on. You step down and wait outside the bus door. (Faith-based School, VA)

Schools typically have policies that pertain to peer-to-peer sexual activity. Depending on the type of school (parochial, independent, or public), which state the school is located in, the age of consent in that state, and whether or not you are operating in a day school or residential community will determine what those policies are and how they are applied. Coming upon students engaged in sexual activity can be tricky to navigate. I've heard teachers describe it as "super cringy," "horrifying," "super awkward," "embarrassing," and "just what kids do." These moments are our opportunity to provide the sexuality education our students deserve—one that emphasizes safety, mutual respect, a healthy perspective on sexuality, and a kind, empathetic, and compassionate handling of the school's policies and what it means to be a teenager who is newly exploring and expressing their sexuality.

All of us respond to being caught, especially in moments of extreme exposure and/or vulnerability, in different ways. The same holds true for adolescents, so we want to remain steady as adults. This may be more challenging for some of us than others. Who the students are, their gender identities, their perceived sexual orientation, and many other variables may factor into our response. We have the power in this moment to have a meaningful impact on a young person's ideas about sexuality.

When Dylan and Jordan step off the bus, they are probably experiencing a host of feelings—anything from embarrassment and/or defensiveness to trepidation, dread, and/or shame. Since it will most likely be uncomfortable, maintain composure and lead with neutrality. You may directly acknowledge, "Well, this is awkward." Different schools have different protocols for how to proceed in these instances. How you proceed will also depend on the age of the students and if there is some aspect of a social power dynamic. These are issues of consent and mandated reporting. Schools have a responsibility to provide training on reporting and the state and sometimes county-specific guidelines for when there is cause for concern and a report is required.

It is typically required that students and their families sign off on having read the student handbook of policies and procedures before a school year starts. In practice, of course, students (and many adults) rarely read the handbook, and/or if they do, are unlikely to remember what the handbook says, even though they put their signature on it. Focus on geography first. Dylan and Jordan are probably together in an area of campus where they're not supposed to be. You may start by pointing this out: "Students aren't allowed to be on the buses without adult supervision." Now transition to a discussion of their sexual activity. This terrain can be tricky to navigate. On the one hand, schools have a responsibility to the law and ensuring student safety. On the other hand, it is actually developmentally appropriate for teenagers to begin exploring and expressing their sexuality with themselves and/or others, as long as it is emotionally and physically safe. How does the greater school culture handle this complexity? What are the technicalities of policy, and how do administrators interpret and apply them?

Conventional disciplinary systems might identify public (even though it probably felt private to the students) sexual activity between students as "vulgarity" by education code, which could, for instance, result in a suspension. But many administrations will instead notify a parenting adult, have a conversation about the inappropriate nature of the student behavior on school grounds, and allow the consequences to be handled as a family matter. Whoever speaks to the student's caretaking adult may have to provide some parenting education. Sexuality is charged for most people, especially when, as a parent, they receive a call from the school about their child's sexual behavior. Again, given our societal history of sexual stigmatization and shame that is typically associated with it, the student's parent may benefit from nonjudgmental recognition that sexuality is a normal healthy aspect of our overall well-being, that teenagers can lose sight of school rules, and that your primary concern is their child's safety. Share what consent information you may have provided when talking to their kid. If a parent would like their student to receive counseling support, the school may have a Health Center on campus that can offer guidance and resources. Or your school may have a partnership with an outside organization that offers therapy and counseling services regarding healthy relationships. The National Center for Youth Law provides a *Minor Consent and Confidentiality: Compendium of State and Federal*

Laws for each state. If the behavior was between students where there is a questionable age gap or specific ages that require a Child Protective Services or Special Victims Unit report, then you or a school administrator or counselor would make that report as required by law. Most sexual activity between and among students does not require a report.

The most important concern at the moment of interruption is Dylan and Jordan's safety—that is, if the relationship and/or sexual activity is consensual. Digital devices can complicate this a bit. If one of the students suspects the other will disclose something that will raise suspicions or implicate them, they may try to coerce what that student will share with you. This can happen in real time through a phone. As you walk the students away from the bus, keep an eye out for phone use, and check in with each briefly. You may say something like, "You know that you can't be in school vehicles without permission or supervision. And I know that sexual exploration among teenagers is developmentally appropriate, as long as it is consensual. It is also against the school rules to engage in sexual activity while on school grounds. What I care about at this moment is how you're feeling about what was happening between you and Dylan/Jordan. Are you okay?"

In my teacher education classes, many educators recognize that "it's really challenging for [them] to address issues of sexuality in supportive and positive ways because [they] never received quality sex education [themselves]." As noted before, the sociopolitical history of sexuality in the US, our generally sex-negative culture (hyper sexualization, stigmatization, body shaming, and objectification), potentially our own negative experiences or associations that we haven't processed or healed from (not many folks are comfortable talking about sexuality—it's everywhere and nowhere all at once), and the total lack of CSE in people's education and professional development can make addressing this topic with young people incredibly challenging. I find that a straightforward narrative that provides information and models language for what consent is and how it might look, sound, and feel within a sexual context is helpful.

Consent is an agreement between people who are of the same mind—both understand what is proposed and accept whatever is agreed upon. It protects people and keeps them emotionally and physically safe. In a consensual relationship (two people relating to each other in some way), both people communicate about how they want to be treated and listen for how the other person wants to be treated. Both people pay attention to the other's wants and needs and work together to treat each other with dignity (like they have self-worth and value). There is mutual respect (treating someone how they want to be treated). This contributes to the context (what's going on with someone internally, and what's going on in their external environment) of consent in a moment.

It's important to relay to students that there are many variables that create the context of a sexual situation. Possible language for conveying these concepts may include, "In a sexual relationship (whether it's established/defined or a hook up), people sometimes will talk about what they want to do sexually before it actually happens. This is a good thing, as long as the context is consensual (wanted and welcome), and even better if it's in person. It's an opportunity to express desires and limits. However, people have the right to change their minds, and sometimes the context of the sexual activity in a moment ends up feeling different or isn't what someone expected. There are lots of variables that create the context of a sexual situation, and they may shift and change when sexual activity is happening. That's why consent needs to be given in the moment and ongoing. It can be revoked at any time. Consent cannot be given while someone is incapacitated (drunk or high) by drugs, including alcohol. Every time someone initiates a new level of intimacy (e.g., going from grinding to taking clothes off), the person who initiates the move needs to ask for the other person's consent and may or may not continue based on their response. They can pause in the moment and say, "this okay?" or "you good?" or "how would you feel about taking this off?"

If the person says, "yes," then go for it; however, if the person being asked seems hesitant in any way (even if they said yes), is drunk (legally they cannot consent), or is not responding to your touch in affirmative ways (like moving towards you, making pleasurable noises, etc.), then stop what you're doing and ask what's up and/or how they are feeling.

If you are the person being asked for consent and you want to give it, do so enthusiastically (help take your shirt off, guide them to what feels good). If you are unsure, say so, and if you want to suggest something else, go ahead and do so; If you don't want to consent, you can say, "no," or "let's just stay like this," or express what you'd like to do instead (including stopping altogether). If you say yes to something and it starts to feel uncomfortable or you don't want it anymore, you can revoke consent or say something like, "this doesn't feel right, let's stop." The person you are with should stop—it's their legal responsibility. If they don't, you may be more assertive with your no, physically get out of the situation, make an excuse like, "I'm going to be sick," or you may say, "If you continue, you will be hurting me/assaulting me."

Sexual communication is normal, natural, and important when people are exploring each other's bodies and sexuality. If something feels awkward (because real-life sexual activity gets awkward sometimes), simply acknowledge it, laugh about it (not at the expense of your partner, of course), and move through it. Consent is what makes sexual activity legal and is most important because it protects the fundamentals of human dignity. Remember though, it doesn't make the sexual activity ethical (taking into account the well-being of the people involved) or "good" (pleasurable and satisfying for both people). Ethical and good sexual activity requires healthy sexual communication and context. That's ultimately the healthy sexual exploration to aspire to, because everybody deserves it to be good.

Scenario work is a tremendous opportunity to pivot from informational learning (simply gaining knowledge and skills) to enriched relational learning (when the educator and students may engage in a reciprocal authentic connection) about the reality and human experience of navigating tricky social landscapes. This work can be transformational learning—that is, engaging cognitive, emotional, and social capacities to actively understand and make sense and meaning of their experiences.[15] Of course, this requires healthy vulnerability on all sides. Using scenarios like those in this book about student experiences is a concrete way to engage in critical thinking, ethical quandary, and reflective thought on various decisions and potential consequences. Scenarios create a degree of separation that allows students to dialogue with each other, share different perspectives, think collaboratively, build off of each other's ideas, identify relevant underlying values and social power dynamics, and practice empathy and effective communication.

In positive relationships, people develop skills and grow with each other, thus deepening the relationship. Issues arise in every relationship, and differences and difficulties can be a catalyst for deeper understanding and intimacy.

CONNECTION (INTIMACY AND LOVE)

A developmental task of adolescence is to figure out how to have a healthy, sustained, intimate relationship. We all know that this is far from easy. This capacity requires us to name, connect to, and understand our feelings and boundaries. In addition, it requires us to be attuned to someone else and their limits and desires, develop and use communication skills, be willing to show healthy vulnerability, and to have the inspiration and motivation to persist and invest time and energy in manifesting all of these skills and qualities. All of us need social connectedness to thrive. As the Nagoski sisters Emily and Amelia write in their book, *Burnout*, "This is the heretical truth: No one is 'complete' without other people—and we mean this literally. To be complete without social connection is to be nourished without food. It doesn't happen. We get hungry. We get lonely. We must feed ourselves or die . . . We mean you need connection in any or all of its varied forms. And it is also true that the lifelong development of autonomy is as innate to human nature as the drive to connect. We need *both* connection and autonomy."[16]

This is true of most intimate relationships: platonic, familial, and romantic and/or sexual. One way teenagers learn to do this is through their friendships. Surviving the gauntlet of adolescence to adulthood can be joyful and fulfilling, it can also be painful and hard. Student social dynamics are a morality clinic on how to be a good person in relationships, often established through trial, error, and consequences.

This has been true for many generations; however, technology adds a new layer of complexity to how kids connect and communicate today. For today's adolescents, who are some of the first true digital natives, it is completely normal and expected that "talking" to get to know someone happens through some sort of app, direct messaging platform, or texting.

SCENARIO: For the last few days, you've noticed that Valentina isn't sitting or hanging out with her usual group of friends and that her participation in class has waned. She's slow to pack up and move on to lunch, when she is usually a part of a group that goes together. You walk over to where she is organizing her backpack and sit in an adjacent desk. "How's it going?" Valentina's affect is flat, but when her eyes meet yours, they are welling with tears, and you're not sure if the feelings behind them are rage or despair. She responds, "I'm alright. Just some bullshit I'm dealing with—that's all." Valentina doesn't usually swear around adults. You offer, "Do you want to talk about it?" She initially responds with, "Nah, I can handle it," then says, "There's these two girls, they wanna fight me over some stupid guy. We're not even together anymore." You ask, "What's the issue then?" She says, "Well, since me and Sean broke up, Gina and Stella were like, you should start talking to Jared, because I guess he likes me. So, I started talking to Jared. Thing is, I didn't know Rita was talking to Jared while I was going with Sean. So now Rita's all pissed at me, and Gina and Stella are acting like they can't believe I'm talking to Jared and Rita should take me on." You mirror what Valentina has said and ask a clarifying question, "Is that the reason you aren't hanging out with them anymore?" She agrees with, "Yeah, I'm just waiting for one of them to say something to me—then it's on. They're all talk—weak is what it is." You pause to clarify, "Is this happening in person or digitally?" Valentina shares, "Our group chat." (Los Angeles County School District, CA)

Popular cultural expectations and norms still socialize us to value women for their appearance (which includes superficial and materialistic possessions) versus other more substantive attributes, like intelligence, humor, creativity, or strength. Many girls report social media tropes of cat fighting and competition, typically for male attention and validation. In addition, societal messages continue to construct our ideas of women as emotional and caretaking protectors of masculinity. Girls are expected to be polite and nice, and if they express anger (the only emotion men are allowed to express), they may be labeled "bossy" or a "bitch." Be aware of reinforcing these stereotypes of girls, and instead, try to affirm and guide them to embrace all aspects of their authentic selves and be connected to each other in some sense of solidarity. That is not to say they will all like each other or should play nice to get along and not rock the boat. But as an educator, you can help them avoid being pitted against each other and develop an appreciation for one another and the capacity to come together in the face of gender-based adversity and discrimination.

Lyn Brown, author, activist, and professor of education at Colby College, observes, "Girls can also be 'mean' or 'tough' because they experience the daily indignities of sexism, classism, and racism. Developing a tough girl exterior is a way for some girls to survive hostile environments or it may be a way for girls to be visible and accounted for. On the other hand, this gritty presentation may just be who a girl is, how she creates space for herself and how she interacts with her friends and the world. Appreciate gender diversity within gender identity and the social and cultural context that may determine what a girl's possibilities and limitations are—this is how we may support girls."[17] Assess what "they want to fight me" and "take me on" means. Is it an actual threat of physical violence? Is it digital posturing or will it manifest in person? Of course, prevention of a physical fight is immediate and important. How we do that is also critical.

As educators, our primary responsibility is to recognize the boundary that's been crossed, which is that students have threatened another student with physical violence. All of the school missions, values statements, and policies I have come across speak to the safety of young people so that they may learn and acquire an education. How this is interpreted and who it includes is being questioned across the United States with anti-LGBTQ+ surveillance and statutes and the exclusion of critical race teachings and laws. It is a human right that all students, no matter their identities, deserve to be safe and protected by all adults in educational spaces. The threat against Valentina has had an impact that you have noticed.

Her affect has changed, her position in the community is different, and she isn't engaged in her learning in the same ways. As I've mentioned before, adolescents tend to focus on the chronology and details of an event: what has happened, what was said, what's been promised, what will happen next, and what they will do in response. What's equally important here is to also understand how Valentina feels. Narrate what you've noticed and ask how she feels: "I noticed you are not hanging out with your friends as much and that your facial expression seems distraught, you're a bit withdrawn and not participating like usual. It seems like my asking is bringing up some feelings too. Are you okay with sharing some of those with me?" Valentina naming what she feels can in and of itself be helpful.

Talk with Valentina about your care for, and responsibility to, support all students, which is a community value. First, ask strategic questions that guide Valentina to articulate and put words to the harm she has experienced. Avoid why questions, which can feel judgmental, and rather, lead with how and what. Pose open-ended questions that inspire self-reflection, and if Valentina needs a feelings wheel or feelings cards (described in previous chapters), then provide them. The goal is to create space for Valentina to describe her emotional embodied experience on her own terms of what has happened and how she is experiencing the impact.

You may then ask if Valentina would like you to directly address the girls who have threatened her. Most likely, she will minimize what's happened to detract from the intensity of what she's feeling, not want to be accused of being a snitch (even if you see it as reporting), and avoid any retaliation or further digital exclusion and/or aggression that may result. Valentina's agency is important, especially because her exclusion probably feels out of control. How can you not make the situation worse for Valentina and still uphold the values of the school and maintain the integrity of the community? A restorative approach centers the humanity of all students involved and honors their emotions (including those associated with harm), the needs of the young people involved, and accountability as to how they met those needs, as well as responsibility for the impact of those decisions on other students and the greater community.[18]

You have observed the impact of the threat—the overall dynamic in the classroom has changed. You went to Valentina first because she presented as isolated, and you could have just as easily addressed this with the friend group. Approach the girls in the friend group before or after class to signal that you are paying attention. You may say, "Hey, I want to check in, because I notice that you are no longer sitting with your friend Valentina. Have you noticed that she seems on her own and less engaged? What's going on?" The girls may provide information, or they may blow you off. Either way, they know you are watching and noticing what happens. This is critical because it communicates, "I see you."

You may continue with, "Here at school, we value care and inclusion, even when we have disagreements." If the girls have shared information that tracks with Valentina's report, you may continue with, "Conflict happens, people have breakups, disagreements, and get mad at each other for all kinds of things. That's an important process for figuring out who we are and want to be in our relationships and how to manage them. *How* we do that matters. It is not okay to threaten someone—that directly compromises people's safety and well-being." It's essential to get to what is behind the behaviors. Speak to the girls individually. Social hierarchies are assured amongst many adolescents and may influence and coerce behavior. Talking to the girls separately, in preparation for a collective talk, will increase the probability that you will have a more productive conversation. As in previous chapters that address decisions that compromise the community, ask, "How did 'x' feel to you?" (conflicted, vulnerable, frustrated, vindictive), and "What were you needing at the time of texting? Was this also true of your in-person interactions?" (recognition, respect, empowered, accepted), and "What did you do, what part did you have in what happened, to get those needs met?" and finally, "What was the cost? To Valentina? Yourself? Our community?" Ultimately, we want all of our students to recognize the interrelatedness of community and how important mutual responsibility and accountability is to an environment where everyone, adults and youth, may realize their potential. This is one of the primary reasons that, throughout this writing, I emphasize the value in cocreating class and community guidelines for cultivating care and mutual respect.

It's possible that the girls will then minimize the threat because a fight hasn't actually happened. You may hear something along the lines of, "Yeah, I told her she sucks because she's talking to my boy, what's wrong with that," and wonder why you're in their business. You may then say, "This is true, and there are words and behaviors that can feel like a physical hit and have a similar impact. So, there are policies that prohibit these behaviors, even if they happen in digital spaces." If your school has not outlined social digital use policies, then it's important to get on that. Remind the girls of school policies and that there are other ways to deal with conflicts than trash talking, ganging up on someone, and threatening violence. It will be just as important to turn towards the emotional and relational aspects of the conflict as well.

A restorative approach aspires to repair the breakdown in community values with the individuals involved. It may also be about restoring the relationships among the girls; however, it may be that they, Valentina in particular, need to reconsider their friendships and choose other people to hang out with. Even if they may not restore their friendship to the level it was prior to the situation, we still want to aspire to their collaboration in making things right amongst themselves and how they may repair and restore their connections to each other as shared community members. Taking an empathic approach and guiding them to understand the benefits of community values for all members is critical—that it's to everyone's benefit that all people in the community feel safe so that they can focus on learning without the stress, fear, and anxiety of distrust and exposure that threatens to compromise people's overall well-being and get in the way of healthy development. Understanding what needs the behaviors expressed and agreement on how the girls will make their situation "right" or better will require bringing them together to discuss what's happened and how to move forward.

We must consider the identities of the students involved and respond accordingly. Race, ability, socioeconomics, native language, and more matter. You may also choose to discuss gender expectations and roles when it comes to romantic and/or sexual relationships. As educators, we have an opportunity to guide how girls might channel their "toughness."

What are the alternative narratives that bring girls together versus drive them apart? What if they turned their strength and purpose towards standing up for what is right and for what they think is in the service of their own development and growth? You may choose to introduce the idea of girl competition over boys as a socialized behavior meant to keep negative gender roles in place. Point out that girl fighting over male attention is about centering boys, not girls proving how strong and empowered they are. In fact, it's quite the opposite.

I've seen the dynamics amongst Valentina and her friends play out among superficial social groups as well as friends who are deeply connected and truly care about and love each other. Support Valentina in assessing how deep and meaningful her friendships are and if she wants and is willing to do what it would take to find a resolution and restore the connection. What might she say so that she feels she stood up for herself while also expressing a desire to stay friends? In regards to the argument with her friends over group chat, you may ask, "What are you ultimately going for?" and/or "Do you think your conversation would go in the same direction if you were to have it in person?" If she is going to have a conversation with any of the other girls, remind Valentina that it should happen in person, because digital conversations prevent us from reading facial expressions and interpreting body language and provide a false sense of security that may shore someone up to say something online that they never would in person. Ask, "What would it take (and look, sound, and feel like) to talk to your friends in person?" and/or "How could you say it in a way that helps resolve the conflict?"

Rosalind Wiseman uses the acronym SEAL to use whenever a student is in a situation where there is conflict, worry, or anxiety:

- *Stop and Strategize.* Breathe, listen, and think about where you want to talk to the person. Do you want to do it now or later—or maybe a little of both?
- *Explain.* Explain what happened that you didn't like and what you want.

- *Affirm.* Admit (*recognize*) anything you did that contributed to the conflict but affirm your right to be treated with dignity by the other person and vice versa.
- *Lock.* Lock in the friendship, take a vacation, or lock the friendship out.

Relationships take work, and learning how to have perspective, regulate our emotions, and productively communicate in the service of those relationships takes time, experience, and practice. When supporting our students in how they may navigate this lifelong process, a brilliant explanation Al Vernacchio shares with his students comes to mind. He told me that "when we assign blame or look for gotcha moments, we aren't putting what's most important first: the relationship. When we strive to 'win' amidst controversy, it's the relationship that loses." In Valentina's case, recognize the hurtful and threatening behavior she has experienced and encourage her to reflect beyond her feelings of anger and possibly betrayal. If she comes to the conclusion that she wants to keep her friendship(s), she will have to consider what it will take to do that. Disappointment and heartbreak happen to all of us. It's how we deal with it that makes the difference in how it impacts us and our capacity to enter and thrive in loving relationships in the future.[19] With adolescence comes an increased focus on our emotions and recognition that feelings progress and we cycle through them. Teenagers can also start to grasp metamoods, such as feeling guilty about feeling angry.[20] As a caretaking adult in Valentina's life, we can guide her to how she may respond in a way that will build that resiliency and skill.

Schools and families are de facto partners in taking care of students so that they may learn and thrive. The spectrum of how that collaboration can manifest itself ranges from affirming and rewarding to exasperating and painful. Any parenting adult knows how challenging it can be to raise a child, and any teacher knows how challenging it can be to educate one. The rewards can be meaningful and bring tremendous satisfaction and joy. Even when teachers and administrators feel at odds with parents and hold completely different points of view, both parties share concern for the child (at least most of the time). How that happens can be challenging for any of us, especially when a student connects with an educator as an ally and there is contention with their parenting adult(s).

SCENARIO: Mr. Collins is a student counselor with a caseload of 350 students. He serves as general support, checks in with students sporadically over the course of the year, and guides them in course selection with the intention of getting kids to high school graduation and poised for success in college. One of his students, River (whose legal name is Ryan), is in the process of figuring out their gender identity. River prefers they/them pronouns and is open to talking about many aspects of their life. Mr. Collins also communicates with families and will reach out to check in about students a couple of times a year. Whenever Mr. Collins emails with River's parents (River is comfortable with him using their chosen name), they will refer to River with their preferred name, but when he speaks to either parent in person, they use Ryan and are reluctant to use River. When Mr. Collins hears that River hasn't been showing up to school, he reaches out to River's parents, who come in for a conference. River's father typically presents as annoyed with the school and refuses to engage in conversation, and River's mother comes across as loving but says this about River's gender expression: "It is what it is, but [she just doesn't] understand." (Jefferson County School District, CO)

Mr. Collins appears to be a trusted resource for River. They feel comfortable talking to Mr. Collins about their life and most likely appreciate how Mr. Collins uses their preferred name and pronouns consistently. This is critical, especially for many LGBTQ+ youth who may not experience acceptance at home and/or in some aspects of school. There are many contexts that LGBTQ+ students must navigate, from having supportive parents but not supportive teachers and peers to nonsupportive parents and/or families and some support from within school. Unfortunately, homophobic language and behaviors are so common in educational spaces that it's inevitable that an LGBTQ+ student will confront discrimination, potential bullying, and exclusion.

Of students who are under the umbrella of LGBTQ+, transgender students face the greatest physical, psychological, and academic risks at school.[21] The current increase in antitrans legislation, especially impacting education, threatens the care and safety educators may provide. The repercussions of this may be devastating. A study by the peer-reviewed journal, Nature Human Behaviour, found that antitransgender laws cause up to a 72 percent increase in suicide attempts among transgender and nonbinary youth.[22] It is our responsibility as educators to support the healthy development of all of our students. Sometimes, school may be the place in which a teenager experiences acceptance from adults and peers, and other times, it may be that home is the place of affirmation and school is not. In others, a teenager may experience some acceptance with their family and at school; however, they are still met with discrimination, aggression, and hostility in other places. All children deserve to be treated with dignity and cared for at school.

Keep in mind the greater context that there are current federal protections of transgender rights, Title IX, enacted as part of the Education Amendments of Act 1972, which prohibits discrimination "on the basis of sex" in education programs or activities receiving federal funding. For more on transgender student and transgender adult employee protections and rights, see appendix C, which provides more in-depth resources that also address the shifting landscape of politics and laws associated with LGBTQ+ issues. Specific to situations like the above for Mr. Collins, what are the state statutes surrounding LGBTQ+ rights in schools and how can educators affirm and/or address students and their colleagues? What are the differences and similarities in how you can treat transgender and nonbinary students as different from LGBQ+ students? What is the overall response to those directives and/or allowances by the school district, your particular institution, and your role as an educator? What identities and experiences do you hold that may activate certain emotions and needs in you as an educator personally? How open and/or discreet can you be when caring for transgender or gender-expansive youth? What are your values and how are you navigating your commitment to caring for all students and your job security? Depending on the answers to those questions, Mr. Collins has some opportunities to support River and their parents.

In my experience as an educator and parent, I find most parenting adults want to feel seen and heard, especially when their child is struggling. It is in everyone's best interest to keep River at the center of

Mr. Collins's and River's parents' collaboration. In her book *The Essential Conversation,* Professor of Education Sara Lawrence-Lightfoot writes, "Every time parents and teachers encounter one another in the classroom, their conversations are shaped by their own autobiographical stories and by the broader cultural and historical narratives that inform their identities, their values and their sense of place in the world."[23] Mr. Collins may inquire as to what narratives may be present and how he may provide information in support of the parents and their relationship with River. River's parents are clearly having a difficult time with the situation. They are inconsistent with how they use River's preferred name and pronouns. They also present as distraught, and River's mother has explicitly said that she doesn't understand. Mr. Collins may reflect this back by saying, "I hear that you are concerned about River and this feels difficult. I appreciate you coming in so that we can figure out a way to support them." Draw upon your experience, speak about River from an asset-based perspective, and discuss how you may collaborate to keep River in school. Highlight River's strengths and contributions as well as their potential. Consider the Strategic Questions from Morter and Peavey that encourage understanding between people without feeling the need to abandon one's values. [24] You may ask, "What are your observations, and what do you think might feel helpful to River?" and/or "What are the obstacles that get in the way of that happening?" River's parents aren't vehement and confrontational, so keep River's well-being and education at the center of the conversation. Appreciate the challenges of parenting and offer to provide resources through advocacy programs that support LGBTQ+ families and their children. For some suggestions, see appendix C.

St ategic Questions may also help River to find places of belonging. Have a resource list of school support. Is there a Gay-Straight Alliance or Gender-Sexuality Alliance (GSA) that River may attend? Are there other LGBTQ+ identifying adults on campus who may reach out to and connect with River (with consent on both sides, of course)? Do River's identities intersect to impact how River may experience marginalization and require attention (e.g., is River also a student of color)? Are there community-based advocacy organizations that may provide affirmation? Have a list of resources prepared with social media suggestions that are positive and affirming of LGBTQ+ youth, as well as resources for kids who are looking for information, understanding, and community. Make sure to include resilience narratives of LGBTQ+ folks—stories as well as historical and current accounts. Explore these options with River first and the possibility of you sharing some of these suggestions with their parenting adults. Sometimes, it can be helpful to families who are challenged to affirm their kid to instead support their kid in connecting to and getting what they need from other folks and organizations.

As River's counselor, you may also establish a "Gender Support Plan" and "Gender Communication Plan." Gender Spectrum provides tools for implementing gender-inclusive practices, like consistent communication among adults about a transgender youth's gender markers, health, safety, "go-to adults," confidentiality, and more.

SAFETY

As educators, we need to cultivate a climate that clearly communicates a moral standard for behavior in which mutual respect among community members is paramount. As mentioned many times throughout this book, it is in all of our best interests, especially our students', to differentiate what kind of harm is happening between or among students. Is it relational aggression (intentional harm of someone's social standing or relationships through deliberate manipulation), mutual aggression (the people involved are intentionally harming each other), teenage conflict or drama (disagreements and arguments that are normal in the developmental process and actually support prosocial skill development), moments of meanness or bullying (intentional verbal or physical harassment that happens repeatedly over time and occurs within a social power differential)? Some folks use *bullying* indiscriminately, to the detriment of efforts to accurately address and hold students accountable for their behavior and how they will learn from it. This can also be a distraction from efforts to prevent gender-based harassment, sexual violence, racism, and other forms of bias-based discrimination. Being clear about terms and definitions and how to respond will make this work more effective. Antibullying efforts are essential; however, we cannot let them distract us from the critical identification of bias-based aggressive and violent behavior and its impact that is too often overlooked when we amass all forms of conflict and aggression under the label of bullying.[25]

All bullying isn't the same, and students who are targeted because of bias are significantly more traumatized by the incidents.[26] It is also essential to assess if there is a digital component and interplay with in-person conflict and vice versa.[27] Cyberbullying has the capacity to make its target feel worthless and can shrink their world through repeated slights, digs, passive-aggressive and aggressive texting, snapping, tiktoking, etc.

SCENARIO: State standardized testing is coming up, so faculty have identified several bulletin boards in the hallways for students to write supportive messages to each other. The students embrace cheering each other on this way—it has always bolstered the community before the big test. Many positive messages, in an array of handwriting, cover the boards; however, interspersed are several notes that say, "Khalil is a fag," and "The Big K is GAY." Students bring this to the attention of teachers, who immediately take the homophobic notes down, but there is already talk circulating about the situation. Khalil is in your advising group, so you reach out to ask how he's feeling and what's happening for him socially. Your plan is to provide support and gather information for the principal, who has been notified and is ready to start an investigation to find out who is harassing Kahlil. Through your conversation, you learn that three boys wrote the notes and have been bullying Kahlil for several weeks with verbal taunts like, "His people are terrorists," and "Camel Jockey." Kahlil doesn't want to reveal names. You are supportive and empathetic and let Kahlil know that you are going to talk to his parents about how you will support him. You are scheduled to meet with the principal that afternoon; however, before the meeting, you hear that during lunch, three students blocked the door of a room Kahlil was trying to exit and were taunting him with more racist slurs and homophobic remarks. All of the boys will be disciplined because Khalil threw a punch at one of the boys to "make him get out of the way." (Fairfax County Public Schools, VA)

If the school has a zero-tolerance policy toward physical aggression, Khalil will most likely face some sort of discipline because he hit someone. While it's important to address violence, instances like this are complicated. Bias-based bullying was taking place—Khalil was being harassed and bullied by intimidation and a barrage of racist and homophobic (whether his identity or not) insults and defended himself. If school educators and administrators were not aware of ongoing harassment of Khalil, it is important that they take the time to understand the larger context. Research tells us that psychological aggression and violence can have the same lasting repercussions and negative consequences as physical aggression and violence, so it is essential that we hold our students accountable to all forms of aggression and violence.[28] And if we are to create true change and facilitate learning, we must be specific and recognize what social power differentials were leveraged to carry out the hostility.

The school is responsible for supporting all of the students involved in the situation. Khalil has been victimized. He will need emotional support for what he has endured, including consideration that he acted in self-defense when implementing policies. He may also be vulnerable to an onslaught of peer-to-peer curiosity and/or retaliation or continued bullying as a result of the incident. Adults can't be everywhere all of the time, and they certainly aren't privy to online aggression that may be going on both in and outside of school. In some cases, students report that adult intervention can make the problem worse.[29] Collaborate with Khalil and his parents to consider restorative practices and approaches, formal reporting, and consequences, as well as ongoing school and therapeutic support. His family may need additional resources outside of school. Some schools have collaborative partnerships with organizations that provide mental health support for youth and their families.

Khalil identifies as Middle Eastern and a person of color. As readers, we don't know what Khalil's thoughts and feelings are about gender and sexual identity, and this incident shouldn't be used to interrogate him about his identity. It is important to recognize that LGBTQ+ youth (who are identified accurately or not) are particularly vulnerable to and disproportionately the targets of bullying. As established in previous chapters, homophobic slurs are commonly used by boys as a means to demonstrate masculinity. An educator or counselor should talk to Khalil about the impact of the sexual harassment and how it is or isn't directly relevant to his own identity, using approaches that do not include questions and/or that victim blame or shame but rather take into account the safety, privacy, needs, agency, dignity and support for varying degrees of trauma.

SURVIVOR-CENTERED PRACTICES

It will also be imperative to talk with Khalil about his experience as a victim and how he may heal and move forward as a survivor. While it is essential to recognize and support him in articulating the harm and/or trauma he has experienced, it is equally important to discuss how he may begin a healing process by reclaiming what agency he does have. How can the school further promote the connections Khalil has with adults and peers that are protective, not only of his school experience but overall mental health? Who were the upstanders in the class who brought the notes to people's attention? These students are important allies and assets. Who was the teacher the students felt comfortable reporting to and who Khalil felt he could talk to about what was happening to him? What values do these folks represent in the community, and how might the school learn more from them about what is working well? What are their ideas for uniting the community against hurtful ways of speaking and acting against others to restore community cohesion and integrity?

If Khalil faces curiosity about the situation from his peers, help him think about what he can say in response. Go over appropriate assertiveness in the form of comebacks/clapbacks/reading (defusing aggression with a countercomment, as in the previous Jason scenario), and/or setting clear verbal and physical boundaries as a part of self-efficacy (standing up for oneself and feeling a sense of agency versus defining oneself by victimhood). Elizabeth Englander, the executive director of the Massachusetts Aggression Reduction Center, outlines "Steps School Personnel Can Take To Help a Target Feel Safer," which includes "Establishing a Safety and Comfort Plan," in her book, *Bullying and Cyberbullying.*[30]

If, in fact, Khalil identifies as LGBTQ+, remember that he may not be out to the community or his family, so respect his privacy. If you are an educator or counselor supporting him, take the time to talk through how he may connect with other youth (either within the school and/or through community-based organizations) who share this aspect of his identity. For LGBTQ+ identifying youth, it can promote healing and empowerment to take on leadership roles in school GSAs and/or community-based advocacy organizations.[31] Encouraging Khalil to consider this may be supportive. Be particularly sensitive to Khalil's comfort levels with what resources would signal or require that may affect his privacy and coming out process.

The school administration must also take responsibility to address the youth who caused harm. In the above scenario, an accurate definition of bullying can support finding an effective solution. Many schools will run the behavior ladder of "if 'x' happened, then 'y' happens next." We must ask, what is the ladder standing on? What are the systemic community cultural issues that need addressing? What did the offenders leverage to cause harm? What power dynamics are the aggressors exploiting? And to fulfill what need they have? What are the missing skills and opportunities for learning within the community relative to power? In the case of Khalil, the bullying was focused on sexuality and race. That is the teaching point for the students who harmed Khalil: racial and sexual justice. This is in addition to the fundamental values of humanity and what it means to be part of a community where all students have the right to equitable access and to engage in their education without fear for their safety. Racist and homophobic discrimination as a means of bullying requires consequences. The type of school you are in will determine what those consequences are, and take a restorative approach whenever possible.

Again, get behind the behavior. What are the offenders expressing negativity about? Sometimes, Pollack writes, "the more insecure a boy feels, the more he compensates with compulsive-masculinity posturing to confirm what he feels is at risk, his masculinity."[32] What are the interpersonal power dynamics amongst the boys? What is their position given their multiple identities in the class and greater community? Is there intersectionality at work? Bring in the boys' families to partner in this exploration and extend these lessons at home. Consider restorative justice practices that aim to reconnect the students who caused the harm with community values. Encourage the boys to think about their actions and talk it through with people who may be effective. How does a breach in the integrity of a community affect all of its members? How are parents and caretaking adults in and out of school impacted? What about the time and energy that must be invested to address the situation with compassion, empathy, and care? Collaborate to come up with an agreed upon plan that will make the wrong, right. Connect Kahlil and the students who caused harm back to the community, and restore a way for the students to work within it again together.

How we address isolated harmful incidents within educational spaces will impact the entire community. Ideally, our response communicates clear boundaries and takes care of all students involved. How we cultivate healthy communities of consent—the foundation for upholding dignity, care, and love—includes how we manage the inevitable moments and events that compromise the connectedness and overall well-being and unity of schools. High school can be a tumultuous time as young people try on and further define their identities and negotiate interpersonal and community social power dynamics. This stage of adolescence is a time of experimentation, risk taking, and discovery. How a school creates space for this and the ups and downs that are an inherent part of growing up with humanity will contribute towards how teenagers will find friends, sustain intimate connections, and act in the spirit of a greater good.

7

Heading into Adulthood

Grades Eleven and Twelve

"I have also decided to stick with love, for I know that love is ultimately the only answer to humankind's problems. And I'm going to talk about it everywhere I go."

~ Martin Luther King, Jr.

As students evolve and prepare to launch into young adulthood, it is ever more important that we continue to model and teach what will encourage their sustained health and well-being. The majority of them will move on from the familiar environment of school—where they have hopefully gained some familiarity and confidence as the oldest students on campus—to communities where they will be the youngest, unfamiliar with their surroundings, as well as less confident about their place there. This can throw any well-prepared young person off balance. So, we must highlight the tools they can employ to steady themselves—the information, skills, and capacities that their education has provided. As young adults, they will be confronted with new independence and responsibilities for themselves and possibly others. This can be exciting, and they may rise to the occasion. The challenges of the world can inspire their passions, for sure, and also be daunting and lead to overwhelm. Draw upon love. The elements of community love—empathy, mutual respect, care, and dignity—that are a part of your school community are what will provide the compass that will guide them as they embark. Finish strong by continuing to see them through and shoring them up with that love along the way.

Developmental highlights:

- Prefrontal cortex development continues.
- Teenagers are in the final stages of puberty.
- Digital spaces continue to be relevant and a primary mode of communication and connection.
- Many teenagers are still working on the developmental task of figuring out how to have a healthy, sustained intimate relationship in their lives.
- Many students are thinking about moving on into adulthood either by attending postsecondary schools (college or university) or going straight to work. Some have no idea what might come next.
- During Senior year, many twelfth graders will reach eighteen years old and be legal adults, yet school policies are applicable relative to state guidelines.
- Eleventh and twelfth grade students need continued health education. They may physically look like adults, they are still in the final stages of puberty and undergoing cognitive development into their twenties.
- Programs designed to improve school environment, address mental health, support students making life transitions, and basically encourage knowledge of self and others all have positive effects on young people.[1]

The 2016 clinical report, reaffirmed in 2022, by the American Academy of Pediatrics—which summarizes evidence-based sexual reproductive health education since 2001—concludes that "developmentally appropriate and evidence-based education about human sexuality and sexual reproduction over time provided by . . . schools . . . is important to help children and adolescents make informed, positive, and safe choices about healthy relationships, responsible sexual activity, and their reproductive health.[2]

BODIES

Young people, particularly those that spend a lot of time on social media (most young people today), are impacted by comparative culture and body image cultural expectations. This is especially true for girls in terms of its negative impact on mental health. Young people growing up today are still socialized to value women for their appearance, as objects for others' consumption, and this is damaging for many young women. Unfortunately, this is increasingly the case for boys as well. There is growing evidence that all teenagers of all genders may experience the negative impacts of media on self-esteem, which can compromise their capacity for authentic connection in relationships. *Muscle Dysmorphia*, or "Bigorexia," is a body dysmorphic disorder characterized by the desire for increased lean muscle mass. Boys and men alike are showing signs of this disorder, fueled by the idea that "bigger is better" and valorizing those who work out intensely and "are all about the gains."[3] A sex-negative culture—one that focuses on body shaming, over-sexualization, and the objectification and dehumanization of bodies—can shape teenage behaviors and how young people explore and express their sexuality with them, in particular these social appearance anxieties.

SCENARIO: You teach an Organic World Language class that always begins with students standing in a conversation circle that morphs into mingling dyads and triads. As facilitator, you introduce current events, pop cultural phenomena, or highlight an event in the community or something you've observed in the classroom as a thread to discuss in Spanish. Students are assembled, about to begin, when Darby nods his head towards Ariel and says with a mischievous grin, "What's that on your neck?" Darby's laughter spreads within the group. You see hickeys on Ariel's neck that she has obviously, but unsuccessfully, tried to hide with cover-up. She is visibly uncomfortable as she tries to cover her neck with her hand. Her boyfriend, Colter, is also in the class and shoots Darby a "cut it out" glare. Darby escalates and teases, "No need to hide it, we all know already. Colter told us about Saturday night." Ariel's downcast eyes get bigger and then narrow as her head snaps in Colter's direction. Colter's glare has softened, and he shrugs his shoulders while mouthing "sorry." Ariel's discomfort intensifies. Then some of the girls say, "Yeah, Ari, get it!" and her expression starts to include a hint of pride. You interrupt the conversation and say, "That's enough, Español!" and pivot to start a conversation about an impending snowstorm. (Independent School, Blaine County, ID)

There are several aspects of this scenario to highlight: the purpose and meaning of hickeys, issues of consent (whether it's consent for the hickey itself and/or the public attention drawn to them and how that makes someone feel), as well as how the relationship dynamics on display impact the experience of the person in the spotlight and community ideas about sexuality overall.

I see a lot of necks with hickies on them when I walk school hallways. My students often observe that hickies are a status symbol that garner attention. They typically think hickies say that someone is "getting play" or engaging in sexual activity, which comes with validation (that one is desired and therefore sexually active) and social currency. The significance of hickies can vary depending on the gender of the participants. To some girls, having a hickey or hickies is "safe," because it fulfills the cultural expectation that a girl be desirable and have some experience, but it doesn't establish how much. And for a guy, there isn't a downside, because hickies confirm that he is getting "action," which affords him "props" and affirms his masculinity. A boy is far less likely to be judged in this situation, because there continues to be a double standard in favor of boys when it comes to sexual activity and judgement. Students will also recognize a hickey on display as someone claiming someone else, which may be interpreted as "stay away, this person is taken." Some girls embrace this status as validating as well, despite the implication of "ownership."

As educators, there are opportunities presented through this scenario. Darby's teasing clearly made Ariel uncomfortable, and the unwelcome attention was of a sexual nature, so it could have been experienced as sexual harassment. It's important for us to say something that can be a simple recognition of what you witness, "Hey, it is disrespectful to make fun of someone's body. Not okay. Stop by my desk after class. Now, let's get to work," and take a stand for community values and shut the teasing/harassment down. Focusing on what's happened any more than that in the moment keeps the uncomfortable attention on Ariel, and making a public example of Darby may be shaming and unproductive. Instead, check in with the students after you've intervened, disrupted the dynamic, and finished class. After class, remind Darby that you'd like to talk for a minute. You may start with, "What was up at the beginning of class? Drawing attention to someone like that, especially about their body and personal relationship, is highly likely to make someone uncomfortable and disrespected," or "What were you going for when you commented on Ariel's body and her relationship?" Darby will most likely respond with something along the lines of, "I didn't mean anything by it. I was just joking—having some fun." You may respond with, "That may have been your intention, but the impact I observed was different. Drawing unwanted attention to someone's sexuality could be experienced as sexual harassment. And when done publicly, it can make other people uncomfortable too. True humor is not at the expense of anyone else. Don't do that in my class again."

You may also follow up with Ariel before you next have class or if you see her on campus when you could have a discreet conversation. You might open with, "Hey, how did you feel about what Darby said to you before class started?" Ariel may blow it off and say, "Oh it was no big deal, he was just trying to be funny." Protecting masculinity, avoiding the perception of being a "snitch," or showing that you were affected are all social norms to avoid for many teenagers (and adults), but at a cost. Darby doesn't learn how not to harass someone, and Ariel may feel like she can't truly express her feelings; this reinforces a message that she needs to just accept the unwanted male attention. Either way, as a caring adult, you can signal that the behavior wasn't aligned with community values for treating each other with dignity. You have also let them both know that you have a standard of respect that you will always uphold when it comes to your classroom and greater community. If Ariel is open to dialogue, listen for and discuss how to assess if a response is warranted and how she might respond to someone making her uncomfortable. For instance, "If you're trying to be funny, that isn't it." Or narrate what's happening, "That doesn't sound like a joke, making people feel uncomfortable in front of others is uncool." She could mirror the impact back to the person by saying, "Did you mean to embarrass/upset me?" These are also statements for a bystander to say in an effort to disrupt the dynamic, block the satisfaction of a response from the person targeted, and discourage further teasing. These skills are critical to maintaining community and may be taught in a Health class.

GENDER AND SEXUALITY DIVERSITY

As we continue to encourage our students to connect with, express, and manage their feelings, it's important to recognize that this doesn't always have to be verbal. Some of the most effective ways to manage our mental health come from being physically active and participating in things like hiking or organized sports. For some, the most powerful expressions of feeling come from the visual and performing arts. Many young people are figuring out ways to express themselves and working on the developmental task of forming and understanding their identity and the feelings that go along with it. Artistic expression can provide an outlet for thoughts and feelings related to gender and sexual identity—a form of internal dialogue, connection, and reflection that may also affect the same in others. For some students, their creativity is an exploration, and for others, it makes a statement.

SCENARIO: Pilar Rojas teaches AP Studio Art. Sydney is a strong and quiet student. She is incredibly expressive through her work and has discussed with Ms. Rojas how she feels her artistic expression reveals so much more about what's important to her than her words. Sydney works hard on her pieces and is curating a powerful portfolio of art that explores the intersectionality of various identities. Sydney completes a large painting with Keith Haring influences of a boy in a dress with hair on the legs and tennis shoes. During peer-to-peer critiques, Ms. Rojas leads the conversation by asking questions such as, "Tell me more. What are you going for with this piece?" Sydney shares that she was interested in bringing attention to societal norms and conformity. Other students respectfully listen, and the group moves on. When it is time for Sydney to select a piece for the AP Art Show, she chooses the painting of the boy in a dress. Ms. Rojas considers herself a "closeted ally" for LGBTQ+ issues and students because the greater school culture is known to be religiously conservative. Ms. Rojas wants to support Sydney but is concerned about how the greater community will react. She speaks to a couple of colleagues who she trusts, and they encourage her to check with the principal before the art show, especially if she wants to keep her job. The principal says that he will "handle it," and asks Sydney to meet with him about the piece first. The principal communicates to Sydney that their meeting is an opportunity to plead her case for including the painting. He asks her if her choice is "for shock and awe, and if it isn't, [he'd] like to hear what it is exactly she is trying to do with the painting." Ultimately, the principal decides it may not be included. Sydney goes to Ms. Rojas deflated, angry, and sad. She is blaming herself for not making a good enough case and acquiesces to select a still life drawing instead. (Faith-based school, Cobb County, GA)

More than ever, educators are put in the unfortunate position of having to navigate job security while supporting the well-being of all of their students. "Handling a situation" where someone puts a young person who is quiet and doesn't feel confident or comfortable expressing themselves verbally, but rather through art, and asking them to defend their choice and expression in a way that feels they are accused of wrong before being able to "make a case" for themselves with an adult administrator creates a social power dynamic on many levels that will undermine Ariel's ability to speak her truth and advocate for herself. It seems likely that Ms. Rojas anticipated the outcome and was wrestling with her own feelings. Ms. Rojas's ambivalence indicates her belief that the principal probably won't support Sydney and her artwork. Needing to ask an administrator in the first place signals that we may be setting Sydney up for disappointment; it might have been better to explain the context and encourage her to choose another piece. This can be particularly challenging because, as an educator, Ms. Rojas wanted to affirm Sydney's talent and meaningful choice on the one hand but also wanted to protect her from the likelihood that the principal would shut her down. If Ms. Rojas was convinced that talking to the principal would be futile and/or even harmful, she could have said, "I wish this was a community where you could put your painting up without issue; however, the reality is different. Let's take some time to talk the possibilities through and make a thoughtful decision in your best interest together."

It is important for Sydney to hear from you that she is not to blame and to contextualize the conversation for her. There are simply some things that are not in our control. Encourage her to resist negative self-talk and focus on her courage in making a bold choice (in terms of the community context) and in talking to someone in a position of power in an effort to stand up for herself and creative expression. Being a supportive presence and validating Ariel's work as a way to understand and express herself and the world around her so that she feels seen and heard by you, if not by the principal or greater community, is important and can make a difference. Inquire about Ariel's family and if they are supportive of how she is exploring social gender constructs. Ask if Ariel is open to finding resources outside of her immediate circles so that she may tap into other positive and affirming spaces where young people are on similar journeys. See appendix C for possibilities. Ask about how and where she will move on into adulthood in a more accepting climate. Might she attend college and/or university or find work that is more open to gender fluid ideas and identities? How can you support her endeavors while minimizing the risk of negative judgement and action? Keep an eye on Sydney, too. Because young people who identify as LGBTQ+ are at greater risk for mental health issues, keep an eye out for any behavioral changes that demonstrate a need for meeting with the school counselor or accessing free telehealth mental health support.

FEELINGS AND VALUES

Despite decades of empirical evidence that tells us comprehensive sexuality education (CSE) supports decision-making that leads to healthier choices and overall well-being in young people, many adults still prioritize political and religious ideologies above student health. And even though most families want schools to provide sexuality education, there are some loud voices in parent bodies, among educators, and community members that often don't have students in school who oppose CSE. These voices shape how some districts and private schools allocate funds (especially if they're limited) in ways that don't prioritize CSE. Many of those who oppose CSE argue that it isn't relevant to academic outcomes and has no place in school, when in fact, research shows that CSE supports student academic success. In fact, students who receive education in self-regulation, resilience, empathy, communication, consent, and healthy relationships—to name a few essential topics—perform better than their peers who do not.

As I've highlighted, there are teachers within school communities who value the benefits of providing young people with medically accurate, age-appropriate information about sexuality. If your school doesn't have a formal CSE offering, there are other ways students may acquire that information.

SCENARIO: Harper is a senior who needs to fulfill her service hours to graduate. She's passionate about art, especially magazine graphic design and "anything having to do with being a woman." She is particularly enthusiastic about a zine called *Go Girl*. It features young women creating art, short stories, as well as a Health section that provides information on sexuality from credible resources. Since Harper's school provides only one day of sexuality education, Harper wants to create a similar zine for the school and put it out in public spaces so students may access important health information that the school isn't supplying. Harper also knows that the school is very conservative when it comes to anything having to do with sexuality—a couple of seniors the year before had tried to advocate for more sex education at school and were shut down. So, she schedules a time to talk the matter through with Ms. Banks, who oversees the service program and signs off on projects. Measured, yet true to her enthusiasm, Harper identifies the need for information on how to navigate sexuality safely and shares that many of the students she knows are not making healthy choices. She references research from credible resources that sex ed is a preventative measure against sexual violence and expresses how much she enjoys the artistic expression of the zine in its many forms. She tells Ms. Banks that she thinks it would be valuable and appreciated by many students in the community. Ms. Banks pauses and carefully says, "I see how passionate you are about this, in particular the creative expression—the artwork of students. Let's feature that on your cover. If you do that, then you may place the zine in places on campus where students may discover it." (NOLA Public Schools, LA)

Ms. Banks is in a unique position to work within the limitations of the school culture to provide what could benefit students. As readers, we don't know how resistant the school is to CSE, nor do we know what kind of efforts Ms. Banks and some of her colleagues may or may not have invested to advocate for CSE programs that they know will benefit students. It's also possible that there is intense surveillance for CSE teachings that would activate resistance and job insecurity. Ms. Banks has supported Harper and her quest to provide students with important information that could provide some protection from uninformed sexual decision-making. Young women are disproportionately affected by sexual violence and issues such as unintended pregnancy relative to their male peers. Informing young women of their agency, how their bodies work, and other information about how they make choices that benefit them and their sexual reproductive health is a human right. Of course, it's beneficial for young people of all genders to understand these issues, because all of us are socialized in gendered social power dynamics. Hopefully the information in the zine reaches students of all identities and inspires them to seek out more evidence-based information for themselves.

It is an unfortunate reality that, today, in many areas of the country, this kind of critical information may only reach students through clandestine efforts. The current context requires educators to get creative and manage the inevitable tensions that arise when navigating what is vital to our student's growth and our own job security.

RELATIONSHIPS (CONSENT, COMMUNICATION, DECISION-MAKING)

Frame relationship education as an opportunity for kids to take charge of who they are becoming and want to be. Neuroplasticity—or the capacity to shape brain development through conscious choice—gives students license to reflect upon who they want to be and aspire to those goals in what they do and how they show up. This applies to relationships! Research tells us that it's not our GPA or ACT scores or the name of the schools we attend that will determine the *quality* of our lives—it's the quality of our *relationships*. So, encourage students to understand that the decisions we make and how we behave in our relationships matters. It counts!

SCENARIO: Twelfth-grade boys Darius and Elijah have History with Ms. Davis during the last period of the day. Ms. Davis is a relatively new and young teacher who is known to be a "chill" and "cool" adult. The boys linger after class to go over their college essays—Ms. Davis has offered to help. After reading through the applications, the conversation transitions to who is asking whom to the Winter Dance. There have been a bunch of public asks akin to "promposals" happening around campus. Apparently, it's been quite the distraction and fodder for gossip. Ms. Davis asks if the boys are going. Darius lets his head drop, and Elijah clicks his tongue and nods towards Darius and says, "Oh, he was being such a pussy." Before Ms. Davis can respond, Darius says, "I'm gonna ask this girl, but she isn't my girlfriend. We're just friends, but I really like her." Elijah immediately jumps in and says, "He's a pussy." Ms. Davis quickly responds, "Hey, I don't like that." Elijah adds, "Oh no Miss, I didn't mean it like that—it's, you know, like a joke." Ms. Davis continues, "You're saying he's weak, right?" Elijah considers the question, "Yeah." Ms. Davis responds, "Well then, you're saying that in reference to female genitalia. What does that mean you're saying about women?" Elijah's eyes get wide, "Ohhh I never thought about it that way. Alright, I'll try not to do that again." (Bronx County Public Schools, NY)

Ms. Davis models how to be an adult with boundaries while also being supportive. She is available to discuss what is happening in their lives beyond just academics while also modeling care and clear boundaries.

When teaching health classes, anonymous questions always reveal what's truly on kids' minds. I often receive questions that ask something along the lines of, "What is patriarchy? Because people say I'm doing it, and I don't even know what it means." So much of the time, I find some folks assume boys are consciously perpetuating misogynist language and ideas, when they are simply reading from cultural scripts. We all need environments free of judgement, ultimatums, and shame to share with open honesty and to learn. Ms. Davis creates this space. Taking the time to support boys in understanding the relevance and impact of their actions—speaking to the caring boy part of them—can go a long way in creating mind shifts and behavioral changes.

There are several opportunities to provide guidance for Elijah and Darius through this scenario. It is to the boys' benefit that they understand the value of using respectful language and learning positive relationship skills. All of these teachable moments will contribute to an overall approach to romantic and/or sexual relationships. Human personalities and values are shaped by repeated experiences, even the minute ones.[4] Darius shows that he is possibly feeling insecure about making himself vulnerable and expressing how he truly feels. Being called a pussy by a friend not only reinforces sexist and homophobic language (pussy and fag is language that communicates you're not "man enough"), it also perpetuates the notion that boys can't experience a spectrum of feelings that are altogether human and available to all of us. We all deserve to have the full range of human experiences. A simple question to Elijah like, "What do you mean by that?" or something a bit more in-depth, "Does your language and body language, which comes across as shaming, support Elijah, who is having a hard time figuring out how to ask someone he likes to the dance?" may inspire self-reflection on how friends should treat each other. You may mention to Darius that "it takes courage to connect with feelings and express them, especially if you're unsure about an outcome. And if you're looking for a real connection, that takes some vulnerability." You can also pose the question, "What's getting in the way of asking, and how could you ask so that you've shown that you like someone without feeling overly exposed?"

I teach a high school class on "How to Ask Someone Out." In the class, we discuss where you might ask someone out—for example, in a spot that is public but also affords privacy. When you ask is also important—not when there are lots of friends around or during a stressful time in school, but when you both are likely to be relaxed. We talk about including a simple "with me" as a part of the ask to indicate true intention without exposing yourself too much. I pose this question to my students: "What would the ask look, sound, and feel like, so that both people, no matter what the answer is, can walk away with dignity?" What's real for boys is typically hidden behind a mask of male posturing, when in fact, many boys experience a confused assortment of desire for connection and fears of rejection.[5] It can also be helpful to reframe rejection as the other person simply concluding that it is not a match. Healthy relationships happen when both people share similar feelings for each other, so if the person you ask says no, they are saying they don't feel the way you do. They're actually saving you a lot of time chasing something that ultimately won't work.

Ms. Davis can help Darius by acknowledging the possibility that his invitation may be declined. Should this happen, encourage Darius to avoid negative self-talk, and ask for examples of how he can manage his disappointment.

In this scenario, Ms. Davis elects to address the chauvinistic language. She states this clearly in her response to the boys. The context of asking girls out has the potential to add a dimension to her observation—that is, if the boys are interested in going out with girls and having healthy, fun, and responsible relationships now and into the future, it's a good start to check their language. Offer that what we say is an expression of who we are, or at least of what we're feeling and what's going on with us. Many male students I know would respond with something along the lines of, "Oh I would never say that to a girl. I respect women. That's just how guys talk." Many boys would say the same thing about homophobic language and a gay friend, arguing that we shouldn't hear their demeaning language as sexist or homophobic because of intention, and in the context of a culture that normalizes harmful behavior, if it's veiled in humor.

This is an opportunity to introduce the concept of personal integrity, or honor, which may resonate with a boy who is at an age and stage where he is figuring out what kind of a man he wants to be. If you reference integrity, take a moment to define it or build a definition out of a question posed to the boys. To raise awareness, ask, "Is integrity/honor something that is variable according to context or is it something that is at the core of who you are all of the time?" How far the conversation goes will depend on your students, their interest, attention, and openness. Let go of definite answers or neat conclusions; instead, invest in encouraging a heightened awareness and self-reflection. There's no reason to think that Elijah isn't sincere in his response to Ms. Davis, and it's also likely that he will continue to say "pussy" to uphold masculine cultural norms in the future. It is also possible that if/when he uses that language again, Ms. Davis's message will be somewhere in his consciousness and steer him towards more respectful language and behavior. It may make a long-term difference.

CONNECTION (INTIMACY AND LOVE)

An important developmental task of adolescence is to figure out how to have a sustained, healthy, intimate relationship. In a culture that all too often pushes young people to disconnect, evade vulnerability, and prioritize performance, students are looking for more connection and guidance. Supporting students with this self-affirming quest can be tricky when families, their values, and priorities, as well as those of other children and/or other families they are connected to, aren't aligned. Of most importance for educators is to maintain perspective on which aspects of this adolescent process are appropriate to discuss and which require important boundaries that respect teacher–student relationships and family values and rights.

SCENARIO: You teach Health, so students frequently stop by your office to seek guidance with their social lives. During lunch, Aiyla and Mason, seniors who have been in a committed romantic relationship since their junior year, stop by and ask to speak with you. They close the door, sit down on the office couch across from you, and Mason starts. He explains that they've been going out for a long time and really love each other. Aiyla is nodding in agreement. Mason shares that a lot of the time they spend together is at school, because Aiyla's parents don't approve of their relationship. Aiyla shares that her parents are conservative and "from a different culture where the parents decide who and when their daughter gets to date." In fact, Aiyla's parents don't want her dating anyone, because they believe it will detract from her studies. Aiyla has one of the highest GPAs in her grade and has already been accepted, early decision, to Yale. Mason explains that when they hang out on the weekend, they go to his house, where his parents fully support their relationship, and Aiyla's friends "cover" for her, since she always tells her parents she's with girlfriends. Both Aiyla and Mason are afraid that, when Mason turns eighteen soon, if Aiyla's parents find out about them, they will charge him with statutory rape to end the relationship. They want to know if this is possible and what they should do to avoid the risk, especially because they want to spend more time together before college and are afraid that this will lead to Aiyla's parents finding out about their relationship. (Independent School in San Francisco County, CA)

Many different adolescent relationships contribute towards the developmental task of figuring out how to have a sustained, healthy intimate relationship. Experience, young love in particular, can be a powerful teacher, and it seems that Aiyla and Mason's connection would support that. However, this scenario is complicated. Honesty within a family relationship is critical as well. An educator's role is limited when a family's values and wishes for their children are in conflict with a teenager's decisions. Aiyla and Mason have come to you because they trust you, but it is important not to get caught up in their situation. Recognize that teachers are not parents or therapists; we can be helpful but only from within those parameters. In the above scenario, even if you believe that achievement pressure can compromise a child's well-being and that a healthy intimate relationship between two teenagers promotes healthy development, we cannot cross a boundary and encourage secrecy in resistance to parental wishes. We can respectfully encourage students to act on their own behalf and respect their privacy when navigating issues with their parents without taking a position that condones dishonest behavior. So be clear in the way you narrate the situation, "I hear how challenging this is for you and am here to listen. *And* as a teacher who also has a responsibility to parents, I cannot take a position on this, but I can help you think through this situation so that you figure out for yourselves what you're going to do next." Inquiry is a powerful tool that allows students to understand, discuss, and take action when faced with adversity.

You may ask Aiyla strategic questions to start her process of being honest about her feelings, her relationship with her parents, and her decision-making process. You can ask, for example, "How does the current situation make you feel?" then simply listen. You may continue with, "How would you, ideally, like the situation to be? What would that feel like?" and follow with, "What would it take to bring about that kind of change? And is there anything you could do to start that process?"

Remind Aiyla that sometimes people are more open to half steps towards a compromise and that using nonjudgmental and personalized language, like avoiding "why" and using "I statements," can be helpful in communicating and connecting when there is disagreement. You may ask, "From a compassionate perspective, where do you think your parent's thoughts and feelings are coming from?" You may also suggest that she practice writing down what she wishes she could say to them and then reflecting on any potential possibilities. It may also benefit Aiyla to discuss the difference between privacy and secrecy in relationships. Privacy typically involves making a conscious decision to protect something by not sharing it—there is a sense of agency. Secrecy in relationships typically signals some sort of shame and happens as a result of someone feeling they have no choice. Self-reflection on this difference can go a long way in deepening understanding, being accountable, and connecting to feelings. Remember, as an educator, you are not in a position to fix anything for Aiyla and Mason but can provide support as they determine what they want to do.

Teachers are also not in the position to provide legal advice. You may say to Mason, "It sounds like you are open with your parents. What about sharing your concerns with them, so that they can help you seek the legal advice you're looking for?"

SAFETY

Unfortunately, sexual harassment and assault is a prevalent issue amongst youth today. In 2023, the CDC released an alarming study, *The Youth Risk Behavior Survey*, that documents record levels of sadness and anxiety in teen girls. Adolescent girls reported high rates of depression, suicidal thoughts, and sexual violence, as did LGBTQ+ youth. The increase in sadness and hopelessness, measured over the last ten years, was present across girls of all races. Reporting focused on the experience of girls specifically, as well as LGBTQ+ youth; however, it is suspected that gender differences may mask the aggressive and violent behavior in boys that can signal depression as well.[6] Of the young adults (18–25 years old) surveyed by the Making Caring Common Project, 76 percent of respondents had never had a conversation with their parents about how to avoid sexually harassing others.[7] One in four girls and one in six boys have been sexually abused before the age of eighteen.[8]

Some consequences of sexual violence are physical—such as bruising and genital injuries, STIs, and pregnancy—and/or others may be psychological—such as anxiety, depression, and suicidal ideation.[9] Additional chronic long-term impact may include PTSD, which can lead to gastrointestinal, cardiovascular, and sexual health problems. Sexual violence survivors are also more likely to engage in risky sexual activity and substance abuse. Sexual violence is also connected to other forms of violence.[10] Girls who have been sexually abused are more likely to become victims of intimate partner violence in adulthood. It is critical that schools be aware of and accountable to this unfortunate dimension of adolescence. The efforts a school makes to prevent incidents of sexual violence and how a school identifies and responds to incidents of sexual misconduct can be vital in supporting the healing trajectory of those young people who experience harm, as well as those who cause it. Educational communities can play a pivotal role in deterring sexual violence for students while they are in their care and, hopefully, beyond.

SCENARIO: Mr. Lee teaches World History and is Devi's (a junior) advisor. Mr. Lee has noticed that Devi hasn't completed the last assignments and isn't as engaged in class conversations. After class, he asks her to stop by his desk to check in. He shares what he's noticed, that it's out of character, and asks if something is going on and if he can provide any support. Devi responds with, "Yeah, there was, but I'm fine now—I'm getting the support I need." Over the next couple of classes, Devi continues to detach and withdraw, so Mr. Lee follows up, but Devi is evasive. Mr. Lee tells her, "Feelings come and go, and I'm noticing what you're going through is sticking around. I'm concerned about you, so I'm going to let Ms. Vazquez, the school counselor, know that you may need some support. She can be really helpful—adults on campus reach out to her sometimes too when they need help figuring something out." Devi responds with, "Really, I'm fine, Mr. Lee," and abruptly leaves. Mr. Lee shares his observations with Ms. Vazquez, who then reaches out to Devi through school email. She recognizes that Devi told Mr. Lee that she is getting support and invites Devi to meet so that she may provide additional support, since whatever is going on seems to be impacting her schoolwork. Ms. Vazquez assures Devi that their interactions are completely confidential and that, of course, it's up to Devi if she'd like to meet. The following week, Devi stops by Ms. Vazquez's office. During Devi's first session with Ms. V, she shares that "there was this guy, and [she] didn't like what happened, and [she] keeps thinking about it and gets distracted but thinks with time it will go away and be fine." Ms. Vazquez also gets a bit of context: There was a party where everyone was drinking, and there was an incident with a student at their school. Devi agrees to return the following week and discloses that, while she was at the party, she passed out for a bit and when she woke up, the boy had his hands down her pants. Devi does not report the boy's name but talks about seeing him in the hallways. (Independent School, Washington, DC)

A sense of safety comes from how the caretaking adults in this situation respond to Devi. Title IX is a federal civil rights gender equity law that ensures equitable access to an education. While public secondary school leaders across the country have an obligation to ensure students are safe at school, districts vary in their sexual harassment and assault prevention measures. Ideally, Title IX holds schools accountable to sexual misconduct reporting and provides guidance about procedure. Feeling safe is relational.

There are multiple layers to this scenario. Mr. Lee notices a student's change in behavior, he refers the student to Ms. V, and Ms. V then responds and offers Devi support. If it is a public school, Devi may choose to make a formal report to the Title IX coordinator on campus, which would set a Title IX investigation in motion. How Title IX is adjudicated depends on the current guidelines of due process that the federal government has in place. This is currently in flux, so it is essential that schools be up to date on the latest guidance. What holds true is that all public schools are legally required to have a Title IX coordinator on their campus to accept and investigate reports.

Mr. Lee is clear about his role as an educator. He is tuned into his students, who they are, and how they behave when engaged and productive in school. He responds when there is a shift or change that signals something is up with a student who may need help. He uses nonjudgemental language to express care about what he sees and is proactive with a response that also allows for Devi's agency. Mr. Lee names behavior in a respectful and caring way while being clear about his professional training and capacities. He is able to recognize what harm looks like; however, he knows that Devi needs to speak to someone who is competent in trauma-informed support so that he won't inadvertently compound the trauma with biased questions and responses that may not be survivor centered. Even though it is not stated, it is also possible that gender and/or other identities may play a role in how Devi will receive his concern. Devi's uncharacteristic behavior and unconvincing assurances makes the school counselor, someone who is qualified to help a young person in distress, an important person to bring in on the situation.

If Devi had initiated the conversation and/or felt moved to disclose more, it would be important for Mr. Lee to explain his responsibilities as a mandated reporter before she shared; those reporting requirements depend on the county and state. It is always an option to call Child Protective Services to check and see if the situation applies to reporting mandates. He might say, "Let's pause for a second, because it's important to let you know about my responsibilities as a mandated reporter . . . that means that . . . I want you to know so you don't set anything in motion that you don't feel ready for right now." If Devi continued to disclose the abuse, Mr. Lee may say, "I appreciate your courage—thank you for telling me. I care about your well-being, and I'm not a trained therapist/school counselor, so let's talk about some options for connecting you with someone who can give you the support you need. I can walk you to Ms. V's office, or I can email her on your behalf to set up a meeting with you, which would you prefer?"

How someone responds to first disclosure can impact a survivor's healing trajectory. It is critical that Mr. Lee believes Devi and takes her seriously. Verification can happen later. These first few moments may impact Devi in the long term. Responding with, "I believe you—thank you for sharing—that takes a lot of courage" sets the tone for the conversation going forward and Devi's overall recovery. Do not ask questions that are victim blaming (such as, "Were you drinking?"; "What were you wearing?"; "Did you lead him on?"; "Are you sure that actually happened?"; "Could it have been a misunderstanding?"). Given the statistics for sexual assault, especially among young people, and how our response can impact their capacity to recover and restore, it is essential that trauma-informed professionals gather Devi's information.

In any school, Devi has the option to call the police. Unwanted and unwelcome sexual touching is considered assault and a felony. This action will also require a name. In fact, if the family or school calls the police in response to a sexual assault, a victim may request an officer who is trained to interact with survivors and is part of a Sexual Assault Response Team (SART), which provides a coordinated response of medical personnel, law enforcement, and sexual assault service providers in the victim's area. Forensic interviews are trauma-informed interviews conducted by an individual who is trained in supporting survivors. The interview is intended to minimize the potential for retraumatizing the survivor with inappropriate questions or by asking them to retell the event(s) multiple times. The interview may then be used for various purposes.

When Ms. Vazquez is made aware of Mr. Lee's concerns about Devi, she takes her time, which in this scenario, she is able to do because she looked in Devi's file and saw that she has a therapist. Her email communicates, "I'm here for you," in addition to providing agency so that Devi feels that she has some choice. Ms. V also communicates her legal responsibilities as a mandated reporter and the level of confidentiality she may hold. Many advocates, including therapists, recognize offering options and allowing survivors to make their own choices as an effective response. The survivor has experienced a traumatic event that has led to feeling disempowered or out of control, so the opportunity to exercise personal choice and reclaim some control is considered a survivor centered practice. This is also an important reason for all teachers to know their school counselors and to receive professional development on student disclosure, mandated reporting policies, and the current state guidelines for Title IX. Both adolescents who experience sexual violence and those who perpetrate it require therapeutic treatment and rehabilitation. Since teenagers spend so much of their time at school, many of these dynamics (between survivor and perpetrator) may play out on campus grounds—during activities, free time, and/or even classes. The impact can affect a student's overall well-being, including academic performance, social standing, and self-esteem.

Ms. V will need to work with Devi or seek consent to communicate with Devi's therapist to assess how she is feeling and how she has been impacted by the abuse. She may need to make a report if Devi's therapist hasn't already. Ms. V will also need to bring Devi's parenting adult(s) into the conversation and support Devi's family. School counselors may offer Devi choices for how to inform her parent(s). Talking to Devi's parents together, talking to them for Devi, or encouraging Devi to do that herself while providing moral support could all be options.

Since Devi is in a private school, she may choose to make a formal report to the Dean of Students or an administrator who oversees student support and discipline at the school. If she does this, she will have to report the boy's name. There are many reasons why she may not. She may be afraid of retaliation, of word getting around and migrating into digital spaces and mushrooming from there, and/or the social dynamics of gossip, taking sides, and cancel-culture in cyber and in-person spaces.

Independent Schools cannot adjudicate under juvenile criminal law (sexual assault is a felony), which is why they are mandated to make a report; however, since the alleged perpetrator goes to the school, they may adjudicate under a sexual harassment policy, since the person's presence is compromising Devi's capacity to learn. Again, it is critical that the number of adults who discuss this with Devi be minimal and that their language and approach be trauma informed and survivor centered as she begins her process. Devi will decide with her family how to proceed regarding the report and what the family has the capacity to decide in collaboration with the school.

If the name of the boy is revealed, it is critical to think about his choices and options too. If he and Devi are in a public school and Devi makes a formal report, he will be accountable to a Title IX investigation and will be required to avoid Devi. Some schools take a restorative justice approach in addition to the investigation, which may require him to meet with a trained caretaking adult who will guide him through an empathetic process that encourages him to be accountable to the harm he caused and hear what the impact of that has had and will be on Devi. Devi, if she chooses, will have the opportunity to express how she feels and what she needs for the two to move forward in a way that is amenable. If the school finds that he is in violation of school policies, there will be consequences for his actions. Again, the Title IX guidelines at the time and what the investigation reveals will determine repercussions.

In addition to the discipline, the boy will also need education in consent and the impact of substances on consent, as well as therapeutic support. This is critical information for young people to learn *before* incidents happen. Consent laws are in place to protect people during moments when they may not be able to protect themselves. Consent education that includes how substances impact consent as well as the legal responsibilities of consent and positive examples of how not to harm someone is valuable and an integral part of cultivating safe educational spaces. Substances impact consent because they impair communication, magnify misperceptions, and are used to justify aggressive behavior. The more of the substance, the more it diminishes our power and judgement. It is important to rehabilitate the young man so that any harm or misguidance he has experienced that led to harmful behavior be addressed and that he may also have the opportunity to change his thinking and behavior, so as not to cause harm again. I know students who learned from the harm they caused and have been inspired to support peer-to-peer education programs in the spirit of sexual violence prevention. However, a young person who has experienced harm may heal, and however the young person who caused harm may live their amends, we caretaking adults play a critical role in the restoration of positive trajectories and access to an education.

* * *

All students—whether they move into adulthood by going straight to work, on to college, or they take some time to mature through other experiences—deserve an education that supports and cultivates their capacity to connect with others in meaningful ways. Connection and true intimacy require trust and a fundamental awareness and ability to manage our emotions. This is critical to empathizing with others, standing in conflict, facing adversity, and fostering care and love anchored in dignity. If we cannot connect with others, we cannot truly spread joy or assume responsibility for causing pain. An education must include a sense of belonging, mattering, and seeing ourselves and the world as it is, so that we may understand, respond, and aspire to one that supports living a fulfilled life. In *All About Love*, bell hooks writes, "To truly love we must learn to mix various ingredients—care, affection, recognition, respect, commitment and trust, as well as honest and open communication."[11] This transformative force of love is what ultimately encourages our students in living to their full potential as individuals, partners, friends, and citizens. To be educators for love, this is what we must teach and model—it is the sexuality education our students deserve.

Appendix A

Taking Care as an Educator: What About Us?

Teaching is hard work—it is heart work. I humbly recognize and appreciate this and all that goes into this demanding profession. Time is a precious commodity in schools and there is very rarely enough available to us during the workday. Having spent over three decades in schools and educational nonprofits, I've seen demands on educators only escalate. We navigate the mental health, youth development, academic achievement, skill building, self-regulation, physical growth, character and moral evolution, interpersonal dynamics, citizenship, and community building of hundreds of students. This meaningful work is far from a cake walk. The comments many of us have heard—"teachers have it easy" or "how hard can it be, you have summers off" or "if you truly cared about kids, you wouldn't worry about the salary"— devalue and demean this difficult work and those who commit their lives to it. And when adults put their political ideologies above student health, our professional expertise and what we know to benefit the well-being of young people is discounted and dismissed. Of course, as in all professions, there are folks who do not fulfill their job descriptions and must be held accountable. But looking back over the last thirty years, the majority of educators I've known are in it for the kids.

I assume if you are reading this book, you are in it for the kids and you want to know how to help them learn how to handle that powerful human force—sexuality—in a way that respects others and themselves. So how do we, as educators, take care of ourselves, particularly when we experience parental and/or collegial hostility, criticism, and even job threats when we introduce comprehensive sexuality education (CSE) in our classrooms?

As discussed in chapter one, CSE has historically been—and still is today—a controversial topic for many people, which is not surprising given our culture's taboos about sex and sexuality. At the same time, as I've discussed, the benefits of CSE across the developmental spectrum are recognized nationally and internationally and are anchored in evidence-based research. Nevertheless, educators are confronted with opposition and resistance from time to time. This type of pushback tends to ebb and flow relative to cultural political shifts and movements. Today, for example, issues surrounding gender and gender pronouns are particularly charged. Most educators believe in youth and community health, which requires us to mediate any concerns and prioritize what we know to benefit all students. It's also important to remember that the majority of parents want their children to receive CSE.

This appendix is intended to offer you, the educator, the same care and dignity you have learned to model for your students throughout this book. Below, you will find common challenging scenarios educators routinely face and guidance for resolution.

SCENARIO: You have been a support teacher for several years in a second-grade classroom and are about to assume the lead teacher role when your colleague takes maternity leave. The transition was announced in the bimonthly newsletter that goes out to parents. You are excited for the opportunity and write a letter to all caretaking adults in the class, introducing yourself and what you are looking forward to in the months ahead. Your signature includes your pronouns. Within hours of the correspondence, your administrator receives a hostile voicemail from a father who is beside himself. He is vehement and confrontational about your use of pronouns and says that he "can't believe this bullshit and that [you] better not be teaching [his] kid this crap." (New Hampshire Public School District, NH)

We all have pronouns. What some people seem to object to is when an individual uses pronouns that are in line with their gender identity rather than the gender they were assigned at birth, which is outside of what some people consider the norm. This father opposes the idea of people identifying their pronouns at all, likely because in conservative circles, doing so is perceived as acknowledging a spectrum of gender identities. But considering pronouns as exclusive to binary genders of male/female can lead folks to make assumptions about others and only one aspect of their larger identity. Recognizing and/or using someone's preferred pronouns is a way to show respect and create an inclusive environment. Proactively identifying our own pronouns reflects this reality and signals awareness and support of a gender spectrum and the rights of others to claim and express their own identities.

Administrators have many responsibilities and are pulled in many different directions. Much of the time, they are working hard behind the scenes to address issues that demand confidentiality. Many teachers/colleagues express appreciation for feeling safe as an individual when they know that an administrator has their back and will support them. In anticipation of community complaints like those in the scenario above, administrators may benefit from a process that clarifies the school's pedagogical rationale and intention regarding "teaching" and "learning" related to gender and sexuality diversity. It is also valuable to remind all community members that this is about supporting and including *all* students.[1] Communication is essential for building trust with families, and evening forums and newsletters go a long way in eliminating surprises and improving communication.[2] Asking for regular teacher-parent communication creates opportunities for shared understanding between school and home, fosters partnerships among all caretaking adults involved in teaching and supporting students, and gives parents and students opportunities to bridge learning between school and home.[3]

Should conflict surface, gather information so you may determine what kind of conflict you are facing. Think back to chapter one and different forms of opposition—reluctance, resistance, organized opposition, and outside agitation—and respond accordingly. In most situations, listening carefully to the concerns that are expressed and trying to find shared values—such as respect and the importance of family, for example—is helpful. Most parents want to feel seen and heard and can be reasonable in dialogue. *Strategic Questioning* by Fran Peavy is an approach that encourages understanding across differences without forcing folks to abandon their own values.[4] This approach creates a path that supports mutual respect within conflict. It is a way to engage in dialogue across differences and look for common ground without abandoning your own beliefs. Strategic questions avoid leading with "why" (when we use "why" we've already made a judgment) and focus on leading with "what" (What are you most concerned about?) and "how" (How has this affected you?).

If a parent continues to be difficult and/or is engaging in bullying behaviors, be assertive and clear about the school's positions and policies. Ultimately, school district mission and value statements create a solid foundation that supports and reflects the belief that schools have a responsibility to *all* of its community members and upholds respect for every individual's identity and how they wish to express that identity.

Given the sociopolitical historical context of sex stigmatization in this country and inconsistent education on the topic (when it exists at all), it's not surprising that peoples' values and attitudes vary widely. Sexuality is a loaded topic, and cultural socialization still steeps many folks in sexual negativity. By that I mean there is a tremendous amount of hypersexualization, lack of knowledge and communication, body objectification and shaming, as well as queer-, homo-, and transphobia. At the same time, years of evidence-based scientific research has established that CSE benefits all of us—young people in particular. Even folks who know this on an intellectual level may have qualms when it comes to how they *feel* about it when it comes to their own child. And even those with the best of intentions may nevertheless be influenced by the way they grew up or by their current cultural environment. What happens and how should we react, then, when our colleagues think and feel differently than we do about what's best for kids or have different values when it comes to how people are treated?

SCENARIO: Fatima teaches in a state that has just passed a "Don't Say Gay" bill, and there is discussion in the faculty room. Her colleague, Diane, says, "Well, I wouldn't want anybody else talking to my kid about that stuff." Fatima notices that Marco, a gay colleague who is pouring himself some coffee, looks uncomfortable. Jana, who works in the registrars' office, comments, "That reminds me, I need to make sure everyone uses the attendance lists—we definitely aren't using whatever names and pronouns the kids want." Fatima considers herself an ally and wants to say something but isn't sure how to handle the situation. (Travis County School District, TX)

Allyship is important in our work to create inclusive and equitable communities of affirmation, care, and dignity for all. Contributing towards cultures of consent supports these values. The very act of saying something in support of those values makes a difference and stands up for inclusion. In fact, it is essential. Strategic questioning provides a way to engage across differences to deepen the understanding of other perspectives, invite openness, empathy, and the movement towards change without making folks feel like they have to abandon their values. This approach pairs well with nonjudgmental language like "I notice . . ." or "Help me understand . . ." (See appendix C to find out more).

Antigay and antitrans legislation recently introduced in many states provides an unfortunate permission structure for intolerance, as this scenario demonstrates. Fatima wants to say something and stand up for her beliefs but can't be blamed for feeling intimidated when intolerance is now state policy. At the same time, as readers, we don't know what social power dynamics could factor into the situation. Is Diane an administrator? Has she been there much longer and does she have more influence at the school? What other identities are present among the folks in the room, and how do they embrace and express them? It's ambiguous whether Diane is referring to human sexuality in general or homosexuality. It's certainly potentially homophobic (despite intention) because "that stuff" is said within the context of a conversation related to a "Don't Say Gay" law, which is homophobic, marginalizing, oppressive, and harmful for students, their families, and school communities.

Still, questions can hold people accountable and invite deeper reflection. Be mindful that inquiry in the moment, in front of others, may be perceived as calling Diane and Jana out in front of colleagues and is likely to feel shaming. However, Fatima may want to signal that she doesn't agree with Diane and Jana to show her support of LGBTQ+–identifying folks like Marco. Or Fatima may encounter resistance and shut down any discussion because Diane and Jana may simply say, "I have to get back to work" and exit the lounge. What is Fatima going for? If Fatima is going for something more meaningful to affect real reflection and change, she may find a time to ask the questions one on one. Fatima might prefer to directly address Diane and Jana's language, especially if it is expressed in religious terms that describe homosexuality as sinful. Religious beliefs do not give anyone the right to take another person's rights away. Fatima can state how the others' comment came across by saying something like "It makes me uncomfortable [or It's offensive] to hear 'that stuff' in reference to people's sexuality," or "That's homophobic and not okay." She might say, "I'd like to better understand your perspective, when's a good time to talk?" Not only what is said, but how it's said is important. Genuine curiosity tends to lead to more openness. If she seeks out her colleagues after the fact, she may start with "When we were in the lounge and talking about the assembly . . ." The strategic questions to ask may be "What do you mean by 'that stuff'?" You may also ask something along the lines of "Which sources do you trust and why?" It's possible that Diane and Jana need reminding about the importance of providing caring, affirming, and loving spaces for all students, including LBGTQ+ youth and their families. Your questions may catch them off guard, they may get uncomfortable, realize their words have an impact on others that could be hurtful; they may potentially shut down, get defensive and leave, or engage in dialogue. Even if they get defensive and cut the conversation short, saying something is important because it reflects and reinforces community values, and your words may have more of a positive influence than is obvious at the time.

It's also possible that there are conflicting values from other communities and aspects of Diane and Jana's identities; for instance, they could belong to a community of faith. In that case, you could get curious with "I notice most faith is rooted in love and am wondering about the relationship of love to . . .?" You could ask, "What do you think about all of the social science that tells us CSE is a critical part of a student's education (backed by the American Academy of Pediatrics, the United Nations, congressional research)?" If they share that they believe they should be the one (and only one) to educate their children on sexuality topics, you might ask, "How's that going? What are your resources and strategies?" If you're able to go deeper. you may ask about the unique opportunities CSE classes offer young people—especially the opportunity to practice dialoguing with peers who are going to be the people with whom they are likely to eventually explore and express their sexuality. Offering opinions versus being judgmental can be an effective strategy.

How you respond and navigate the moment is context dependent and dependent on what works for you and what you're going for at the time. I find that moving from conflict to connection by calling someone in and investing in strategic questions and dialogue affects change in community-building ways. I also find that direct and explicit statements shine light on demeaning behavior and puts the responsibility on the actor to figure out and seek understanding themselves. Whether that person acts to do so or not is up to them. In this case, unfortunately, Diane and Jana have the backing of the state, and if Fatima speaks up, they may well dismiss her objections or push back more or less aggressively. Even if they do, Fatima has stood up for her values, her students, and the larger community, and the ideas she has expressed are more likely to affect change (or plant the seeds of change) than remaining silent. At the same time, it's a lot to expect educators to risk their positions in the community, their jobs, or even their safety, and in some contexts, silence may be the wisest choice. In the end, speaking up or not will depend on your beliefs and how you put courageous love into action to affect change and ensure dignity for all.

Increasingly, educators express fear and feel they lack training and skills for how to manage the politicization of gender and sexuality in schools. It is a minority of parents and educators who support these kinds of attacks, but too often, they have the loudest voices and get away with it.

SCENARIO: Soraya is the founding administrator of a four-year-old faith-based school. There is controversy brewing among the elementary school faculty and the parents. A kindergarten teacher was wearing an Elton John t-shirt in class when a curious student asked, "Who is that?" The teacher briefly explained that Elton John is a famous musician who has created a lot of meaningful music and that the shirt is from his last concert tour. The student follows with, "How come it's his last?" The teacher responds that Elton John has expressed wanting to take time away from his job to spend more time with his husband and children. The information that Elton John has a husband makes its way home, and there is expressed concern that the school is teaching gender and sexuality at an inappropriate age. News travels quickly, and there is a faculty member who agrees with the criticism and others who are also incensed. Soraya, the head of school and a woman of color who shares the faith the school is founded on, is trying to navigate the discord and hear each perspective, the teachers (all self-identified white feminists who don't share the same faith as that the school is founded on) believe it is appropriate to talk about gender and sexuality diversity in elementary school classrooms. They question her, "How can you be a leader in a school that has a mission of equity and loving humanity and not stand up to this homophobia?" The teachers threaten to leave if Soraya doesn't stand up to the relatively small group of resistant parents and the board chair, who also shares her faith, and says, "What are you going to say on the day of judgment if you allow this kind of teaching to continue?" Soraya is challenged to bridge the two factions in a way that feels equitable to both sides as the board chair warns, "The school doors will be closed by Fall because of what you're doing." (Faith-based independent school, Cook County, IL)

In my interview with Soraya, she expressed how deeply painful it was to be in a contentious position within the learning community she deeply loved and cared about. It was divided, people took sides and expected that she would do the same. In response, she held community meetings, was present for many conversations, endured judgment, personal verbal attacks, and ultimatums. Soraya believed in both her faith and the value of gender and sexual diversity equity within the context of age-appropriate

CSE. In hindsight, she shared that she had lost sight of what she thinks might have provided effective solutions. There were actually many large pockets of support for her as a head of school in a difficult situation. Those folks believed in her capacity to make good decisions and had faith that, as a professional, she would make the best decision in the interest of the children and school. Soraya's take away was that she had become so overwhelmed by the loud and powerful minority that she forgot about cultivating and seeking support from those who had faith in her leadership abilities.

Soraya's advice, when confronted with impatience and distrust, is to take the time to educate folks who are apprehensive but willing to learn. Consult with fellow educators and leaders outside of the immediate community to maintain a sense of perspective and make decisions not from a place of fear or in reaction to other people's fear. Have more one-on-one conversations to avoid mob mentality and gain a better understanding of the problem. Bolster those connections and rapport so that you may build trust and create consensus. Identify the different forms of resistance and specific strategies for addressing them, as addressed in chapter one. As we advise students, whenever we face overwhelm, chunk it up. Parcel what's happening and methodically address each part of your larger issue. Ultimately, the school closed because of the conflict, which was obviously devastating for the majority of the community. Soraya shares this scenario in the hope that her learnings may help others navigate similar situations more effectively while letting administrators know that it is possible to seek and find support and solidarity in what are seemingly impossible situations.

Sometimes the colleagues we may seek support from are not helpful and reinforce stigmatized ideas about sexuality that impact us personally.

SCENARIO: Deja is the puberty educator for her unified school district. She travels between different schools on a rotating schedule and teaches a two-week puberty and SEL unit in all of the middle schools. In one of the classes, middle school student Carl is easily distracted. During a class discussion about identity, Riley, who goes by they/them pronouns, shares how they feel about gender norms and expectations. Carl impulsively states, "Yeah, well I identify as a snowplow." Carl's friend group erupts in laughter, and there is a verbal altercation between Riley and Carl. Deja sends Riley and Carl to the school counselor to work it out. After class, Dr. Angela Rose, the vice principal, requests a meeting to gather information on the incident. Gloria, a visiting administrator from a neighboring school, is also present. Throughout the conversation about Riley and Carl, Dr. Rose refers to Riley with he/him pronouns. During a pause in the conversation, Deja says, "you know, Riley goes by they/them pronouns." Dr. Rose pauses and sighs. At this point Gloria asks, "What does that even mean?" Dr. Rose explains that "more and more students are making a point to identify themselves other than she/he." Gloria laughs, shakes her head, and says, "that's just crazy —kids these days!" Deja assumes Dr. Rose will affirm the inclusion of different genders, but says, "Yes, it's grammatically incorrect to use 'they' as a singular pronoun. Sometimes I don't even know what they're thinking." Dr. Rose and Gloria continue to laugh. Deja, who identifies as queer and has a gender nonbinary partner, provides the information they ask for and leaves. She is distraught that an administrator would disrespect a student's identity and make assumptions about hers, so she texts her union mentor about the situation and asks if there is anything she can do. Deja's mentor encourages her to follow up with Dr. Rose and express how she felt about what happened. When Dr. Rose and Deja meet, Dr. Rose reveals the text that Deja had sent to her mentor in confidence. (Suffolk County School District, MA)

Situations like this can activate an entire spectrum of thoughts and feelings, especially when contextualized within a social power dynamic. Dr. Rose is an administrator who engaged in disrespectful, minimizing conversation with another administrator—both have influence and power that Deja does not when it comes to her job security. They are oblivious to and assume Deja's sexuality and/or how she feels about inclusive pronouns no matter her own identity and/or don't care that she identifies as queer. If we offer grace, it's possible that Dr. Rose has had a difficult day. Administrators often mitigate and mediate a lot of challenging contexts and are required to manage sometimes vehement and confrontational situations, many times in isolation due to strict confidentiality policies. This is a possible explanation, but not an excuse. Even if the administrators' intention is seemingly benign, their impact is not.

Not only is the interpersonal interaction fraught, Deja's supposed union ally has betrayed her trust by sharing her private text with the very person she was feeling exposed by. Deja's union contact has not taken her report/concern about her work environment or grievance seriously. Her contact has dismissed the grievance as something inconsequential—a trivial notion of political correctness. When teachers feel unsafe and unsupported while acting responsibly for educating people on how misgendering and minimizing people's identity markers is an issue, the union isn't serving its purpose.

This is further complicated by the current escalating anti-LGBTQ+ and anti-DEIJ surveillance in many districts. Deja may contemplate what to prioritize: the well-being of students in her immediate care, the internal administrative issue, or the irresponsibility of the union contact. What to take on and in what order? She has to decide if she's going to move past the situation, make a bigger move to file a union complaint, or find another job. I often hear teachers say they stay in work environments that feel consistently exasperating and hostile because they feel "the kids need someone to advocate for them." While this desire to be an affirming adult is honorable, our well-being as caretaking adults is just as important. I have an administrator friend who advises teachers in similar situations with "None of us are a child's last opportunity to learn something; we need to let go of that burden so that we can do our work in the ways we can and sustain ourselves too."

There are other factors for Deja to consider as well.

Schools can be political places, and Deja is called to teach a curriculum or feels a responsibility to teach the curriculum in a way that is inclusive of all students. Since that approach isn't supported, she has a decision to contemplate. There is the contained verbal incident and then there is the overall culture of the school, which is a community effort administrators are responsible to cultivate. Furthermore, Deja's job is peripatetic in nature.

Where is her safe haven? Moving from place to place makes it difficult to establish trusted rapport with work colleagues. If she stays, does she compromise her personal integrity? And if she doesn't have a cohort of people she can connect with because she's moving around so much and isn't supported, is her well-being in this work context sustainable? This is an inevitable problem when there aren't established health education programs, which is true in many school districts. It can be hard for teachers to be as effective or sustain themselves when their jobs are so fragmented.

How might Dr. Rose have approached the scenario differently? My own experience as a teacher informed my approach as an administrator. When cultivating cultures of consent where all people feel seen and heard, the first question to ask might be "How are you doing?" and then follow with "What happened? What's your perspective?" The approach an administrator uses to understand the problem can build trust. Valuing rapport and connection by bringing humanity and humility to the conversation contributes towards cultivating empathy and cultures of consent. How we listen can preserve dignity. Seeing the person in front of us and seeking to understand who they are and whom and what they care about with genuine curiosity and respect increases the preservation of dignity.

This is true whenever the administrative issue involves a teacher as part of the presented problem as well.

SCENARIO: Jason is a popular teacher in his late thirties. Many students appreciate his teaching and humor. In addition to teaching history, he oversees affinity groups on campus, coaches a sport, and is attentive to his advising group. The development office at his school has requested that he support the current capital campaign by connecting with former students through social media. The development team is trying to encourage young former students' engagement and financial support for the school. A couple of months into the process, Jason receives an email from Mike, the head of school, requesting a meeting the next day. At the meeting, Mike states that he has received an email from an alum reporting that Jason had a romantic sexual relationship with a former student and that Jason is friending alums through social media to groom them for sex. Jason is gutted by the accusation. He tells Mike that he has "never, ever had a relationship with a former student, and that it is against [his] personal code of conduct." With full transparency, Jason immediately offers his phone with his social media accounts and shows Mike the DM's he has had with alums. He points out that several alums got too personal, so he replied with polite but firm messages with clear boundaries. One alum asked Jason about interracial dating, to which he responded, "I can't be talking to you about relationships, so I am not going to." Mike emails the alum who made the complaint (through the anonymous account that the alum had created) to say that he and the school have taken the accusation seriously, conducted an investigation, and have found no wrongdoing. Mike also welcomes any additional information the person would like to report but never hears from them again. However, the issue is far from resolved for Jason emotionally and professionally. He seeks therapeutic support for how to maintain rapport with his students and continues to feel anxious about his demeanor and language. It takes months for Jason to regain his perspective and confidence, and he ultimately moves on to another school. (Independent School in San Francisco County, CA)

Situations like this one are complicated. Of course, school administrators must investigate allegations of sexual misconduct, and an investigative process for any educator is going to be a challenge and have an enormous impact. I've been included in investigations where the accused has been culpable and where the accused has been without fault. In one case, there was no infraction, but the accused's behavior was outside of the acceptable norm. Whatever the circumstances, process and outcome, how an investigation takes place reveals how much a school values cultures of consent and dignity.

Cultures of consent and dignity are proactive about policies and training for adults and students alike. Just because Jason's case was dismissed as over doesn't mean that the effect of it will be too. Will Mike follow up to check on Jason? Does Jason feel connected to another colleague or administrator who could provide a regular check-in to see how he's doing post-investigation? What are/were Jason's feelings and needs during and after the investigation? What will it take to restore his faith in his work with young people and the school?

Protective factors such as explicit policies about digital communication and citizenship are critical, especially among adults and students. There are school specific apps for texting with students, and schools need to be clear about the boundaries of when it is appropriate for an alum or a faculty member to friend and follow each other on social media platforms.

As schools catch up with the ways young people connect, communicate, and network through digital platforms, what safety measures need to be in place *before* a situation arises? If a school's development strategy includes reaching out to its young alums through social media, a culture of consent would mean sending out correspondence to let people know what to expect, how the procedure will be handled, and that teacher participants have been through training. The notice must be welcoming and grant the former student the choice to accept the connection, or not. The teachers tasked with the outreach need scripts and/or guidance for how to initiate that digital connection. Social media platforms are notorious for sexual innuendo and content, it is not a matter of if but when a teacher may encounter a student exchange that pushes the boundaries. Schools must provide teachers with language and scripts for how to respond accordingly. They need to have conversations about the what-ifs and clearly documented requests, expectations, and responsibilities. Teachers may consider creating their own paper trail.

This is particularly important given current statutes that limit integrated, inclusive, and diverse identities. Even lawyers have shared with me that they currently have a difficult time advising their teacher clients because definitions for what falls under the categories of "don't say gay" and "divisive anti-DEIJ" programming are so inconsistent. In Deja's case, described earlier, if she wants to pursue her complaint, it would be prudent to build a record and paper trail chronicling all conversations and interactions.

Expectations for behavior are clearly stated in handbooks; however, many of us know that students and parents rarely read through the extensive document that they sign and pledge accountability to. It's important to educate students on community norms regularly and underscore the values behind each guideline. To be clear, the onus of these community responsibilities doesn't fall on teachers alone, especially when contextualized within hierarchies of power and authority. Administrators must lead the way and walk their talk. In Jason's situation (the last scenario described above), the approach came across as too routine and lacked assurance for Jason as Mike verified his non-offence. And once the investigation was over, Mike didn't appear to consider the longer-term impact on Jason or offer support. How administrators care for others, including adults in schools, matters.

It was a great privilege to write this book. I had the humbling and inspiring opportunity to interview many educators from across the country. If there's one thing I've taken away from this experience, it is that what teachers do matters. Teaching continues to be challenging, and it certainly isn't getting any easier. As identified in the opening paragraph of this section, educators are increasingly expected to meet the growing needs and demands of young people, their families, and their communities, especially in light of the current political and systemic challenges to education. Despite feeling at times undermined, disrespected, taken for granted, and disheartened, teachers are resilient and show up to their jobs every day because they love, care about, and appreciate kids. The majority are in it to affect change for the better, *for all of us*. They believe in and are dedicated to their work of supporting the transformation of children's lives for the better.

I heard countless educators talk about how much they learn from their students—most have boundless compassion and respect for students who are dealing with unimaginable circumstances yet get themselves to school regularly. Many talked about how invested they are in professional development so that they may meet the complex needs of their students. Teachers spoke of being inspired by student resilience and strength—how students challenge teachers to practice empathy, patience, and stability. When I asked what's keeping them in a profession that is underpaid, underappreciated, and suffering from attrition, they talked about holding on to the investment they're making in the future, the reward of the students who express how they've made a difference, and the fulfillment that comes when a child sees themselves at their best in their teacher's eyes.

All of the above is true, and at the same time, burnout for educators is real. The phenomenal educators who contributed to this book wholeheartedly understand how a colleague would leave the profession; when asked what can help to stay in it, they shared their strategies. Many spoke of establishing clear boundaries so they can carve out time for themselves and, as a result, have more to give to their students. Schools are places that house tremendous need. It is easy to feel like we have to meet all of those needs at the expense of our own well-being. Boundaries with time, energy, and care are paramount. Seeking collaborative partnerships and relationships with colleagues was also consistently noted. Social connectedness in solidarity as educators was a huge lifeline for many folks. More student-centered pedagogical practices and collaborative advocacy for change led to feeling strength and support. It's also important to remember why we became teachers. I have a box with all of the notes students have written to me. Every now and then I'll pull it out and become nostalgic and restored. And finally, there *is joy-snacking*—a dear administrator friend of mine shared that, when her role as principal gets super challenging, she initiates silly banter with colleagues and goes to visit kindergarten. We are all nourished by joy—seek it out where it exists in your school and snack away.

Appendix B

Courageous Conversations

I am deeply indebted to the many students, parents, teachers, and administrators who so generously shared their time, stories, and wisdom with me during the many interviews that took place, so that I could write this book. The following scenarios are derived from these interviews, saved and presented as enrichment opportunities. Our learning for how to approach these conversations within education communities is endless. Here are mini case studies to inspire courageous and continued conversation with colleagues. So much of my perspective has been shaped by such discussions. Dialogue in which we wrestled, shared, listened, and got really curious with each other. It was during the most uncomfortable and challenging ones that we grew the most.

You may discuss these scenarios first and then read the book to see if what is shared here affirms or adds to your approach, or you may read the book first and then practice applying the information and suggestions offered and modeled. Whatever path you choose, please know that the folks who shared them are on this journey with you. We all are and appreciate how we share at least one thing in common: we care about education and kids.

K–2nd SCENARIO: Madison and Lucia are amongst a small group of first graders at lunch. Emmie is sharing about what she did for Easter: an Easter egg and candy hunt, Easter egg dying, and the details of her new bunny stuffy that was in her Easter basket. Lucia shares that she went to church and that during Sunday School, they had treats. Madison contributes, "I don't believe in God but get a basket anyway." After lunch, during quiet time, Lucia turns to Madison and audibly says, "You don't believe in God?" Madison replies, "Nope," to which Lucia responds, "How can you not believe in God?" Madison is annoyed and raises her voice to say, "I just don't, okay?" A few kids close by shush them, and you make your way over to see what's up. (Blaine County School District, ID)

K–2nd SCENARIO: Bret is in kindergarten and building a block tower during free-choice time. He started it yesterday. You helped him place a note in front of it that said, "please save," because he wasn't finished and wanted to see how high he could build it. He expressed excitement, because this was the tallest tower he has built, including when he works on them at home. Ryan is antsy and walks the classroom, indecisive about how he wants to spend his time. He is intrigued by Bret's tower and walks by a couple of times to size it up. His next time past, he walks up to the tower and swipes at it so that it comes crashing down and says, "Boom!" Bret is shocked for a moment and then furious and starts crying. (Santa Clara County Charter Schools, CA)

K–2nd SCENARIO: Every kindergarten class typically has a couple of students who often have one of their hands down their pants. When you notice this, you usually ask if they need to use the bathroom. In most cases, the child realizes what they're doing, mumbles a yes or no, and takes their hand out of their pants and moves on with their activity or takes a trip to the bathroom. Timmy has a difficult time with the indirect request and will typically say "nope" about using the bathroom, while continuing to keep one of his hands in his pants. A couple of other students have noticed and pointed it out. (New York City Public Schools, NY)

3rd–4th SCENARIO: You excuse your fourth-grade students for recess. You typically walk them out of the door as they transition down the hallway, but a student has lingered to ask about the work she missed while absent. After the class files out, you hear commotion coming from the open door. You swiftly get to the hallway, and a few students are standing over Jared and Milo, who are wrestling on the floor. Just as you arrive,

Milo pushes Jared off and says, “Get off of me, what are you, gay?” and Jared retorts, “Nah, but I know you are.” (Allegheny County School District, PA)

3rd–4th SCENARIO: You receive a phone call from a mom whose third-grade son is in your class. She found a note in her son’s backpack that she thinks is from a girl because of the quality of cursive and hearts drawn. The inscription says, “Will you be my boyfriend?” with two little XXs. The mom thinks her son is too young to be involved in romantic relationships and doesn’t want him to feel pressured to say yes. (Los Angeles County Unified School District, CA)

3rd–4th SCENARIO: You typically facilitate an art activity gift and card for Mother’s Day and Father’s Day during the Spring term. You receive an email towards the end of the Winter term. It’s your student Crystal’s mom, Gail. Gail and her wife, Jordan, anticipate that there may be gendered assignments for these holidays, so would like to give you a heads up that Crystal usually likes to create two Mother’s Day cards, and they provide the names of people in Crystal’s life who serve as father figures. You didn’t realize that Crystal has two moms and send a reply thanking Gail for the anticipatory information and guidance. You wonder if this will bring up questions in class about how it’s possible to have two moms and realize that you’re uncomfortable with even thinking about the possibility. (Middlesex County Public Schools, MA)

3rd–4th SCENARIO: A group of students in your third-grade class have taken to gendered games of tag during recess. It’s boys versus girls. It seems the tag is fun for all in the beginning, and then it devolves into an argument. You are on yard duty and see the contention between Olivia and Leroy. There is a small audience of kids, and they are taking sides. As you approach, Olivia says with intensity, “We don’t want to play tag—they keep chasing us.” Leroy quickly retorts, “You were still running and having a good time.” “No, we weren’t.” “Yes, you were! And unless you say, ‘time out,’ the game keeps going.” You interject, “Okay, hang on, let’s talk this out. We need a talking object so we can take turns.” Leroy is quick to pick up a rock and start, “Unless you say time out, the game keeps going. You kept running.” Your students are familiar with this talking structure, so Leroy passes the rock to Olivia. Olivia shares, "It doesn't matter, I was saying 'no, stop,' and you still kept chasing me." Without waiting for the rock, Leroy quickly retorts, "But you kept running!" Several other students who are gathered around jump in to support a side. (Whatcom County School District, WA)

3rd–4th SCENARIO: Third-grade students Rosa, Lashonda, Riley, and Noah are working together as a small group on Valentine's Day cards for some of the adults in their school that they appreciate. You are milling about the classroom to ensure students are on task. When you approach, you overhear Riley ask Noah, "Is teacher Davis a Ms. or Mrs.?" Noah replies, "She's a Mrs." Lashonda affirms this, and Riley says, "Oh yeah, then she must have a husband." Rosa chimes in, "My Auntie is married to a woman. Maybe she has a wife." Riley makes a scrunched-up face and says, "That's just weird." Rosa retorts, "No it's not!" Riley's gaze meets Rosa's intense look, and with a shrug of the shoulders, her focus goes back to writing down "Mrs. Davis." Rosa's look softens into sadness. (Long Beach Unified School District, CA)

3rd–4th SCENARIO: There is an all-gender game of tag going on during recess. Mariana gets aggressively focused on Danny and incites everyone to keep going after him. Danny quickly gets tired and slows down, so he keeps getting tagged and struggles to tag anyone back. Exasperated, he stops and says he isn't playing anymore. Mariana taunts him, "You can't give up, you're it. Quit being a baby." Other kids start laughing and taunting Danny, who is now quietly crying. A couple of the students pile on and call Danny a crybaby and a sissy. Kyle shouts to the other kids to "cut it out" and "leave him alone." Kyle walks in between Danny and the other kids and says, "Let's get to class" and walks with Danny to your classroom. (Long Beach Unified School District, CA)

5th–6th SCENARIO: As the district sexuality educator, you visit a classroom to provide puberty education to a group of fourth graders. After passing around an anonymous question box, you read aloud what students have asked and provide answers. You read the following: "I'm bi but can't come out to my friends because I'm afraid they won't accept me—what should I do?" Before you can form a response, Janelle speaks up, “Who is this person?” There are other nods and curious looks amongst the students. You answer, “This is anonymous, and we want to protect people’s privacy. It sounds like they may be feeling and dealing with a lot, so we don’t want to expose them.” Janelle follows with, “No, I want to know so I can be their friend.” There’s murmuring and several kids start jumping in with, “I’ll be their friend,” and “I will too,” and “yeah, me too.” (Suffolk County School District, MA)

5th–6th SCENARIO: You are about to start class, and the room is settling down. Suddenly, Becky whips around and, in a raised and frustrated voice, tells Sam to “cut it out!” Sam has a mischievous grin on his face as he sinks back down into his seat, and Becky says, “Sorry Mr. Howard,” and composes herself, but with a furrowed brow. During some small-group work, you discreetly ask Becky to stay after class. Becky reports that “some of the boys will surprise us—moan in a girl’s ear. You know, like they’re having sex.” (San Francisco County Independent School, CA)

5th–6th SCENARIO: You take roll at the beginning of class, and there is a gender nonbinary student you aren’t aware of. You call out their legal name, and they speak up to ask you to use their chosen preferred name, Avery, and share that they use they/them pronouns. Whispering and side conversations as well as giggling erupts. Another student blurts out, “What’s that mean? Are you gay?!” There is immediate laughter and “oh my God’s!” in response. The energy in the room is escalating. Avery’s face is hot, and their mouth is now turned down in a frown as they look down at the desk and sink further into their chair. Their eyes are welling up, and their arms are crossed. They look as though they want to leave, but they are seated without easy access out of the room. (St. Louis County Public Schools, MO)

7th –8th SCENARIO: You receive a call from a concerned parent. Their child, Callum, has been friends with Jimmy, another student in the class, throughout middle school, but recently, there has been a shift that is making Callum uncomfortable. Callum has reported to his parents on multiple occasions that Jimmy has become needy and clingy, that he isn’t picking up on Callum’s social cues to give him some space (he will try to move away from Callum or shrug him off, but Jimmy keeps moving towards him and touching him). Callum has also reported that Jimmy's parents have started to say negative things about Callum. Callum feels Jimmy has become overwhelmingly possessive and tries to isolate him from other friendships. Jimmy will say things like, "If you don't do 'x' with me, then I'm not going to be your friend and neither will anyone else." Jimmy has also told Callum that Jimmy's mom has said that "Callum is a horrible friend if he won't play with you—what an awful kid." (Maricopa Unified School District, AZ)

7th–8th SCENARIO: You dismiss your class and notice that Trey is looking distressed. You request he check in and observe "that [he] didn't participate as much as usual" and wonder if there's anything going on. Trey's gaze is fixed on the ground, and he is shifting his weight back and forth, lightly kicking the leg of a desk. After some thought, he shares that "someone just wrote something about me on the bathroom wall. It's no big deal, though. It's just that someone took a picture, and now everyone's looking at it and talking about it." Trey forces a smile, looks up at you and says, "I'm good though—it's all good—I gotta get to class." You have a free period so survey the bathrooms and find this scrawled on the bathroom wall: "Trey has a micro-dick" along with a drawing of a tiny phallus. (San Francisco County Independent School, CA)

7th–8th SCENARIO: You and the other seventh-grade teachers organize an outdoor field trip that includes service learning in a national park on a Friday. The class will be working to weed out invasive species and restore native plants. Students are divided into small groups of four. You oversee three groups of four. Connor's group seems to be getting along particularly well and having a wonderful time. When you are all together again Monday morning, you have a debrief session where students are expected to share about their experience. Connor expresses that "it was horrible. [He] hated it and never wants to do something like that again." After the debrief, you meet with Connor one on one. You express curiosity, because on Friday he seemed to have so much fun, and then on Monday he said he didn't. You ask what changed. Connor shares that he was disappointed to not be in the same small group as Brit (one of his best friends). When one of his other friends, Jake, saw his disappointment and asked why he was so bummed, he "stupidly" shared that "no one understands that I'm totally in love with her" and swore his confidant to secrecy. Over the weekend, Jake spread the word and "everyone was talking about it. Jake ruined my whole experience." (Los Angeles County Independent School, CA)

7th–8th SCENARIO: Two of your students, Maia and Aliyah, are escorted by the playground monitor back to your classroom after recess when they should be at Music Class. She reports that she observed the two students physically fighting on the yard, and a ring of students gathered around them chanting, "FIGHT! FIGHT! FIGHT!" Principal Tanaka has requested they wait with you until he is done with his meeting. The girls are anxious and eager to talk to you. After the monitor leaves, they launch into their account. They swear that they were play fighting. They thought it would be funny to brawl and see if anyone noticed and believed if it was real. When you ask how they started it, they sheepishly state that they started yelling at each other. When you request specifics, they share phrases like "Hey, Bitch" and "Fuck you, Ho." They reveal more about how they were actually "cat fighting" and going for each other's hair and shoving (but not so that it really hurt—[they] were careful). When you inquire about their inspiration, they reference an Instagram reel. (Hawai'i County Public Schools, HI)

9th–10th SCENARIO: You teach Science and are the dorm parent on duty, signing students in for interdorm visitation. Eleventh-grade boy, Logan, is approaching with a tenth-grade girl, Jaylin, and there is a flirtatious dynamic between the two. Logan is in your class and missing several assignments that you discussed with him earlier that day. He committed to working on the assignments that evening but is obviously socializing instead. He and Jaylin step up to the table to check in. (Independent School, Windham County, VT)

9th–10th SCENARIO: You're driving a school van to a sports team competition and hear several students on their phones talking about the "Who's Hot and Who's Not" list in the back. You hear two boys say, "She's an eight out of ten. She has a nice rack and a nice ass, but her face isn't so nice, but that's what paper bags are for." And then a girl says, "Why is

Gloria on the list? She's flat as a board." And another girl says in a quieter voice, "Hey Jen, you're number three. I thought you were top of the list. WTF?" (San Francisco Unified School District, San Francisco County, CA)

9th–10th SCENARIO: A tenth-grade girl, Kaylah, emails you to discuss the math class she takes from you. When the time comes and she enters your office, another student in the class, Maria, is with her. They are holding hands as they enter, ask if they can close the door, which you agree to, and then take a seat on the couch across from you. You greet them and ask, "What's up?" with a curious look. Maria looks at Kaylah who nods in response. Maria then shares that she "had a really awful experience" with a boy who is in the same class. It's really uncomfortable for her, and she would like to request that she not be assigned to any partnered or small-group work with him. (Independent School, San Francisco County, CA)

9th–10th SCENARIO: You're a dorm parent and hear some laughter and commotion in the Commons as you walk the hall between classes and the beginning of afternoon activities. You walk in to find several girls clustered. You say, "Hey, what's going on?" and they immediately come to attention. One is smiling, one is wide-eyed looking down at the floor. Another composes herself and says, "Oh nothing we're just getting ready to go," and they quickly move by you and disperse towards their rooms to change. You scan the room, and everything seems to be fine, until you see a "hottest teacher" list on the white board. There seems to be some fresh pen representing the new, young, single English teacher and soccer coach. (Independent School, Arlington County, VA)

11th–12th SCENARIO: You are in your dorm parent apartment and overhear a conversation that is traveling the hall. It sounds like several Senior girls having a good time hanging out in someone's room. There seems to be a couple of students playfully teasing another about the freshman "project" she has going on. You hear the name of a ninth-grade boy. You've seen him on campus. He is getting a lot of attention because he is tall and, from what you can tell, considered "hot" but has no clue. Word is that he is an excellent basketball player and should make varsity.

Apparently one of the girls is "showing him what's up." (Independent School, Ventura County, CA)

11th–12th SCENARIO: There are several students talking outside your office. Your door is open just a crack and your blinds are closed because you made a private phone call. It doesn't look like you're there. You can vaguely hear a conversation that's happening in hushed voices: Bella, Sophie, and David are talking about Nelly and the weekend. She got really drunk and hooked up with someone. The rumor is that she regrets it and is alluding to being "taken advantage of." David says, "I don't believe it. She's always looking to hook up." Bella says, "Tell me about it. Next time someone should get pics and post. That'll wake her up." Another friend, Vic, says, "Wouldn't be hard, there's sure to be someone on her radar again soon." (Palo Alto Unified School District, Palo Alto, CA).

11th–12th SCENARIO: You've just finished teaching your eleventh/twelfth Math class and are walking the hallway to make copies in the faculty lounge. The hallways are typically packed during the passing period, so you move along the wall to avoid crowds. As you come up on a small group of eleventh-grade boys, you hear laughter drift up from the center, and someone audibly says, "Damn, that girl's head game is fire." Another shouts, "Throat G.O.A.T.!" before one of the boys facing the hallway inadvertently makes eye contact and elbows the kid, Pete, who said it. All the boys look, see you close by, put their heads down while snickering. Pete says, "Oh shit" while scrambling to pick up his backpack to leave. (Berkeley Unified School District, Alameda County, CA)

Appendix C

Resources

Guidelines for CSE across K–12th grades:

Sexuality Information and Education Council for the United States (SIECUS) National Sex Education Standards

Evidence-based Approaches to Sexuality Education: A Global Perspective edited by James J. Ponzetti, Jr.

Teaching About Sexuality and HIV: Principles and Methods for Effective Education by Evonne Hedgepeth and Joan Helmich

Health and Sexuality Education Curricula, Programming, and Training:

Advocates for Youth

Alabama Campaign for Adolescent Sexual Health

Amaze

Amplify Youth Health Collective (Oklahoma)

Answer: Sex Ed, Honestly

Common Sense Media: Digital Literacy and Well-Being Curriculum

Education Training Research (ETR or etr.)

Ever Forward Club

EyesOpenIowa

Health Connected

Healthy Teen Network

Futures Without Violence: Coaching Boys to Men

Girls Leadership

Less Awkward

Making Caring Common Project

Our Whole Lives (OWL)

Outspoken Sex Ed

Re-Set School

RULER: Social and Emotional Learning

The Representation Project

The Sex Education Collaborative

Teen Health Mississippi

Trailhead Institute

Unhushed

Sexuality Information Resources:

BISH (UK)

Guerrilla Sex Ed

Outspoken Sex Ed

Planned Parenthood

Scarleteen

Sex, etc. (.org)

Strategic Questioning by Fran Peavey

Talk About Sex (sponsored by SIECUS)

Teen Health Today Newsletter by Christopher Pepper

Sexuality Diversity in Schools:

Boston Alliance of LGBTQ+ Youth (BAGLY)

Communities United Against Violence

Gender Spectrum (.org)

GLSEN Changing the Game; Sports Project

Lavender Education

National Center for Lesbian Rights: It Takes a Team!

National Center for Transgender Equality

Re-Set School

Safe Schools Coalition

Transgender Child and Youth: Understanding the Basics

Transgender Training Institute

Bodies:

The Body Positive (.org)

The Body Project by National Eating Disorders Association (NEDA)

Sexual Violence Prevention Resources:

A Call to Men (.org)

Center for Changing Campus Culture

End Rape on Campus (EROC)

I Have the Right To (.org)

It's On Us (.org)

One Love Foundation

Know Your IX (Advocates for Youth)

Learning Courage (.org)

National Sexual Violence Resource Center

National Women's Law Center

Nest Foundation

Promoting Awareness Victim Empowerment (PAVE)

Equimundo (Healthy Masculinity Gender Equality)

Rape, Abuse & Incest National Network (RAINN)

Safe Bae

Restorative Justice Resources:

Impact Justice Restorative Justice Project

National Center for Restorative Justice

The Ahimsa Collective

Zehr Institute for Restorative Justice

Individual Consultants and Advisors:

Elissa Asch (Consent Wise)

Shelly Bar, M.D. (Eating Disorders)

Kelly Bhatnagar, Ph.D., FAED (Wellness, Eating Disorders)

Ashanti Branch (Healthy Communities, Masculinity)

Jennifer Bryan Ph.D. (Centering Well-being, Gender, and Sexuality Diversity)

Jessica Colvin, MSW, MPH, PPSC (Wellness programs and centers at SWELL)

Charis Dennison (Health Educator)

Sarah Huss (Health Educator, CoMethod)

Cait Kamins (Health Educator, CoMethod)

Amy Killy LCSW, LICSW, LCSW-C (Psychologist at Weaver and Associates)

Christopher Pepper (Health Educator)

Deborah Roffman (Sexuality Educator)

Elizabeth Scott, LCSW, CDES-S (Embodiment, Eating Disorders)

Nadine Thornhill Ed.D. (Sexuality Educator)

Kimm Topping Ed.M. (LGBTQ+ Educator, Historian, Artist)

Rosalind Weissman (Living with Dignity)

Fiona Zecca M.A. (Early Childhood Development and Behavior Specialist)

Podcasts for All Caretaking Adults:

Ask Lisa: The Psychology of Parenting

NAIS podcasts

Peace at Home Parenting podcast

Raising Good Humans

This Is So Awkward

The Longest Shortest Time

Books for All Caretaking Adults:

10 to 25: The Science of Motivating Young People by David Yeager, Ph.D.

A Guide to Gender: The Social Justice Advocate's Handbook by Sam Killermann

Ace: What Asexuality Reveals About Desire, Society, and the Meaning of Sex by Angela Chen

All About Love: New Visions by bell hooks

Always My Child: A Parent's Guide to Understanding Your Gay, Lesbian, Bisexual, Transgendered, or Questioning Son or Daughter by Kevin Jennings

American Hookup: The New Culture of Sex on Campus by Lisa Wade

Atlas of the Heart: Mapping Meaningful Connection and the Language of Human Experience by Brené Brown Ph.D., MSW

Becoming Cliterate: Why Orgasm Equality Matters—and How to Get It by Laurie Mintz, Ph.D.

Boys & Sex: Young Men on Hookups, Love, Porn, Consent, and Navigating the New Masculinity by Peggy Orenstein

Come As You Are by Emily Nagoski Ph.D.

For Goodness Sex: Changing the Way We Talk to Teens About Sexuality, Values, and Health by Al Vernacchio

From Diapers to Dating: A Parent's Guide to Raising Sexually Healthy Children—from Infancy to Middle School by Reverend Debra W. Haffner

From the Dress-Up Corner to the Senior Prom: Navigating Gender and Sexuality Diversity in Pre-K–12 Schools by Jennifer Bryan, Ph.D.

Generation Queer: Stories of Youth, Organizers, Artists, and Educators by Kimm Topping, Ed.M.

Girls on the Brink: Helping Our Daughters Thrive in an Era of Increased Anxiety, Depression, and Social Media by Donna Jackson Nakazawa

Girls & Sex: Navigating the Complicated New Landscape by Peggy Orenstein

Masterminds and Wingmen: Helping Our Boys Cope with Schoolyard Power, Locker-Room Tests, and the New Rules of Boy World by Rosalind Wiseman

Middle School Matters: The 10 Key Skills Kids Need to Thrive in Middle School and Beyond—and How Parents Can Help by Phyllis L. Fagell, LCPC

Never Enough: When Achievement Culture Becomes Toxic—and What We Can Do About It by Jennifer Breheny Wallace

Permission to Feel: Unlocking the Power of Emotions to Help Our Kids, Ourselves, and Our Society Thrive by Marc Brackett, Ph.D.

Pornography and Public Health by Emily Rothman

Queen Bees and Wannabes: Helping Your Daughter Survive Cliques, Gossip, Boys, and the New Realities of Girl World 3rd ed. by Rosalind Wiseman

Sex, College and, Social Media: A Commonsense Guide to Navigating Hookup Culture by Cindy Pierce

Sex Ed for the Stroller Set by Karen Rayne and Laura Hancock

Sex Positive Talks to Have with Kids: A Guide to Raising Healthy, Informed, Empowered Young People by Melissa Pinto Carnagey, LBSW

Sexploitation: Helping Kids Develop Healthy Sexuality in a Porn-Driven World by Cindy Pierce

Sexual Citizens: A Landmark Study of Sex, Power, and Assault on Campus by Jennifer S. Hirsch and Shamus Khan

Strange Bedfellows: Adventures in the Science, History, and Surprising Secrets of STDs by Ina Park M.D., M.S.

Talk to Me First: Everything You Need to Know to Become Your Kids' "Go-To" Person About Sex by Deborah Roffman

Talk to Your Boys: 16 Conversations to Help Tweens and Teens Grow into Confident, Caring Young Men by Christopher Pepper and Joanna Schroeder

Teaching When the World is on Fire edited by Lisa Delpit

The Body is Not an Apology: The Power of Radical Self-Love by Sonya Renee Taylor

The Body Keeps the Score: Brain, Mind, and Body in the Healing of Trauma by Bessel Van Der Kolk, M.D.

The Emotional Lives of Teenagers: Raising Connected, Capable, and Compassionate Adolescents by Lisa Damour

The New Puberty: How to Navigate Early Development in Today's Girls by Louise Greenspan, M.D. & Julianna Deardorff, Ph.D.

The Parents We Mean to Be: How Well-Intentioned Adults Undermine Children's Moral and Emotional Development by Richard Weissbourd

The Transgender Child by Stephanie Brill and Rachel Pepper

This Is So Awkward by Cara Natterson M.D. and Vanessa Kroll Bennett

To Raise a Boy: Classrooms, Locker Rooms, Bedrooms, and the Hidden Struggles of American Boyhood by Emma Brown

Under Pressure: Confronting the Epidemic of Stress and Anxiety in Girls by Lisa Damour, Ph.D.

UnSelfie: Why Empathetic Kids Succeed in Our All-About-Me World by Michelle Borba, Ed.D.

Untangled: Guiding Teenage Girls Through the Seven into Adulthood by Lisa Damour, Ph.D.

Yes, Your Kid: What Parents Need to Know About Today's Teens and Sex by Debby Herbenick, Ph.D.

You Are Your Best Thing: Vulnerability, Shame Resilience, And the Black Experience edited by Tarana Burke and Brené Brown

Books for Educators:

Adolescents at School: Perspectives on Youth, Identity, and Education edited by Michael Sadowski

Belonging and Becoming: The Power of Social and Emotional Learning in High Schools by Barbara Cervone and Kathleen Cushman

Bullying and Cyberbullying: What Every Educator Needs to Know by Elizabeth Kandel Englander

Care Work: Dreaming Disability Justice by Leah Lakshmi Piepzna-Samarasinha

Culturally Relevant Pedagogy: Asking a Different Question by Gloria Ladson-Billings

Culturally Responsive Teaching: Theory, Research, and Practice by Geneva Gay

Emotional Intelligence for School Leaders by Janet Patti and Robin Stern

Families with Power: Centering Students by Engaging with Families and Community by Mary Cowhey

Justice on Both Sides by Maisha T. Winn

Language, Culture, and Teaching: Critical Perspectives by Sonia Nieto

Learning While Black and Queer: Understanding the Educational Experiences of Black LGBTQ+ Youth by Ed Brockenbrough

LGBTQ Youth and Education: Policies and Practices, 2nd ed. by Chris Mayo

Owning Up: Empowering Adolescents to Create Cultures of Dignity and Confront Social Cruelty and Injustice by Rosalind Wisemen

Respect by Sara Lawrence-Lightfoot

Safe is Not Enough: Better Schools for LGBTQ Students by Michael Sadowski

Sex Ed for Caring Schools: Creating an Ethics-Based Curriculum by Sharon Lamb

Sexuality Education Wheel of Context: A Guide for Sexuality Educators, Advocates, and Researchers by Dr. Sara Nasserzadeh and Dr. Pejman Azarmina

Sexuality and Relationship Education for Children and Adolescents with Autism Spectrum Disorders by Davida Hartman

The Facts of Life and More: Sexuality and Intimacy for People with Intellectual Disabilities by Leslie Walker-Hirsch

Trans Studies in K–12 Education: Creating an Agenda for Research and Practice by Mario I. Suárez and Melinda M. Mangin

Notes

Chapter 1

1. D. Kirby, *Emerging Answers 2007: Research Findings on Programs to Reduce Teen Pregnancy and Sexually Transmitted Diseases* (The National Campaign to Prevent Teen and Unplanned Pregnancy, 2007), 4, http://www.thenationalcampaign.org/EA2007/EA2007_full.pdf.
2. "United Nations Population Fund (UNFPA)," *International Technical Guidance on Sexuality Education: An Evidence-Informed Approach* (UNESCO, 2018), https://www.unfpa.org/sites/default/files/pub-pdf/ITGSE.pdf.
3. Carol Cassell Hedgepeth and John A. Helmich, *Teaching Responsibility: Sex Education and the Responsible Behavior Curriculum* (ETR Associates, 1996), 2.
4. Sexuality Information and Education Council of the United States (SIECUS), *Guidelines for Comprehensive Sexuality Education: Kindergarten–12th Grade*, 3rd ed. (SIECUS, 2004).
5. Marla E. Eisenberg, Dana H. Bernat, Linda H. Bearinger, and Michael D. Resnick, "Support for Comprehensive Sexuality Education: Perspectives from Parents of School-Age Youth," *Journal of Adolescent Health* 42, no. 4 (2008): 352–59, https://doi.org/10.1016/j.jadohealth.2007.09.019.
6. Eisenberg et al., "Support for Comprehensive Sexuality Education."
7. American Academy of Pediatrics, "The Importance of Access to Comprehensive Sex Education," 2023, https://www.aap.org/en/patient-care/sexuality-education/resources/the-importance-of-access-to-comprehensive-sex-education/.
8. Sexuality Information and Education Council of the United States (SIECUS), *On Our Side: Public Support for Sex Education* (SIECUS, 2017), https://siecus.org/wp-content/uploads/2018/07/On-Our-Side-Final-Web.pdf.
9. "Review of Key Findings of 'Emerging Answers 2007' Report on Sex Education Programs," Advocates for Youth, 2007, https://www.advocatesforyouth.org/resources/health-information/review-of-key-findings-of-emerging-answers-2007-report-on-sex-education-programs/.

10. UNESCO, *International Framework for Sexuality Education: International Technical Guidance* (Paris: UNESCO, 2015), 9, https://unesdoc.unesco.org/ark:/48223/pf0000234806.
11. E. Yankah and P. Aggleton, "The Manufacture of Consensus: The Development of United Nations Technical Guidance on Sexuality Education," in *The Palgrave Handbook of Sexuality Education*, ed. L. Allen and M. L. Rasmussen (Palgrave Macmillan, 2017), https://doi.org/10.1057/978-1-137-40033-8_3.
12. Yankah and Aggleton, "The Manufacture of Consensus," 27.
13. Guttmacher Institute, "Adolescent Pregnancy and Its Outcomes Across Countries," August 2015, https://www.guttmacher.org/fact-sheet/adolescent-pregnancy-and-its-outcomes-across-countries.
14. Karin K. Coyle, Patricia M. Anderson, and Barbara A. Laris, "School-Based Sex Education and HIV Prevention," in *Adolescent Sexual Development, Sexual Behavior,* and *Sexual Health*, ed. Lynn T. Warner and Bradley R. Entner Wright (Praeger, 2015), 147.
15. Charles H. Cooley, *Human Nature and the Social Order* (Scribner's, 1922).
16. Beverly Daniel Tatum, *Why Are All the Black Kids Sitting Together in the Cafeteria? and Other Conversations About Race*, revised edition (Basic Books, 2017), 19.
17. Tatum, *Why Are All the Black Kids Sitting Together*, 7.
18. Bobbie Harro, "The Cycle of Socialization," in *Readings for Diversity and Social Justice*, 4th ed., ed. Maurianne Adams et al. (Routledge, 2018).
19. Deborah Roffman, *Talk to Me First: Everything You Need to Know to Become Your Kids' "Go-To" Person about Sex* (Da Capo Lifelong Books, 2012), 7.
20. Hedgepeth and Helmich, *Teaching Responsibility*, 62.
21. Hedgepeth and Helmich, *Teaching Responsibility*, 37.
22. Marla E. Eisenberg et al., "Support for Comprehensive Sexuality Education and Adolescent Access to Condoms and Contraceptives: An American Public Opinion Study," *Journal of Adolescent Health* 70, no. 3 (2022): 486–493, https://doi.org/10.1016/j.jadohealth.2021.10.018.
23. Eisenberg et al., "Support for Comprehensive Sexuality Education," 2008.
24. Leslie M. Kantor and Nora J. Levitz, "Parents' Attitudes and Beliefs about Sex Education in Schools," (Planned Parenthood, September 2017), 2, https://www.plannedparenthood.org/uploads/filer_public/80/ae/80ae978d-83a7-4087-828c-bae68befb409/2017-parents-sex-ed-survey-results.pdf.
25. Elizabeth Bowlsby, "Strategies for Communicating with Parents about Sexuality Education," in *The Sex Education Debates*, Advocates for Youth, 2023.
26. Hedgepeth and Helmich, *Teaching Responsibility*, 85.
27. Debra Hauser, *A Guide to Implementing Sex Education Programs: Executive Summary* (Advocates for Youth, 2017).
28. Hauser, *A Guide to Implementing Sex Education Programs.*
29. Hedgepeth and Helmich, *Teaching Responsibility*, 110.
30. Jennifer Bryan, *From the Dress-Up Corner to the Senior Prom: Navigating Gender and Sexuality Diversity in PreK–12 Schools* (Rowman & Littlefield Publishers, 2012), xxi.
31. Cara Natterson and Vanessa Kroll Bennett, *The Puberty Podcast Presents: This Is So Awkward* (Rodale Books, 2023), 285.
32. Stephanie Brill and Rachel Pepper, *The Transgender Child: A Handbook for Families and Professionals* (Cleis Press, 2008).

33. Kate Bornstein, *My New Gender Workbook: A Step-by-Step Guide to Achieving World Peace Through Gender Anarchy and Sex Positivity*, 2023 ed. (Routledge, 2023).
34. Michael Sadowski, *Safe is Not Enough: Better Schools for LGBTQ Students* (Harvard Education Press, 2016), 13.
35. Sadowski, *Safe is Not Enough*, 15.
36. Marc Brackett, *Permission to Feel: The Power of Emotional Intelligence to Achieve Well-Being and Success*, (Celadon Books, 2019), 11.
37. Kathleen A. Ethier, "Girls, LGBTQ Youth Face Historic Levels of Violence, Suicide Risk in CDC Survey," CDC Newsroom, February 13, 2023, https://www.cdc.gov/media/releases/2023/p0213-yrbs.html.
38. Brackett, *Permission to Feel*, 19.
39. Centers for Disease Control and Prevention (CDC), "Social Connection," last reviewed March 3, 2023, https://www.cdc.gov/social-connection/index.html.
40. Robert Waldinger and Marc Schulz, *The Good Life: Lessons from the World's Longest Scientific Study of Happiness* (Simon & Schuster, 2023).
41. Irvin Scott, "2024 Convocation Address, Harvard Graduate School of Education," delivered at Harvard University, Cambridge, MA, May 22, 2024.
42. American Academy of Pediatrics, "10 Tips for Parents to Teach Children about Body Safety and Boundaries," HealthyChildren.org, 2023, https://www.healthychildren.org/English/safety-prevention/at-home/Pages/Tips-for-Teaching-Children-Body-Safety.aspx.
43. H. B. Chin et al., "The Effectiveness of Group-Based Comprehensive Risk-Reduction and Abstinence Education Interventions to Prevent or Reduce the Risk of Adolescent Pregnancy, Human Immunodeficiency Virus, and Sexually Transmitted Infections: Two Systematic Reviews for the Guide to Community Preventive Services," *American Journal of Preventive Medicine* 42, no. 3 (2012): 272–294, https://doi.org/10.1016/j.amepre.2011.11.006.
44. John S. Santelli et al., "Evidence-Based Approaches to Adolescent Sexual and Reproductive Health Education: Updated American Position Paper," *Journal of Adolescent Health* 62, no. 5 (2018): 595–598, https://doi.org/10.1016/j.jadohealth.2018.03.001.
45. Hedgepeth and Helmich, *Teaching Responsibility*, 83.
46. Geneva Gay, *Culturally Responsive Teaching: Theory, Research, and Practice*, 3rd ed., (New York: Teachers College Press), 2018.
47. Gay, *Culturally Responsive Teaching.*
48. Gay, *Culturally Responsive Teaching.*
49. Gay, *Culturally Responsive Teaching.*
50. Maisha T. Winn, *Justice on Both Sides: Transforming Education through Restorative Justice* (Harvard Education Press, 2018).
51. Winn, *Justice on Both Sides.*

Chapter 2

1. Shari L. Dworkin and Alina Martyniuk, *A Framework for Sexuality Education Across the Lifespan* (United Nations Development Programme, 2011), 3.
2. Damon E. Jones, Mark Greenberg, and Max Crowley, "Early Social-Emotional Functioning and Public Health: The Relationship Between Kindergarten Social Competence and Future Wellness," *American Journal of Public Health* 105, no. 11 (2015): 2283–2290, https://doi.org/10.2105/AJPH.2015.302630, 105.

3. Rebecca D. Taylor et al., "Promoting Positive Youth Development Through School-Based Social and Emotional Learning Interventions: A Meta-Analysis of Follow-Up Effects," *Child Development* 88, no. 4 (2017): 1156–1171, https://doi.org/10.1111/cdev.12864.
4. Celene E. Domitrovich et al., "Promoting Social and Emotional Competencies in Elementary and Middle School Students: The Impact of the Social and Emotional Learning Program," *American Journal of Community Psychology* 60, no. 3-4 (2017): 386–403, https://doi.org/10.1002/ajcp.12190.
5. Christina Cipriano et al., "The State of Evidence for Social and Emotional Learning: A Contemporary Meta-Analysis of Universal School-Based SEL Interventions," *Child Development* 94, no. 5 (2023): 1181–1204, https://doi.org/10.1111/cdev.13968, 31.
6. Cipriano et al., "State of Evidence for Social and Emotional Learning," 32.
7. Cipriano et al., "State of Evidence for Social and Emotional Learning," 34.
8. Ellen Frans, *International Technical Guidance on Sexuality Education: Review of Evidence and Experience* (UNESCO, 2015), 53.
9. Deborah Roffman, *Talk to Me First: Everything You Need to Know to Become Your Kids' "Go-To" Person about Sex*, (Hachette Book Group, 2012), 76.
10. Roffman, *Talk to Me First*, 19.
11. "Characteristics of Primary Learners," Teaching Strategies, accessed April 22, 2024, https://teachingstrategies.com/blog/characteristics-of-primary-learners/.
12. SIECUS, *Sex Education Collaborative, National Sex Education Standards: Core Content and Skills, K–12*, 2nd ed. (SIECUS, 2020), https://siecus.org/wp-content/uploads/2020/03/NSES-2020-web-updated-1.pdf.
13. "Characteristics of Primary Learners."
14. "Characteristics of Primary Learners."
15. Hallie Martyniuk and Emily Dworkin, "Child Sexual Abuse Prevention: Programs for Children," National Sexual Violence Resource Center, 2011, https://www.nsvrc.org/sites/default/files/Publications_NSVRC_Guide_Child-Sexual-Abuse-Prevention-programs-for-children.pdf.
16. Sandy K. Wurtele, Melissa Melzer, and Lindsay C. Kast, "Teaching Preschoolers to be Smart About Avoiding and Reporting Touching Problems," *Journal of Child Sexual Abuse* 24, no. 8 (2015): 873–890, https://doi.org/10.1080/10538712.2015.1091092.
17. Martyniuk and Dworkin, "Child Sexual Abuse Prevention."
18. Martyniuk and Dworkin, "Child Sexual Abuse Prevention."
19. Roffman, *Talk to Me First*, 67.
20. Julie M. Alleva et al., "Body Image Education: A Review and Future Directions," *Body Image* 26 (2018): 131–139, https://doi.org/10.1016/j.bodyim.2018.07.004.
21. Debra Haffner, *From Diapers to Dating: A Parent's Guide to Raising Sexually Healthy Children* (Beacon Press, 2004), 92.
22. Roffman, *Talk to Me First*, 109.
23. Roffman, *Talk to Me First*, 108–13.
24. Jennifer Bryan, *From the Dress-Up Corner to the Senior Prom: Navigating Gender and Sexuality Diversity in PreK–12 Schools* (Rowman & Littlefield Publishers, 2012), 7.
25. Catherine S. Tamis-LeMonda, "Gender in Early Childhood," in *Handbook of Parenting: Volume 1: Children and Parenting*, 3rd ed., ed. Marc H. Bornstein (Routledge, 2021), 516–20.
26. Bryan, *From the Dress-Up Corner to the Senior Prom*,160.

27. Richard Weissbourd, *The Parents We Mean to Be: How Well-Intentioned Adults Undermine Children's Moral and Emotional Development* (Houghton Mifflin Harcourt, 2009), 11.
28. Marc Brackett, *Permission to Feel: The Power of Emotional Intelligence to Achieve Well-Being and Success*, (Celadon Books, 2019), 30.
29. Brackett, *Permission to Feel*, 11.
30. Carol Cassell Hedgepeth and John A. Helmich, *Teaching Responsibility: Sex Education and the Responsible Behavior Curriculum* (ETR Associates, 1996), 41–43.
31. Weissbourd, *The Parents We Mean to Be*, 27.
32. Howard Kirschenbaum, *Values and Ethics in School Counseling*, 2nd ed. (American School Counselor Association, 2013), 189.
33. John J. Ratey, *A User's Guide to the Brain: Perception, Attention, and the Four Theaters of the Brain* (Pantheon Books, 2001), 247.
34. Michael Riera and Joseph Di Prisco, *Uncommon Sense for Parents with Teenagers* (Perigee Book, 2002), 172.
35. Weissbourd, *The Parents We Mean to Be*, 6.
36. Michael Thompson and Catherine O'Neill-Grace, *Best Friends, Worst Enemies: Understanding the Social Lives of Children*, (Ballantine Books, 2001), 8.
37. Thompson and O'Neill-Grace, *Best Friends, Worst Enemies*, 10.
38. Thompson and O'Neill-Grace, *Best Friends, Worst Enemies*, 12.
39. Thompson and O'Neill-Grace, *Best Friends, Worst Enemies*, 40.
40. "Characteristics of Primary Learners."
41. Doug Zesiger, "Stinky Tales," https://www.stinkytales.com.
42. "Characteristics of Primary Learners."
43. Thompson and O'Neill-Grace, *Best Friends, Worst Enemies*, 38.
44. Roffman, *Talk to Me First*.
45. Roffman, *Talk to Me First*, 85.
46. Edward M. Hallowell, *The Childhood Roots of Adult Happiness: Five Steps to Help Kids Create and Sustain Lifelong Joy* (Ballantine Books, 2001), xii.
47. Hallowell, *The Childhood Roots of Adult Happiness*, 9.
48. Melissa E. Hancock and Kelly Rayne, *Understanding and Responding to Problematic Sexual Behavior in Children: A Guide for Parents, Teachers, and Professionals* (Jessica Kingsley Publishers, 2023), 118.
49. Christina E. Andrea et al., "Evaluation of the Stewards of Children Program for Child Sexual Abuse Prevention and Response," *Child Abuse & Neglect* 34, no. 11 (2010): 865–875, https://doi.org/10.1016/j.chiabu.2010.06.003.
50. Elizabeth Townsend, *Child Sexual Abuse: Information for Parents and Caregivers* (Darkness to Light, 2016).
51. Hancock and Rayne, *Understanding and Responding to Problematic Sexual Behavior in Children*.
52. Cory Silverberg, *Sex Is a Funny Word: A Book about Bodies, Feelings, and YOU* (Triangle Square, 2015).
53. Silverberg, *Sex Is a Funny Word*, 97.
54. Silverberg, *Sex Is a Funny Word*, 110.
55. Hancock and Rayne, *Understanding and Responding to Problematic Sexual Behavior in Children*, 109.

56. Hancock and Rayne, *Understanding and Responding to Problematic Sexual Behavior in Children,* 117–18.

Chapter 3

1. Kathleen M. Myers and Linda C. Mayes, *A Practical Guide to Child and Adolescent Psychiatry for Pediatrics and Primary Care* (WashingtAmerican Psychiatric Association Publishing, 2023), 13–14.
2. Oksana Sopher, "The Science of Puberty: What Educators (and Parents) Need to Know," *Edutopia*, 2023, https://www.edutopia.org/article/science-puberty-educators-parents.
3. Sopher, "The Science of Puberty."
4. Sopher, "The Science of Puberty."
5. Sopher, "The Science of Puberty."
6. Louise Greenspan and Julie Deardorff, *The New Puberty: How to Navigate Early Development in Today's Girls* (Rodale, 2015), 67–9.
7. Sydney de Jesus, "Period Poverty: 1 in 5 American Girls Miss School Due to Lack of Access to Period Products," *Healthline*, February 6, 2024, https://www.healthline.com/health-news/period-poverty-american-girls-school.
8. Marc Brackett, *Permission to Feel: Unlocking the Power of Emotions to Help Our Kids, Ourselves, and Our Society Thrive* (Celadon Books, 2019), 105.
9. David C. Lewis et al., "LGBTQ+ Youth: Promoting Well-Being and Affirmation in Families, Schools, and Communities," *Annual Review of Clinical Psychology* 15 (2019): 465–487, https://doi.org/10.1146/annurev-clinpsy-050718-095435, 861.
10. Michael Sadowski, *Safe is Not Enough: Better Schools for LGBTQ Students* (Harvard Education Press, 2016), 81.
11. Sadowski, *Safe is not Enough*, 94.
12. Sadowski, *Safe is not Enough*, 42.
13. Catherine M. Clark, Joseph G. Kosciw, and Eva M. Hurley, *The 2021 National School Climate Survey: The Experiences of Lesbian, Gay, Bisexual, Transgender, and Queer Youth in Our Nation's Schools* (New York: GLSEN, 2022), 73.
14. Catherine S. Tamis-LeMonda, "Gender in Early Childhood," in *Handbook of Parenting: Volume 1: Children and Parenting*, 3rd ed., ed. Marc H. Bornstein (Routledge, 2021), 504.
15. Tamis-LeMonda, "Gender in Early Childhood," 506.
16. Tamis-LeMonda, "Gender in Early Childhood," 510.
17. Tamis-LeMonda, "Gender in Early Childhood," 512.
18. Brackett, *Permission to Feel*, 20.
19. Brackett, *Permission to Feel*, 13.
20. American Psychological Association, "Resilience," in *APA Dictionary of Psychology*, 2nd ed. (American Psychological Association, 2018), https://dictionary.apa.org/resilience.
21. Mary K. Alvord, Raquel A. Gurwitch, and Judy Freedman, *Resilience Builder Program for Children and Adolescents: Enhancing Social Competence and Self-Regulation: A Cognitive-Behavioral Group Approach* (Research Press, 2012).
22. Myers and Mayes, *A Practical Guide to Child and Adolescent*, 36.
23. Catherine Newman, *What Can I Say? A Kid's Guide to Super-Useful Social Skills to Help You Get Along and Express Yourself* (Storey Publishing, 2022).
24. Newman, *What Can I Say?*, 10.

25. Newman, *What Can I Say?*, 11.
26. Elizabeth Englander, *Bullying and Cyberbullying: What Every Educator and Parent Needs to Know*, 2nd ed. (Harvard Education Press, 2023), 26.
27. Claudia Morter and Fran Peavey, *Strategic Questioning: An Approach to Creating Personal and Social Change* (The International Institute for Social Change, 1997).
28. Myers and Mayes, *A Practical Guide to Child and Adolescent Psychiatry*, 35.
29. Myers and Mayes, *A Practical Guide to Child and Adolescent Psychiatry for Pediatrics and Primary Care*, 40.
30. L. Monique Ward and Jennifer S. Aubrey, "Watching Gender: How Stereotypes in Movies and on TV Impact Kids' Development," *Common Sense Media*, June 2017, https://www.commonsensemedia.org/research/watching-gender-how-stereotypes-in-movies-and-on-tv-impact-kids-development.
31. Howard N. Snyder, *Sexual Assault of Young Children as Reported to Law Enforcement: Victim, Incident, and Offender Characteristics* (US Department of Justice, Bureau of Justice Statistics, 2000).
32. Michael B. Robb and Trisha L. Mann, *The Common Sense Census: Media Use by Tweens and Teens, 2023* (Common Sense Media, 2023), https://www.commonsensemedia.org/research/the-common-sense-census-media-use-by-tweens-and-teens-2023.
33. Robb and Mann, *The Common Sense Census*.

Chapter 4

1. Emily Nagoski, *Come As You Are: The Surprising New Science That Will Transform Your Sex Life, Revised and Updated* (Simon & Schuster, 2021).
2. Intersex People: OHCHR and the Human Rights of LGBTI People," United Nations Human Rights Office of the Commissioner, accessed October 14, 2025, https://www.ohchr.org/en/sexual-orientation-and-gender-identity/intersex-people.
3. Alexander M. Czopp, "The Problem of Positive Stereotypes: When Praise Becomes Prejudice," in *The Social Psychology of Good and Evil*, 2nd ed., ed. Arthur G. Miller (Guilford Press, 2015).
4. Kathleen M. Myers and Linda C. Mayes, *A Practical Guide to Child and Adolescent Psychiatry for Pediatrics and Primary Care* (American Psychiatric Association Publishing, 2023), 13–14.
5. Oksana Sopher, "The Science of Puberty: What Educators (and Parents) Need to Know," *Edutopia*, 2023, https://www.edutopia.org/article/science-puberty-educators-parents, 107.
6. Myers and Mayes, *A Practical Guide to Child and Adolescent Psychiatry*, 115.
7. Myers and Mayes, *A Practical Guide to Child and Adolescent*, 112.
8. Marc Brackett, *Permission to Feel: Unlocking the Power of Emotions to Help Our Kids, Ourselves, and Our Society Thrive* (Celadon Books, 2019), 107.
9. Brackett, *Permission to Feel*, 30.
10. L. M. Ward and J. S. Aubrey, *Watching Gender: How Stereotypes in Movies and on TV Impact Kids' Development* (Common Sense Media, 2017), https://www.commonsense-media.org/sites/default/files/research/report/2017_commonsense_watchinggender_executivesummary_0620_1.pdf.
11. B. J. Casey, R. M. Jones, and T. A. Hare, "The Adolescent Brain," *Annals of the New York Academy of Sciences* 1124 (2008): 111–126, https://doi.org/10.1196/annals.1440.010.

12. Casey, Jones, Hare, "The Adolescent Brain."
13. Cara Natterson and Vanessa Kroll Bennett, *This is So Awkward: Modern Puberty Explained*, (Penguin Random House, 2023), 137.
14. Catherine Newman, *What Can I Say? A Kid's Guide to Super-Useful Social Skills to Help You Get Along and Express Yourself* (Storey Publishing, 2022).
15. Brett Laursen and Rene Veenstra, "Toward Understanding the Functions of Peer Influence: A Summary and Synthesis of Recent Empirical Research," *Journal of Research on Adolescence* 31:4, December 2021, https://doi.org/10.1111/jora.12606.
16. William Pollack and Mary Pipher, *Real Boys: Rescuing Our Sons from the Myths of Boyhood*, (Owl Books, 1999), 13.
17. Victoria Rideout et al., *Common Sense Census: Media Use by Tweens and Teens* (Common Sense, 2022).
18. Rideout et al., *Common Sense Census: Media Use by Tweens and Teens.*
19. US Department of Justice, Civil Rights Division, "Title IX of the Education Amendments of 1972," 2000, https://www.justice.gov/crt/title-ix-education-amendments-1972.

Chapter 5

1. Elizabeth Englander, *Bullying and Cyberbullying: What Every Educator and Parent Needs to Know, Second Edition* (Harvard Education Press, 2023), 2.
2. US Surgeon General, *Social Media and Youth Mental Health: The US Surgeon General's Advisory* (2023), https://www.hhs.gov/sites/default/files/sg-youth-mental-health-social-media-advisory.pdf.
3. Elizabeth Hamel et al., *Generation M2: Media in the Lives of 8–18-Year-Olds* (Kaiser Family Foundation, 2010), https://www.kff.org/other/report/generation-m2-media-in-the-lives-of-8-18-year-olds/.
4. Victoria Rideout, Alanna Peebles, Supreet Mann, and Michael B. Robb, *Common Sense Census: Media Use by Tweens and Teens* (Common Sense, 2022).
5. Rosalind Wiseman, *Masterminds and Wingmen: Helping Our Boys Cope with Schoolyard Power, Locker-Room Tests, Girlfriends, and the New Rules of Boy World* (Harmony Books, 2014), 8.
6. Jennifer Bryan, *From the Dress-Up Corner to the Senior Prom: Navigating Gender and Sexuality Diversity in PreK–12 Schools* (Rowman & Littlefield Publishers, 2012), 204.
7. Englander, *Bullying and Cyberbullying*, 40.
8. Cris Mayo, *LGBTQ Youth and Education: Policies and Practices* (Teachers College Press, 2022), 56.
9. Lyn Mikel Brown, *Girlfighting: Betrayal and Rejection Among Girls* (New York University Press, 2005), 217.
10. Englander, *Bullying and Cyberbullying*, 41.
11. Englander, *Bullying and Cyberbullying*, 38.
12. Englander, *Bullying and Cyberbullying*, 14.
13. Brown, *Girlfighting*, 106.
14. Brown, *Girlfighting*, 128.
15. Bryan, *From the Dress-Up Corner to the Senior Prom*, 57.
16. Mayo, *LGBTQ Youth and Education*, 53.
17. Joseph G. Kosciw et al., *The 2021 National School Climate Survey: The Experiences of Lesbian, Gay, Bisexual, Transgender, and Queer Youth in Our Nation's Schools* (GLSEN, 2022).

18. Kosciw et al., *The 2021 National School Climate Survey.*
19. CJ Pascoe, *Dude, You're a Fag: Masculinity and Sexuality in High School* (University of California Press, 2011), 54.
20. Mayo, *LGBTQ Youth and Education*, 53.
21. Wiseman, *Masterminds and Wingmen*, 25.
22. CJ Pascoe, *Dude, You're a Fag*, 53.
23. Wiseman, *Masterminds and Wingmen*, 31.
24. Wiseman, *Masterminds and Wingmen*, 45.
25. Paolo Freire, *Pedagogy of the Oppressed: 50th Anniversary Edition* (Bloomsbury, 2018), 72.
26. Michele Borba, *UnSelfie: Why Empathetic Kids Succeed in Our All-About-Me World* (Touchstone, 2016), xix.
27. Al Vernacchio, *For Goodness Sex: Changing the Way We Talk to Teens About Sexuality, Values, and Health* (HarperWave, 2014), 22.
28. Borba, *UnSelfie*, xiii.
29. Borba, *UnSelfie*, xiv.
30. Bruce D. Perry and Maia Szalavitz, *The Boy Who Was Raised as a Dog: And Other Stories from a Child Psychiatrist's Notebook* (Basic Books, 2011), 12.
31. Brené Brown, "RSA Short: Empathy," animated by Katy Davis, RSA, YouTube video, December 10, 2013, https://www.youtube.com/watch?v=1Evwgu369Jw.
32. Cara Natterson and Vanessa Kroll Bennett, *This is so Awkward: Modern Puberty Explained*, (Rodale Books, 2025), 64.
33. Natterson and Kroll-Bennett, *This is so Awkward*, 67.
34. Jacqueline Grennon Brooks and Martin G. Brooks, *In Search of Understanding: The Case for Constructivist Classrooms* (Association for Supervision and Curriculum Development, 1999), 47.
35. L. M. Ward and J. S. Aubrey, *Watching Gender: How Stereotypes in Movies and on TV Impact Kids' Development.*
36. "Sexual Assault Safety & Prevention," RAINN, accessed April 27, 2024, https://www.rainn.org/articles/sexual-assault-safety-prevention.
37. Bobbie Harro, "The Cycle of Socialization," in *Readings for Diversity and Social Justice*, 4th ed., ed. Maurianne Adams, Warren J. Blumenfeld, Carmelita (Rosie) Castaneda, Heather W. Hackman, Madeline L. Peters, and Ximena Zúñiga (Routledge, 2018), 28.
38. William Pollack, *Real Boys: Rescuing Our Sons from the Myths of Boyhood* (Henry Holt, 1998), 66.
39. Pollack, *Real Boys*, 33.
40. Wiseman, *Masterminds and Wingmen*, 318.
41. Edward M. Hallowell, *The Childhood Roots of Adult Happiness: Five Steps to Help Kids Create and Sustain Lifelong Joy* (Ballantine Books, 2001), xi–xii.
42. Phyllis L. Fagell, *Middle School Matters: The 10 Key Skills Kids Need to Thrive in Middle School and Beyond—and How Parents Can Help* (Sourcebooks, 2019).
43. Howard Gardner and Katie Davis, *The App Generation: How Today's Youth Navigate Identity, Intimacy, and Imagination in a Digital World* (Yale University Press, 2014), 105.
44. Brown, *Girlfighting*, 203.
45. Brown, *Girlfighting*, 130.
46. Brown, *Girlfighting*, 200.
47. Wiseman, *Masterminds and Wingmen*, 216.

48. Hallowell, *The Childhood Roots of Adult Happiness*, 3.
49. "California Education Laws Related to Safe and Supportive Schools," National Center for Safe Supportive Learning Environments, 2023, https://safesupportivelearning.ed.gov/.
50. "Frequently Asked Questions | Protecting Student Privacy," US Department of Education, https://studentprivacy.ed.gov/faq.
51. Pollack, *Real Boys*, 33.
52. Richard Weissbourd et al., "The Talk: How Adults Can Promote Young People's Healthy Relationships and Prevent Misogyny and Sexual Harassment," 2017, https://mcc.gse.harvard.edu/reports/the-talk.
53. Weissbourd et al., "The Talk."

Chapter 6

1. Kathleen A. Ethier and Jonathan H. Mermin, *Youth Risk Behavior Survey Data Summary & Trends Report: 2013–2023* (Centers for Disease Control and Prevention, 2024), https://www.cdc.gov/healthyyouth/data/yrbs/pdf/YRBS_Data-Summary-Trends_Report2024_508.pdf.
2. Elizabeth Englander, *Bullying and Cyberbullying: What Every Educator and Parent Needs to Know*, 2nd ed. (Harvard Education Press, 2023),14.
3. Lu Luo, Chuansheng Ma, and Jun Dang, "Prosocial Behavior Protects Adolescents from Negative Effects of Daily Stress," *Journal of Adolescence* 97 (2023): 1–3, https://doi.org/10.1016/j.adolescence.2022.12.008.
4. Rosalind Wiseman, *Queen Bees and Wannabes: Helping Your Daughter Survive Cliques, Gossip, Boyfriends, and the New Realities of Girl World* (Harmony, 2009), 244.
5. Howard Gardner and Katie Davis, *The App Generation: How Today's Youth Navigate Identity, Intimacy, and Imagination in a Digital World* (Yale University Press, 2014), 119.
6. Jennifer Bryan, *From the Dress-Up Corner to the Senior Prom: Navigating Gender and Sexuality Diversity in PreK–12 Schools* (Rowman & Littlefield Publishers, 2012), 33.
7. Ed Brockenbrough, *Learning While Black and Queer: Understanding the Educational Experiences of Black LGBTQ+ Youth* (Harvard Education Press, 2024), 94.
8. Kimberlé Crenshaw, "Mapping the Margins: Intersectionality, Identity Politics, and Violence against Women of Color," *Stanford Law Review* 43, no. 6 (1991): 1241–1299.
9. Brockenbrough, *Learning While Black and Queer,* 108.
10. National Center for HIV/AIDS, Viral Hepatitis, STD, and TB Prevention (US) and Division of Adolescent and School Health, 2023.
11. Simon Rice, Ronny Purcell, and Patrick D. McGorry, "Adolescent and Young Adult Male Mental Health: Transforming System Failures into Proactive Models of Engagement," *Journal of Adolescent Health* 62, no. 3S (2018): 11, https://doi.org/10.1016/j.jadohealth.2017.06.023.,1.
12. National Center for HIV/AIDS, Viral Hepatitis, STD, and TB Prevention (US) and Division of Adolescent and School Health 2023.
13. Beverly Daniel Tatum, *Why Are All the Black Kids Sitting Together in the Cafeteria? And Other Conversations about Race* (Basic Books, 1997), 7.
14. Michael Sadowski, ed., *Adolescents at School: Perspectives on Youth, Identity, and Education* (Harvard Education Press, 2020), 4.
15. Eleanor Drago-Severson, *Leading Adult Learning: Supporting Adult Development in Our Schools* (Corwin, 2009).

16. Emily Nagoski and Amelia Nagoski, *Burnout: The Secret to Unlocking the Stress Cycle* (Ballantine Books, 2019), 135.
17. Lyn Mikel Brown, *Girlfighting*, 216.
18. Maisha Winn, *Justice on Both Sides*, 26.
19. Carol Dweck, *Mindset: The New Psychology of Success* (Ballantine Books, 2007), 145.
20. Christopher Peterson and Martin E. P. Seligman, *Character Strengths and Virtues: A Handbook and Classification* (Oxford University Press and American Psychological Association, 2004), 349.
21. Michael Sadowski, *Safe is Not Enough*, 81.
22. Cody Lee et al., "Association of Anti-Transgender Legislation with Suicide Risk Among Transgender and Nonbinary Youth," *Nature Human Behaviour* 8 (2024): 2096, https://doi.org/10.1038/s41562-024-01889-0.
23. Sara Lawrence-Lightfoot, *The Essential Conversation: What Parents and Teachers Can Learn from Each Other* (Ballantine Books, 2004), 3.
24. Claudia Morter and Fran Peavey, *Strategic Questioning: An Approach to Creating Personal and Social Change* (The International Institute for Social Change, 1990).
25. Emily Bazelon, *Sticks and Stones: Defeating the Culture of Bullying and Rediscovering the Power of Character and Empathy* (Random House, 2014), 298–99.
26. Englander, *Bullying and Cyberbullying*, 14.
27. Englander, *Bullying and Cyberbullying*, 28.
28. Tonja R. Nansel et al., "Bullying Behaviors Among US Youth: Prevalence and Association with Psychosocial Adjustment," *JAMA* 285, no. 16 (2001): 2094–2100, https://doi.org/10.1001/jama.285.16.2094.
29. Englander, *Bullying and Cyberbullying*,121.
30. Englander, *Bullying and Cyberbullying*,123.
31. Sadowski, *Safe is Not Enough*, 64–65.
32. William Pollack, *Real Boys: Rescuing Our Sons from the Myths of Boyhood* (Henry Holt, 1998), 150.

Chapter 7

1. Christopher Peterson and Martin E. P. Seligman, *Character Strengths and Virtues: A Handbook and Classification* (Oxford University Press and American Psychological Association, 2004), 351.
2. Cora C. Breuner and Gina M. Mattson, "Sexuality Education for Children and Adolescents," *Pediatrics* 138, no. 2 (2016): e20161348, https://doi.org/10.1542/peds.2016-1348.
3. Jason M. Nagata, "Bigorexia, or Muscle Dysmorphia, Is an Increasing Problem Among Boys and Men," *American Academy of Pediatrics*, https://www.aap.org/en/news-room/news-releases/aap/2023/bigorexia-or-muscle-dysmorphia-is-an-increasing-problem-among-boys-and-men/.
4. Dan Kindlon, Michael Thompson, and Teresa Barker, *Raising Cain: Protecting the Emotional Life of Boys* (Ballantine Books, 1999), 258.
5. William Pollack, *Real Boys: Rescuing Our Sons from the Myths of Boyhood* (Henry Holt, 1998), 151.
6. Kathleen A. Ethier and Jonathan H. Mermin, *Youth Risk Behavior Survey Data Summary & Trends Report: 2011–2021* (Centers for Disease Control and Prevention,

2023), https://www.cdc.gov/healthyyouth/data/yrbs/pdf/YRBS_Data-Summary-Trends_Report2023_508.pdf.

7. Richard Weissbourd, Trisha Ross Anderson, Whitney Allgood, and Emily Bernstein, *The Talk: How Adults Can Promote Young People's Healthy Relationships and Prevent Misogyny and Sexual Harassment* (Making Caring Common Project, Harvard Graduate School of Education, 2017), https://mcc.gse.harvard.edu/reports/talk-adults-promote-healthy-relationships.
8. Shanta R. Dube et al., "Childhood Abuse, Household Dysfunction, and the Risk of Attempted Suicide Throughout the Life Span: Findings from the Adverse Childhood Experiences Study," *JAMA* 286, no. 24 (2001): 3089–3096, https://doi.org/10.1001/jama.286.24.3089.
9. Kathleen C. Basile and Sharon G. Smith, "Sexual Violence Victimization of Women: Prevalence, Characteristics, and the Role of Public Health and Prevention," *American Journal of Lifestyle Medicine* 5, no. 5 (2011): 407–417, https://doi.org/10.1177/1559827611409512.
10. Basile and Smith, "Sexual Violence Victimization of Women."
11. bell hooks, *All About Love: New Visions* (William Morrow, 2001).

Appendix A

1. Jennifer Bryan, *From the Dress-Up Corner to the Senior Prom: Navigating Gender and Sexuality Diversity in PreK–12 Schools* (Rowman & Littlefield Publishers, 2012), xxiii.
2. Michael Sadowski, *Safe is Not Enough: Better Schools for LGBTQ Students* (Harvard Education Press, 2016), 185.
3. Bryan, *From the Dress-Up Corner to the Senior Prom: Navigating Gender and Sexuality Diversity in PreK–12 Schools*, 157.
4. Claudia Morter and Fran Peavey, *Strategic Questioning: An Approach to Creating Personal and Social Change* (The International Institute for Social Change, 1990).

Acknowledgments

Many people think my work is primarily about consent, but in truth, it's about love and connection. I am humbled and grateful to be blessed by the love and connection I feel from the family I was born into as well as the family I have discovered and cultivated along the way. This community of people brings meaning to my life and sustains me. In particular, I am thankful for the folks who have supported the writing of this book. Whether it was through an interview, a spontaneous question while writing, talking through concepts, verifying information, or cheering me on when I needed to sustain the grind, my colleagues, family, and friends have showed up for me in the most generous and thoughtful ways.

Gretchen Brion-Meisels, Michael Vázquez, and Kimm Topping: You are superstars in the constellation of folks doing this work. I am forever learning from you about the meaningful process of people feeling cared for and like they belong and matter in educational spaces—it is truly an honor to be in your good company.

Peggy Orenstein: P, you are a dear and cherished friend. The texting (OMG our texting), the conversations, meals, hikes, and travel bring so much perspective and joy. Thank you for always engaging with heart *and* mind as we aspire to "all about love" together.

Rick Weissbourd: Your work is an inspiration. How you always uphold the great importance of morality, care, dignity, and love is a constant guide for how my work evolves—I am ever grateful to learn from you.

Debbie Roffman: Queen, fifty years of teaching and still going strong! A steadfast mentor, you never cease to inspire and amaze me. Always up to date and ready to address what's most relevant, your work is forever focused on keeping kids at the center of education and parenting—always with integrity, always with love.

Debra Wilson: Thank you for your unwavering support in *every* context. Despite being in demand and one of the busiest people in the world, you always find time to be present and show up as a caring, affirming and steady force. GRATEFUL!

Cindy Pierce: The levity and grace that you bring to the most challenging of conversations is astounding and appreciated. Courage, care, and faith—you are da bomb!

Jenn Epstein: Our twenty-plus years of partnership and solidarity means more to me than I could ever express in words. I couldn't ask for a better work wife and friend. Thank you for always taking the time to understand and give love.

Charlotte Worsley: Thank you for always supporting me and ensuring the justice and equity we all deserve. I couldn't have realized this dream without it.

Zoe Duskin: A rock star who makes a difference in the lives of children and their families every day. You manifest all of the blessings that come with community. Thank you for your friendship and love.

Ivy Chen and Helen Chen: Sexuality Education Sisters! You don't even know how much I appreciate our regular hang out seshes. Whether it's connecting over work, family, friends, celebrating big birthdays, or swooning over all of the pups, hanging out with you is always a highlight. Thank you for always being there for me.

Cara Natterson and Vanessa Kroll-Bennett: Powerhouse women who are flipping puberty positive. I appreciate your commitment, unbelievable persistence, solidarity, professional prowess, and friendship. Thank you for including me in your endeavors to make this world more joyful and loving for kids and their families.

Amy Killy: Our friendship that has grown out of our first work together at the Consent Summit means so much to me. I appreciate you and all that you bring to your tremendous work with young people.

Clarke Weatherspoon: I can always count on you to keep it real. I value our friendship and professional collaborations to no end. Knowing that we always have each other's backs brings peace to life for which I am deeply grateful.

Erin Skiffer: BOTH . . . AND . . . !! You are both a valued friend and colleague. Always ready to fiercely take on what needs to be done and with such incredible grace and care. My admiration for you runs deep—I look forward to the multitude of both/and conversations we have yet to share.

Sarah Huss: Girl, you are appreciated beyond measure. I can always count on you to keep it real and for the kids. The love and light you emanate is astounding.

Connie Matthiessen: I am so deeply thankful for your time, talent, patience, and care. I couldn't ask for a more supportive writing partner and friend. Our collaboration over the years has taught me so much. Thank you for all of the thoughtful generosity with which you provide your feedback.

Ashanti Branch: Your work with adolescents, young men in particular, is truly transformative and restores humanity among young people through the cultivation of authentic connection, care, and love. Respect and thanks.

Christopher Pepper: It is such a privilege to know your work and have had opportunities to collaborate. Your commitment to student health is amazing, and your capacity to affect change—an inspiration. I look forward to *Talk to Your Boys* (cheers to Joanna Schroeder too)—it is sure to make the world a better place for all of us.

Al Vernacchio: I am a super fan and deeply value the opportunities we've had to work together. You make such a difference—thank you for all that you have done and do as an advocate for healthy sexuality and love.

In addition to the folks above, I couldn't have written this book without the educators, students, and parents who have shared their stories and wisdom as well. I was constantly moved and humbled by these folks, who were so responsive, generous with time, and openly shared about their experiences with schools. I am delighted to thank John Spears, Dawn Colwell, Mike Casey, Gaby Grebski, Geoffrey LaPlant, Brian Rhodes, Maria Brown, Dharinne Perera Myers, Kirsti Jones, Carrie Sheinberg, Whitney Phippen, Mary Aden, Agnes Lo, Robyn Perry, Greg Daniels, Danny Chui, Zayne Sibley, Nedaa Alwawi, Quinn Reno, Tessa Shepard, Andy Milne, Stacy Walden, Claudia Gonzalez, Danika Wong, Emily Rhodes, Karin Soriano-Bilal, Meg Zuttermeister, Doug Zesiger, Julie Stone, Drew Miller, Tamila Taylor, Emily Zien, Heidi Nichols, Brit Hoyt, Victoria Adams, Jesús Galindo, Nitzayah Schiller, Zoe Jiran, Sophie Weissbourd, Calysta Phillips, Emily Straight, Amy Alamar, Libby Spears, and Alison Blair. Your open honesty, care, and dedication to the well-being of young people is what will sustain spaces for kids where they can be seen, heard, and cared for in connection with others. I express my heartfelt gratitude for how each of you found the time, presence, and courage to share the joy and challenges of what it means to be part of a school community.

Jennifer Bryan PhD, Dr. Rachael Gibson, Dr. Sara Nasserzadeh, Laurie Mintz PhD, Karen Rayne PhD, Elizabeth Scott LCSW & CEDS, Fiona Zecca, Jamie Forbes, Leaf Seligman, Mary Keating, and Michael Tafelski: Your work is tremendous and something I aspire to everyday. Thank you for sharing your time and expertise—it enriched my perspective and writing exponentially.

Shannon Davis and the Harvard Education Publishing Group team: Thank you, Shannon, for recognizing the value of this work and cultivating the opportunity to connect and embrace the ways we overlap through HGSE. Your patience, understanding, open mind, and heart have supported me and this project in so many ways. I appreciate you standing by it to make it a reality.

I am also blessed to have so many dear, cherished friends who are phenomenal teachers and school people. They have contributed to my knowledge as an educator and informed my writing as well: Suzanne Alpert,

Nínive Calegari, Joanna Ro, Alec Lee, Samantha Sanderson, Heather Rogers, and Eugenie Chan.

My friends and colleagues at the Urban School: I am so proud that you are my colleagues and friends. Your scholarship, dedication, creativity, and love for young people inspires me every day. I am so fortunate to work in such a phenomenal community where education is so much more than just school.

Of course, I also give thanks to my adored and appreciated friends and family—especially my parents and brother, who are the foundation of my life and provide the joy, love, and support that makes it all so special.

To my children, Mei Lan, Kyle, and Maddie, I am in awe of how you are evolving into young adults of integrity and purpose. You are my favorite people on earth and still inspire me to bring my best loving self to every day, especially whilst you serve up that humble pie. I value nothing more than being your mama.

And to my husband, Brian. Your support, partnership, and love are the foundation of our family. It is truly the greatest blessing to be living this adventure together. Cheers to a lifetime, my love.

About the Author

Shafia Zaloom is a health educator, parent, consultant, and author whose work centers on human development, community building, ethics, and social justice. Her approach involves creating opportunities for students and teachers to discuss the complexities of teen culture and decision-making with straightforward, open, and honest dialogue. Shafia has worked with thousands of children and their families in her role as teacher, coach, administrator, board member, and outdoor educator. She has contributed articles to *The New York Times, The Washington Post*, and numerous parenting blogs. Shafia's book, *Sex, Teens, and Everything in Between*, has been reviewed as "the ultimate relationship guide for teens of all orientations and identities."[1] Shafia is currently a health teacher at the Urban School in San Francisco, teaches at the Harvard Graduate School of Education, and develops curricula and trainings for schools across the country. She was honored by the San Francisco Giants Foundation in 2018 for her work with Aim High—a program that expands opportunities for students and their teachers through tuition-free summer learning enrichment—and was recently granted CAHPERD's Health Teacher of the Year Award for 2021. Her work has been featured by many media outlets, including *The New York Times, USA Today, NPR, KQED,* and *PBS*.

[1] (Zaloom 2019)

INDEX